Princess
New York — Key Biscayne

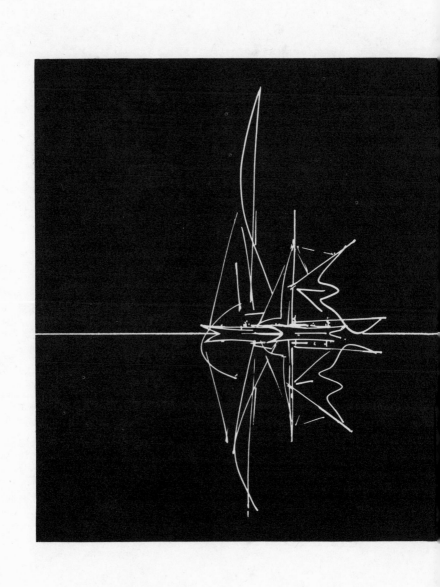

Princess

Joe Richards

Illustrated by the author

David McKay Company, Inc.   *New York*

BOOK ONE
New York

I

I bought a Friendship sloop in the early spring of 1938. She was lying in a boatyard in Flushing, Long Island. Her name was *Princess*. It was neatly lettered on her transom in the arc of an eyelid. "NEW YORK" formed the lower lid. Where you might imagine an eyeball there was a two-inch iron pipe that broke through the lovely oval of her counter. She had been crying, too; the rusty stains dripped down to her water line.

She had power. A two-cylinder engine of unknown vintage lay under her mahogany bridge deck. She had one of those old-fashioned, bathtub-shaped cockpits, an icebox, and a stove which bore the name "MARINE HOUSEHOLD." She slept two. There was a small bookshelf, and even a pipe rack.

I wish I could tell you what I thought of her at the time. I

3

can't. Ask any man after all those years to tell you how he felt when he first set eyes on his wife. Now don't get me wrong. We have been through a lot together, and we are still in love. She has thrown a lot of pots and dishes at me, and I have stayed up with her through all kinds of bad times both ashore and afloat. Remember, I was twenty-nine when we met and *Princess* was over sixty, but she had the spirit of a kid.

I looked the other way when I first saw her. Something told me, "This girl is not for you."

I was looking over a little weekender with bilges like a coffin, a dead-rise dog with an ugly wooden outboard rack bolted to her flat stern that had recently come off the forms of a local yard. She too was for sale. I had climbed up and was inspecting her when I caught another glimpse of *Princess*. It was perhaps the sheer of her deck, the clipper bow, the gentle reverse curve of her forefoot, or the well-fed look of her fat-bellied chine that did it. I was a goner.

The negotiations for the transfer of title to *Princess* were straightforward and simple. I found the owner through the yard manager. Over a cup of coffee I asked for the truth. Then I handed over pieces of green paper, backed up by the Government of the United States, for a sloop which I was told was "as sound as a dollar." I went home and fell into a beautiful sleep with the title to *Princess* under my pillow.

You know where you could have found me the next morning. I sat on her port bunk and feasted my eyes. I remembered tales I had heard as a child in Maine of the uncanny sailing qualities of a Friendship sloop, and this was the real McCoy—built by Wilbur A. Morse, twenty-six feet long, over nine feet of beam, deep in the water, and balanced like a bird in flight.

There were little lockers under the stove. I found a hammer with one claw, a sailmaker's palm stiff with salt, odds and ends. It was fun to poke around and find the evidence of voyages made, departures and landfalls, leaves of an old log, rusty fishhooks and sinkers, beer openers and bobby pins. She had lived!

It was a lovely morning. I sat with the hammer dangling in

my hand, leaned back against the ceiling, and gave the old girl an affectionate rap. "Holy Cow!"

The hammer went through her ceiling like a one-inch auger bit through cheese. There were four eyes now: the eye on the transom, the hole in the ceiling, and both of mine, now wide open. I rapped her again, and there were five. I dug up the floorboards in a frenzy like a man looking for money that had been stolen. I was that man all right; there were no frames in sight. I began to tear away at the ceiling. It came off in black, rotten masses. In an agony of frustration and despair, I ripped away with that crippled hammer at the pristine whiteness of the ceiling till the whole story of corruption and fraud lay exposed to the light of the clean spring sky. Never did a young crusading D. A. attack the substrata of entrenched vice with more ferocity than I set to on that poor cancerous old frump.

The pitiful evidence of framing came loose in long sections to the touch or broke apart like toasted muck. The ceiling was out, lying alongside in a pile that rose to the water line. The white icebox and the black stove were perched on top like carrion birds on a crazy nest when, brandishing the lone claw of the hammer, I went after the yard manager with blood and flecks of dry rot in my eye.

The yard manager was deaf. I am not joking. He was really deaf! He wore a faraway smile and an earphone which I suspected was tuned in to KDKA. Somehow I managed to convey my state of mind.

"Well, I thought you paid a mite too much for her," said the yardman, who had some sort of anonymous name like Smith, "but you have a fine model there, and we will give you a hand if you want to rebuild her." I began to take heart. "You should have looked into her before you bought her." The yard manager Smith puffed his pipe.

The words "dry rot" had meant very little to me. I had heard the phrase in pompous speeches by politicians in connection with the decay of the moral fiber of society. So this is where they got the word. My head was spinning like an outboard prop. I

5

could see myself on the floor of the Senate, waving a rotten rib and shrieking, "See what happens!"

"Whatever held her together up till now?"

"Force of habit and a bit of paint," said Smith. "As a matter of fact, they took her down to Montauk last fall in a gale so strong that all three of them had to hang onto the tiller to keep her from coming about."

"That's not for me."

"Clean her out and we'll give you a hand," said Smith. "Frame her up and she'll give you a lot of pleasure."

I went back to *Princess*. She still looked beautiful on the surface. It took a few days to get started. What bits and pieces of frames still clung to her belly were left undisturbed. They were used as a pattern to bend new ones. The steam box used to soften oak for bending was stoked up.

The following weekend there were thirty frames bent over a form that followed the curve of *Princess*. They cost a dollar apiece. There's a strip of deck planking along the edge of the boat called a waterway. I might have pried it up and made it easy to slide the frames into place, but, let's face it, I'm an artist, not a boatbuilder. I learned the hard way.

Each frame was dragged down into the damp hull and set into a notch in the keel. The curve of the contour was a great big beautiful S. The frames were bent to fit perfectly amidships, and as I moved forward a different part of the S fitted into place. There seemed to be a reason for it.

Suddenly down there in the dark I knew. This was calculus. S was a symbol, a mathematical thing. The pieces I cut off from the bottom of the S to make it fit were longer as I moved forward. But always by the same amount. Then it hit me: The boat itself was a slide rule, the granddaddy of all slide rules, and still a better one than most. Small wonder that this was one of the finest designs for a hull that man has ever known.

What with her years and odd bulges, *Princess* was a little out of line. The curved frames, like whalebone stays of a lady's corset, had to be pressed into position. I rigged automobile jacks to do the job, and broke half a dozen in the process. Like the man said, "Anything for progress."

The old nail holes in the planks were cleaned out, and bronze screws were used to lock the frames in place. The new wood was slightly green for bending, and the screws were driven home without drilling. I have muscles to prove it, but no brains. When I released the jacks, they went off like the crack of doom. For hours I was as deaf as Mr. Smith.

That weekend I installed two frames. There was an unbelievable difference in the feel of her when I climbed aboard. After I pulled the ceiling out she shivered like a jellyfish when I went near her. Now she began to stiffen up. I began to stiffen up, too. Lying in that damp hull was giving me rheumatism, but I was back at it the following weekend.

Working all day Saturday and most of Sunday, I broke my record, the Sabbath, and all of my fingernails. I installed three frames. That made five. I had only twenty-five to go.

It was getting along toward July, about the time I was getting suspicious of a patch of cement on the inside of her stem, that a beautiful little red seaplane landed in the bay and taxied up to the water's edge. The flyer got a can of gas from the yard, filled his tank, and, buzzing me goodby, disappeared into the heavenly sky. I went back to the mines. Probing pay dirt in the stem, I reached clear through and felt the warm sunlight on my empty hand. You can find some funny sights around an old boatyard—like me, lying disconsolately in the dank bottom of a half-rotten vessel with my arm poked through the stem in the place of a figurehead.

The fourth of July found me with a pick and shovel digging a big hole in the rock-studded earth under the bow. I had to have room to drive out the iron driftpins that held her stem to the keel. The planks had been pried loose from the stem at a tremendous cost of time and patience and were stretched out fore and aft, creating an enormous maw with festoons of caulking cotton

7

caught in its teeth. The bowsprit, still dangling by the forestay, was loose and hung alongside the shrouds. The knightheads were rotten and fell apart to the touch.

When I had dug a big enough hole to turn around in, one of the boys in the yard came by. "So you're going to bury her after all!" I threw the shovel at him.

As it got later in the season, I began to play hooky in the middle of the week. I was desperate. I had to get that stem out. I came out and cut the tie rods that held the stem to the first deck beam, and the dry weather helped me drive the driftpins out.

As I worked along, an old man employed by the yard sat on a barrel near *Princess* during his lunch hour and shot the breeze. He had actually worked for Morse, and he would tell me about the yard in Friendship, Maine—how they went back into the woods and cut the timbers for the vessels; how they fed their steam-driven sawmills with the scraps of wood around the yard; about the disgruntled cousins and relatives who broke away and tried to build real Friendship sloops but could never make it. "There was no one like Wilbur A. Morse, except an old hunchback feller who used to do all the designing for him," said my friend.

It does seem incredible now that one man could have known so much about a boat. They are all gone now, gathered to their fathers, but they knew how to fashion a vessel, God bless them.

I showed my friend the rotten stem that finally came loose. "You'll never find one like that around here," he said. "That one we got right off the tree." But the old man helped me build a new one. We scarfed it together. "This will be better than the original," he said. "It'll never warp." I looked at the old stem. It was warped an inch or two out of line. I paid the yard thirty dollars more for the oak, bolts, and the old man's time, and I took the stem out and set it in place. Everything cost thirty dollars in those days.

The stem fell into place. I borrowed a big auger and lay in the bottom of the hole and drilled up for the bolts. Then I cut new

8

knightheads and fastened them to the stem. There didn't seem to be anything you couldn't do on a boat if your back was as strong as the obsession.

That night at home, hammering and sawing and pounding in my imagination, as boat people do for hours after the tools have been put away, I remembered the slightly cruddy ends of the planks that I had planned to refasten to the stem. Would the screws hold them? I had visions of the bow opening up in a seaway and gulping down a bellyful of salt water.

The more time you spend working in a boatyard, the more fearful you become of the power of the sea. You are really at war with the sea, armed with a puny caulking iron and a silly-looking long-headed mallet, and the longer you make war without actually coming in contact with your adversary, the more fearful you become. "You build 'em and I'll sail 'em," says the hearty mariner.

Yet there is plenty to say for the sailor who knows his vessel. Among seafaring people that knowledge is called sea savvy. I was getting plenty of savvy and damn little sea!

Washers! I said to myself in the middle of the night. That will do it! I'll put washers on all the screws that hold the planks to the stem. Washers, by God!

Next day I bought washers, a whole gross of them, all shiny and made of brass. They would teach that old devil sea a lesson. I got hold of an electric drill and spent the whole evening countersinking the holes in them. In the morning I set out for the yard. It was getting to be August.

I started with the garboard and pulled her into place. The washers were fine. Tremendous strength in those washers. No danger of splitting wood. About that time the old man who had served his apprenticeship in the boatyard of Wilbur A. Morse hobbled over to see how I was getting along with the new stem.

"Washers!" he growled.

"What's wrong with washers?" I asked. "Nice and strong."

"Washers," he said with a spurt of tobacco juice. There was a wild look in his eye. I waited.

There may be a code of etiquette that makes yachting

9

pleasant, and there are unchanging customs that rule all men who go to sea. But the code of the real boatbuilder is a law that permits no infraction, that will tolerate no variation. It is as unyielding as North.

"Take 'em off, or I'll never talk to you again," said the old man. I took them off. Years later I was still finding washers in the bilge, all countersunk. I bought a smile for myself with every one.

2

My affair with *Princess* became a marriage of convenience. Every hour spent traveling out to the boatyard, every moment spent digging out dry rot, even the time spent trying to figure out what to do next, froze the knot a little tighter. I had married her for money—my money.

The fever that drives a man to rebuild a sixty-year-old vessel can make him lose sight of the reason for doing it. The surge of the tide down along the water's edge was lost on me. The clean westerly tugged at the shrouds and I heard nothing. A new part added to the vessel made the old parts look worse. The accomplishment of one day became a command for the next. I fell into a panic lest the cycle would take so long that I would have to start on the first again by the time the last job was done. I would be doomed, caught in an endless chain of dry rot and disintegration.

Then I discovered Cuprinol. I filled a bucket with the stuff and swabbed her every hour on the hour. The boat smelled of Cuprinol, I smelled of Cuprinol, my studio smelled of Cuprinol, even my English bulldog smelled of Cuprinol. "What is that smell?" my friends would ask.

"Cuprinol," I would answer. "I love it!"

Princess began to perk up. The planks were drawn into place and fastened. She looked like a boat again. Now I could return to the business of reframing her. I fell into the easy rhythm with which I am sure she was first put together in the Down East boatyard of Wilbur A. Morse. When I got off the bus in Flushing, I was back in the days of canvas.

I tried to drag my friends into this world of knightheads, king planks, driftpins, stringers, and rabbets. They looked at me. One real pal I had known since those days up on the hill when as kids we had scooped out a giant sea among the rocks. When the rain came, we built a navy powered by rubber bands. He alone consented to come along and help me work on the boat. Being a man with the greatest reverence for tools, he didn't like the way I leaned a handsaw on its head or the way I put a plane down on its blade. The way I tossed a chisel around had him frothing. He was a purist. He liked things clean. I caught him with a stiff wire brush gouging away at the soft wood planking, and talked him out of it. Then I went around and drove more screws into the last of the frames.

I had her reframed now from the forward end of the bridge deck right up to her bow. I didn't like the way she looked aft, but I wanted to feel her in the water. Here it was the middle of August. I had my sights on Labor Day. All at once I heard a sharp rapping and tapping on the other side of the vessel. My friend had got hold of a flat file and inserted it between two planks at the bow, and was driving it aft with a hammer. I caught him about three feet abaft the chain plates. "What are you doing, Mac?"

"I'm cleaning out her seams." The inner lips of those planks were gone forever. For years and years it was always a little wet along the bunk on the port side, no matter how hard I caulked her. It came to be known as McLennan's Leak.

The hardest thing about rebuilding an ancient ark is the decision you have to make about the things you are not going to do. There were some strange repairs made years before which I just had to show the old man who had worked for Morse.

He shook his head, unbelieving. Some of that reconstruction employed everything from cardboard to little blocks tacked together. From the inside it looked like a mock-up boat, the kind you see set up on a TV stage for a Sunday afternoon show.

The sternpost, for instance, a structural member as important to a vessel as a ridgepole is to a roof, had been cut clear through to provide additional space for the cockpit floor. The whole keel must have swung like a barn door in a seaway. There is a special God who takes care of those who go down to the sea with ignorance and with faith.

And then someone had gone to considerable pains to figure out the worst way in the world to mount the engine, the forward end of which was supported by a timber laid athwartships with its ends resting neatly on plank ends and doing double duty as butt blocks. This created a bovine condition on the underbelly of *Princess*. I left buckets under her on both sides in the earnest expectation of getting a little milk.

The old boatbuilder's reaction was fine. "Well," he said, "some poor fisherman did the best he could, had to earn a living for his wife and kids, couldn't afford to hire anybody, did it himself."

"Was this boat really used for fishing?"

"Was she?" He stared. "Why, I've seen her coming home heeled over in a gale in the dead of winter, men hanging on, covered with ice and full of fish."

They were sailed hard, these Friendship sloops. There was money in fish. Then they were sold to yachtsmen when power became the thing. They were tough. The deck beams, now riddled with rot, had been fashioned with incredible perfection. Mortised at every joint and flowing from the king plank back along into the lovely oval of her transom, they were stout enough to sustain the weight of barrels of fish. I became more and more determined to match her bit by bit, new wood for old, when it happened like a bolt out of the blue.

In fact, it was a bolt out of the blue. I was so deep in work that I hardly noticed the late summer sky cloud overhead. When the rain came, I made a break for the shed. There was not much shelter under deck planks that had shrunk like dry string beans. I had just about closed the door of the office when the place lit up with a shaft of lightning and rocked with a simultaneous crack of thunder. It struck *Princess*.

The yard was flooded. Then the sun came out as if nothing had happened. Nothing had: *Princess* was unharmed. The lightning had been grounded by the sloppy shrouds and stays that were dangling all around. I was lucky, but it got me thinking that if I had to die I would rather drown than be fried by lightning in a boatyard. I went back to the office and with sound and motion indicated that I wanted to launch *Princess* by the first of September. Mr. Smith had heard the lightning strike even without his earphone, and he understood.

From that day on I gave up the incidental business of making a living as an artist. Back from their nest of discarded rotten ceiling went the stove and the icebox. A couple of floors fashioned out of two-inch oak were lagged deep into the keel with bronze. Then the bunks were set in place. I brought out a suitcase full of personal gear and a couple of pans and eating tools and set up housekeeping.

It was fun. A long water pipe that stretched far across the surface of the yard picked up the heat of the sun and delivered hot water for three minutes and twenty-five seconds at full throttle. That was long enough for a bath. Then it became ice water, which, if your timing was right, made it just as nice as my studio at the Beaux Arts. My aim seemed to be an eighty-four-hour week, no commuting and no salary, which anybody can have if he really wants it.

The working conditions were ideal. It was great to get up at the crack of dawn, do a full day's work before breakfast, and after another long day's work loll around in the cool of the evening and do still another day's work by artificial light.

I developed a personal method of caulking that would have got me fired from any fourth-rate yard. There were lots of old nail holes to be plugged and broken bits of nails to be extracted. A pair of shoemaker's clippers, which I had learned to manipulate, persuaded the most stubborn ones to come out.

A dentist friend came by one day. "You're just the man I'm looking for!" I set him to work with the clippers. I watched him struggle in vain for an hour to extract one little nail. You learn a lot about people from a boat.

My English bulldog came out and made himself at home on the port bunk. He was a creature to whom God and Nature had denied the primary condition of survival. He was completely lacking in the most elementary protective device—he was utterly devoid of fear. His name was Sonny Boy, being no doubt a product of the Jolson era, and he had belonged to a motorcycle cop who had trained him to ride the bike and fight. His reaction to anything that touched bottom with all fours was cataclysmic. He was a social menace. With the acquisition of *Princess* I was beginning to suspect that I had a certain affinity for that kind of thing.

His devotion to me was abject to a point of embarrassment. Unlike most dogs that I have known, he didn't know how to bark or cry. When he was excited he would holler, and when he was sad he would sing. The rest of the time he snored. Every time I went down to do some work on the bottom, Sonny Boy would dive off the deck and land with a crunch that made me fear for his bones. When I went back on deck, he would get hung up on the ladder or fall, time after time, on his back until I carried him up. In this world of boats whatever fear he had was all for me. He had to be right there every minute lest this strange sea creature gobble me up. If I tried to tie him down, he would sing a wild dirge that was calculated to wake the dead. I had my hands full.

My *Princess* really looked lovely with her chain plates and bowsprit back on and a gleaming white coat of gloss on her top-sides. I installed the magneto on the motor and filled her gas tank, which looked very much like an old hot-water boiler that had escaped from somebody's kitchen and gone to sea in the engine department. It was no trick to get the engine going. A couple of turns on the flywheel with the carburetor choked, and she was primed. Another turn and off she went. At least there was no shriek for attention from this quarter. She ran cool and with surprisingly little vibration at half-throttle. I didn't bother to open her up for fear of shaking apart that section of the vessel that had not been rebuilt. I was contented and grounded her off.

From the early days of spring I had watched the boats go down into the water. One by one the yard had emptied itself of its foul-weather friends. The excitement of launchings, the beer parties, the plans for rendezvous, the high spirits were all consigned to the past. Now the sun beat down and the wind swept dust and chips of wood and bits of caulking cotton across the yard. Only *Princess* was left. She huddled next to the shed as if she were a little afraid of the sea. With a disease like hers I would have been afraid to go swimming myself.

Now at last it was her turn. My heart beat fast. The boys came over, put down the greased planks, and snatched her away. It seemed incredible that the thing I had looked forward to for so many months, that I had labored so long and so hard to have happen, could take place so quickly and with so little fuss.

There followed a ritual, however, that has persisted down through the years. It is symbolic of the length of work and the shortness of time. It has taken place at every launching of *Princess* since; it has been observed in Flushing, City Island, Edgewater, Cape May, Annapolis, Norfolk, Oxford, Moorehead City, Charleston, St. Augustine, Palm Beach, and College Point. It is a simple ceremony unmarked by either frills or dignity. She had me chasing after her into the water with a last brushload of paint.

3

There she lay beside a floating dock in Flushing. Her thirsty planks nursed at the water that cradled her. She dribbled like a baby while the wood swelled. I pumped. Any boatman has a right to be proud of a tight, dry hull. I had a wonderful pump.

The persistent little sea that collected between the floors and under the old engine was referred to as *mare nostrum*, and was returned regularly by the scruff of the neck to the system of oceans, like a stray pet. There was hope, of course. Not the kind of hope that grows into a big, fat fantasy while you sit around and twiddle thumbs. The skinny critter I'm talking about was being fed with long, thin wisps of caulking cotton while I crawled around in the wet bilge with a lantern. Gently, very gently, the strips were being inserted in the larger leaks between the planking with a nail file. One wrong move, one sharp thrust, and the whole gasket of cotton would be shoved right out of the bottom, and I would have to beach her. The pressure of the water was my friend on the other side. We got along. The third night it rained, and the miracle happened: The fifty-year-old planks, now firmly tied with bronze to the new frames, squeezed themselves together and closed the last remaining gap.

Somewhere on the coast of Maine old Wilbur A. Morse, builder of *Princess*, had he known, would have breathed easier. She was dry. All up and down the Atlantic Coast, in among the Lakes, scattered in surprising corners of the world, recognizable bits and pieces of little vessels constructed in this old man's yard are rotting in a tidal marsh or crumbling in the sun. Some are still afloat, endlessly butted together and full of strange repairs, inept and loving.

In their day these little boats beat their way into far harbors and turned the heads of boatbuilders. A man who knows boats can tell by the look of a vessel whether she is right. All down through the Caribbean into Central and even South America, the "American Boat" looked right, and native builders strove to copy her. Many of them did a better job than Charley Morse, who worked right up the bay in Thomaston. The trouble with Charley was that he was too close to the prophet, and his transom was too big.

A good sailing vessel is a thousand boats in one. She is a different hull on every different course and in every degree of tilt as she heels over. Within a moment in a changing seaway she may present a score of different contours to the water. This was the last dream of a great generation of boatbuilders, and, like men carving little models of great ships that have foundered long ago, they poured out their skill, their knowledge, and their love. They named them sweetly too—like *Princess*.

The magic moment that marks the end of a long job can creep up on you. The job of rebuilding was far from thorough, but suddenly I knew that for now she was ready. I didn't have time to be excited about it. I just went down below and started up the engine. All hell broke loose!

Sonny Boy, constantly underfoot and giving every evidence of being a landlubber regardless of who rules the waves, had been eying the smelly little engine from the time he first set paws on *Princess*. Now he lashed out and attacked it with all the ferocity of an inveterate canvas man. All was quiet again when he finished chewing off the ignition wires. Then he sat in the bilge and grinned from ear to ear, literally.

Somebody was going to have to make a decision. I looked around. There was nobody but Sonny Boy and me. The kind of decision that Sonny Boy would make would have us both in Fiddler's Green. It was up to me. I called his godmother, an old landlady who let me have him when he took to shacking up in my studio, and back went Sonny Boy. It was sad but not hopeless. I was determined to rig something, find a way to make a sailor out of him. It wasn't that he was afraid of the sea. Sonny Boy was afraid of nothing. But the sea is itself a clumsy rough dog, and you have to outwit her at every turn. The direct approach is loaded, and nothing can be more direct than an English bulldog. For the moment I needed both hands free for *Princess*.

First I squared things away down below. The ignition wires were replaced, and a good thing, too. The icebox and the little black stove that said "MARINE HOUSEHOLD" on the oven door were secured to the hull with the spare turnbuckles. Everything worked for its passage on *Princess*.

I rigged her. A lot of it was wrong. In fact, some of the errors have become standard practice aboard my vessel. The forward shroud is still, after all these years, the after one. The most meticulous yachtsmen have never said anything about it, and if the mast knows it is too polite to mention it. The cockpit was a masterpiece of cleats and some Old World cabinetmaker's art. I could never quite figure out whether it was supposed to be Louis the Fourteenth or Chippendale. From the condition of it, I guess it was mostly Chippendale.

The sails were bent on. The big main, all stretched out of shape and baggy along the foot from endless tension on the outhaul, the clubfooted staysail that trimmed itself, and the working jib were made ready. It was morning, and there was a little breeze. I raised her staysail, freed her lines, and moved out into the bay. In the afternoon it blew.

Princess cut through the water like a thing alive. She pivoted on a point and clawed into the teeth of the wind. The long boom that stretched out over her counter and reaching bowsprit held a proud expanse of sail. She was slippery, all right, and there was hardly a ripple aft. I had myself a boat!

I sailed past the old fort up to Stepping Stones and back. The wind blew steady from the west. A light spray whipped across and washed the yard dust from her deck. With that enormous mainsail she carried a strong weather helm, which is as it should be. Among the things that a fisherman can't afford besides season tickets to the opera is a jibe with a deckload of fish while he's tending his lines.

Years before I had heard about the way a Friendship handles herself, about the miraculous balance that keeps her on her course hour after hour with no one at the helm. Now I would find out whether all the lies they told were true. I lashed the tiller. She was steady. I watched the compass card for long minutes. It seemed glued to the glass. I stretched my legs along the deck, stepped out on the bowsprit to watch her bow slice the water, went down below to see if the freeboard planks had made up yet. Why are planks so bashful? Then, like the old shipmaster checking over the helmsman's shoulder, I looked again. She was as steady on her course as if she carried an invisible pilot. I had the old-time wooden version of an Iron Mike. Now if she could only cook!

I couldn't resist preening my fine feathers, slightly mildewed maybe, in front of the boatyard back in Flushing. I swung in between the moorings and the two dolphins and came about smartly by the floating dock. There was a man standing there alone, watching. It was the man who sold me the boat.

It is now twenty-five years since I first went off to sea as a deckhand on the S. S. *Tuscaloosa City*, an ambivalent ship bound, according to its articles, for "port or ports in India." That ship lies now at the bottom of the North Sea. There are no more decisions for her to make. There are many other ships I have known, from great tankers to the tiny tugs that I risked brain and being— mostly being—to deliver in the far Pacific. The memory of ships and places tends to congeal into a luminous thing that I can hold before my eye. This of all things I remember—the sea washes out in an hour all the ugly memories of the land. I invited my poor fabricating friend for a ride. Did I say poor? I was glad to have him aboard. At least till we got out in deep water.

We sailed in silence back over the same course. This man, who had taken my hard-earned money in exchange for a worthless wreck, sat for free on the bridge deck and stared down below at the rows of new framing and the hard stout stem clamped with gleaming bronze. "If I could only have done it," he said.

My foot was getting warmed up kicking the tiller. I did a lot of listening. "If I could only have done it," he said. "I can't even drive a nail."

"Screws," I said, "bronze screws." *Princess* turned, close-hauled, and tore back. I dropped him on the end of the long dock, where the J. P. Morgan yacht used to lie. He stood on the end of the pier watching as the wind took us away. I never saw him again.

I took my ship to the floating dock and put a harbor furl in her sail. It was high time for a celebration. I called everybody I could think of, collect, iced her up, and took on a general cargo, generally beer.

The next morning I stretched out on the deck in the sun, read the newspaper, and waited for the gang to show up. I hadn't had time to read a paper in weeks. According to what I read, the old world was still aspinning. Some monkey by the name of Hitler was kicking the gong around. The Giants were trailing in the National League, and wheat was $1.50 a bushel in Chicago. Was this the world I lived in? It was hard to believe. I read every little word like a man just returned from a brief ten-year visit to the North Pole. My eye fell on a wee item that jumped out at me like a front-page streamer: "HURRICANE HEADING THIS WAY."

A tropical hurricane that originated in the Caribbean, with winds estimated to be over one hundred and twenty miles an hour, is reported to be traveling north at a speed of approximately ten miles an hour. It has bypassed Florida. Warnings are posted along Cape Hatteras. Unless it veers sharply to the East, it will strike the vicinity of New York and New England sometime Wednesday.

This was Sunday morning.

On my trip to India ten years before we had been belabored by a hurricane. More than the danger and the sight of a steel deck bending like wet paper, I remembered the solemn expression on the face of a weather-beaten Swede who always tied the paint can on the deck to a stanchion, even if the sea was as calm as a lake. Hurricane! I remembered walking on one bulkhead and then on the other as we broached, turning, to run before the wind.

A steel vessel had seemed to be a thing of infinite strength.

It isn't. In relation to its size it is an eggshell. If my little boat was enlarged in every respect from twenty-six feet to about five hundred, the planking would be twenty inches thick and the frames would be twenty-by-forties of solid oak. No ship is that strong. If he could stand being rolled about in a barrel for days on end, a man could survive anything in *Princess*.

The gang showed up one by one, and we restowed some of the iced cargo waiting for the stragglers. It was one of those lazy days. We ghosted out into the Sound. Now and then someone dove overboard, and most of us went after him. There was no ladder. We doused the mainsail and rigged the gaff as a derrick to hoist the fat ones back on deck.

Later the wind strengthened, and we settled down to some serious sailing. With nine of us aboard, the old girl felt more at home. She strutted.

Past Execution Light and on up along the mainland side, she was almost a match for the racing machines. This didn't set so well with the racing folk. They expected to pass me as if I had snagged a lobster pot. When I passed them, which I did now and then in half a gale, they lost all interest in the history of American yacht design and changed their course.

It was near dark when we rounded the long pier and prepared to make her fast. Everybody wanted to go home, but right away. They always do. The cargo I had stowed had enough specific gravity to make me part mule. Being a simple soul, a fact attested by a document proving my ownership of a sixty-year-old boat, I believed what I read. I had read about a hurricane.

"What hurricane?" they taunted, the infidels, pointing at the innocent sky. I could hardly hear them for the wild roar of the Indian Ocean. I was the last one ashore in my silly little punt with its six inches of freeboard. I pulled it up on the floating dock and took one last look at *Princess* in the failing light. An anchor cable was fast to one dolphin, and a delightful daisy chain of frayed hemp and rusty links around her rudderpost held her stern to the other. We all went home.

Sonny Boy greeted me like a missing soldier home at last. I

was unimpressed. He did the same thing every time I went out for a pack of cigarettes. I looked at all the unfinished paintings in my studio. I had art and financial fences to repair.

On the other side of the great window that swamped the place with north light, the days grew gray and it rained. Out in the park a badly planted tree toppled over in a gust of wind. The barometer looked demented. It must have been tapped on the head once too often. I went about my business. Then the phone rang. "Better get out here in a hurry! Your boat—." The phone went dead.

I ducked into a subway. There was a gale in the street. Out in Flushing the buses were few and far between. When I found one, it struck a wet reef and disgorged its fares. I clawed my way from tree to tree against the ripping weight of the wind. It was a trek through tossed salad garnished with live wires.

By the time I made it to the yard the crest of the storm had passed. There was still a foot of floodwater, but the wind had backed around. I saw the old man.

"What happened to my punt?"

"Where was it?"

"On the dock."

"Hell, the dock's gone!"

Princess was still afloat, tethered to the dolphins fore and aft. "How did she ride it?" I asked.

"She rode it like a duck," said the old man from the State of Maine.

When the sea receded, I was taken out to *Princess*. She was what you call utterly unperturbed. The beach was littered with wreckage. The bay was jammed with a flotilla of debris. Trees were broken and uprooted. Some had gone to sea. As if in retaliation, an armada of boats had invaded the shore to the extent of a mile and a half. It was as if Nature in a sudden temper of dissatisfaction had decided, like an impetuous painter, that the picture was all wrong and smeared it over for a fresh start. From the look of things, there were going to have to be a lot of fresh starts. The boat carpenters were undoubtedly busy sharpening their tools.

24

The fascination of disaster held me to the place for hours. From my studio, deep in the city, the hurricane had seemed no more than a stiff breeze. This was carnage.

It was long after dark when I left the place. As I walked through the streets, circling and climbing over the wreckage, it seemed unreal that *Princess* should have survived. What storms she had known, what rocks had grazed her keel, the strange inanimate determination of the tight-lipped planking that had kept her afloat for sixty years of hard usage, I would never know. But there she was, tossing her pretty little tail in the teeth of havoc, all unscathed. There was something beyond my ken in all this, something about the will of man, endlessly resurgent, beating back the inexorable persistence of nature—something to think about in the subway.

4

When I was a kid, I used to sleep on the back porch in the summertime. In the early morning the sunlight glanced along the stucco wall and made pictures. I remember giant seas smashing against rocks, and wonderful cloud formations. As the sun rose the scene slowly changed till at last the sun fell fair upon the wall and it was nothing but white.

We lived twenty miles from the coast, and a little river that twisted along under the hill was all I knew about the water. I remember collecting barrel hoops for ribs and building a boat with tar paper swiped from a building going up across the street. It looked good in the magazine, but it didn't stay afloat long enough to let me get on board.

When I was sixteen, I obtained dubious title to a sailing

dory in Boothbay Harbor, Maine, for five dollars. What with the beard of marine life that was attached to its bottom, and a general absence of lateral resistance, she wouldn't even run across the wind, to say nothing of tack. Nevertheless, I made elaborate plans for a singlehanded voyage clear out to Monhegan Island, which lay twenty miles to the east in the open sea. She was provisioned —a jug of water, a loaf of bread, and a rock tied to a line for ground tackle. I took off in the morning with a gentle breeze.

About an hour later, after traveling a mile or so down past the little private island and heading for the point, I was overtaken by a man with a great white beard, rowing a skiff. He headed straight for me. I recognized him. He was the old man, well past ninety, who sat on a porch day in and day out and stared. I thought of him as an invalid. What was he doing out in a boat?

Without a word he grabbed my painter. Invalid or no, he was definitely off his rocker. Maybe it was a joke. I hollered at him. He paid me no mind, made my painter fast to a thwart on the skiff, and towed me all the way back to the dock.

While he made my dory good and fast to a piling, and while I fumed over this infringement of the freedom of the seas, a fog rolled across and covered us like a quilt, thick and impenetrable. I meant to thank him; I couldn't even find him.

Princess was the natural culmination of these things.

After surviving the hurricane and yielding a paltry couple of weekends of sailing, she decided to spring a leak. It wasn't a bad leak, although I have yet to hear of a good one. It wouldn't sink her—that might well have been a mercy. It was just bad enough to keep me enmeshed in a vague sense of apprehension as I tried to go about my business. In the middle of my day I would get panicky and dash all the way out to Flushing to take care of her.

When I got out, I'd find a mere six inches of water slopping about her floorboards. Never any more. It baffled me till at last I discovered what old Archimedes had found out while floating properly inside a tub. As soon as the ton of inside pig iron ballast in her bilge was flooded, it lost in weight the equivalent of the weight of the water it displaced, and water, as you know if you've ever been hit with a paper bag full, is very heavy stuff.

It is also wet and kind of deep here and there. I began to think about hauling her out. But first I wanted to find the leak. It's as hard to find a leak in a boat up on the ways as it is to find one in a roof when it isn't raining. It had no intention of spending a whole winter weighing the pros and debating the cons about that leak.

My stock of patience was getting low, and I was fresh out of South Sea Islands divers with leather lungs and long hair that drifts into the leaks. I broke out my trusty flashlight and a bucket and a sponge, and took to the bilge for a nice afternoon's crawl.

At two o'clock in the morning I was still playing hide-and-go-seek with that leak. I was just getting warm—to use the word in a strictly technical sense, as I was numb with cold—when the leak stopped. You can expect miracles of mercy but very little fair play from the sea. "There are more things in heaven and earth, Horatio, Than are dreamt of in your philosophy," said Hamlet. What he forgot to mention was that there are also a few things floating half-submerged in the sea that decide all of a sudden to make like a cork.

Now, at least the nice, clean salt water that was so anxious to get into the filthy bilge could content itself in constantly crowding that blessed bit of flotsam into the hole. I wanted to sail right on into November, just as long as the Sound didn't ice over.

I had the coal stove set up with a Charlie Noble that got tangled up in the mainsheet so often that it lost most of its nobility. Bent and battered as it was, it created a fine draft for the little stove. Being a green hand in the coal business, I was intrigued by the relative ease of igniting and, particularly, of obtaining soft coal. There were barges around overflowing with the stuff. Also, at this stage of the game, my being more or less impervious to the opinions of people, there was no mirror on *Princess*. The colder it got, the darker my complexion became. I was getting a bituminous tan. Then, as they say in the ads, I switched to anthracite. My friends began to recognize me again.

One old shipmate—I had sailed to India with him on a

freighter—decided to get the low-down on this boating business. He was in the black gang, an oiler. We called him Slivers. I picked him up off a wharf and set a course to the east. Slivers went down below and drew the hatch cover over him. The wind was fair, it was late in the afternoon, and I settled down at the tiller. The Charlie Noble began to belch forth a continuous long cloud of smoke. Slivers was stoking her up.

Now and then a tattooed arm reached out from the cabin and handed me a cup of coffee or a crude sandwich. I was warm and snug in a big sheepskin coat, the *Princess* was steering herself. The stars came out all shiny, and the lights along the shore were like lights along any shore at night. It could have been Karachi or Ceylon. Bombay was no different in the dark. I could almost smell the fragrance of the tropical jungle sensed far out at sea that often spoke a landfall long before the eye could see a light. Or was it that stove? He sure had a head of steam down there.

We were heeled way over now, driving toward Middle Ground. I had picked up the light at Stratford Shoal blinking every ten seconds. The name of a light repeated and repeated, over and over again, by interval of time between winks is a thing a sailor can watch by the hour without being bored. It is like the name of someone he loves spoken in a long corridor of darkness, endlessly constant, endlessly comforting.

Princess was whipping along now to the limit of her lines. It occurred to me that all the power in the world could hardly add a knot to her speed. All at once she began to vibrate and give forth with a rapid put-put-put. The engine department had resisted temptation for as long as it could be endured. In my world of canvas, power had reared its ugly head. Slivers had started the engine. I let him run it to keep him happy.

I decided to backtrack and hole up for the night in Stamford Harbor. It was long past midnight, and since Slivers showed no inclination for the great outdoors, I was shorthanded on deck.

I had good reason to humor Slivers, who was toasting himself down below between the heat of the stove and the engine. More than ten years before Slivers had had occasion to command a ship from the engine room. It was only for a second, but it was enough. It saved the ship, its cargo, and a whole mess of reputations.

I was at the wheel. According to law, no ordinary seaman may act as quartermaster within a hundred miles of land. I was an ordinary seaman. I liked to steer, the mate thought I was good, and the tape in the chartroom that records the course seemed to prove it. The old-timers knew better. "When the kid is at the wheel," they'd say, leaning on the taffrail, "the steering engine uses more steam than the turbine."

The crew's quarters were right over the steering engine, and it was a long way to the bridge. Those were the days before the left-and-right-rudder law. The order was starboard when the pilot wanted port and port when he wanted starboard, which to a man who understands a tiller is the most natural thing in the world.

It was hot, as I recall, and the wind was aft, blowing off the desert. We were taking the ship through the Suez. I had been at the wheel for more than an hour, holding her right on the ranges every moment. The pilot, seeing how I handled her, relaxed and got into a bull session with the old man. Suddenly, as we came into the lake, he turned and said in impeccable English, "Starboard your helm."

The wheel looked like a wheel to me. It wasn't a tiller and it wasn't a cow's tail. Starboard was to the right, so I threw the wheel over to the right and that was that.

The ship lurched into a soft bank. A split second before the telegraph rang the engine stopped, and by the time anyone could signal full astern she was thrashing her way out of the trap. Slivers was down below at the controls. He felt her strike and just anticipated the orders a little bit. Good old Slivers! Ships which cannot be refloated in twenty-four hours after going aground and blocking the canal are blown away with dynamite.

The ship was freed. I received a polite request from the mate after my temporary banishment from the bridge not to divulge my status to any snooping English pilots. Henceforth I was

30

to be a dumb able-bodied seaman instead of a promising ordinary one, a title to which I seemed eminently qualified. The skipper of that ship became the Coast Guard inspector out in Texas before he passed away. Fortunately, I sat for my mate's ticket in Charleston. As for the ship, she sank later under very suspicious circumstances. It seems there was a war going on.

It was two in the morning when *Princess* rounded The Cows and nosed her way in between the jetties. The wind had dropped to a whisper. I doused her sails and banged on the deck to stop the engine. When the hook was down I went below. What I found beggars description. Slivers, a strange denizen of the nether world of engine rooms, had hiked the temperature of the cabin up to around a hundred and thirty degrees Fahrenheit. The paint on the overhead was all bubbled up; the top of the stove was pink and sagging with the heat till it looked like a washbasin. Slivers was fast asleep, snoring fit to wake the dead. I dragged a mattress and blanket out on the bridge deck and went to sleep.

5

The honeymoon was slowly drawing to a close. For a girl old enough to be my grandmother, *Princess* had been a terribly balky bride. But she was getting younger every day, and I was getting older. The way I figured it, by the time I was her age I would have replaced enough frames, beams, and planks to make her practically a debutante. Then it would be my turn to balk.

Between little voyages to the near reaches of Long Island Sound I lay on the bunk and studied her anachronistic carcass from the inside.

The deck was gone. Looking up from the inside gave the illusion of being in a cage. Between the shrunken strips I could watch the clouds go by. I could also tell immediately when it rained. I got in the habit of sleeping under an umbrella. In dry weather little bits of the rotten deck beams continually dropped into the bunk. *Princess* ate crackers in bed!

My short little voyages turned into journeys of exploration. Wrecking can be as much fun as building, and I got that old itch for the feel of a pry bar. I was in search of a place nearer home where I could devote less time to commuting and more to slum clearance.

City Island seemed the answer. I turned in behind the north end of the island against a strong tide and a fresh wind. The place was jammed with little boats moored with hardly room to swing. The lesson of the hurricane had been lost on this gang, but the pedagogic old blowhard would be back someday.

I tacked back and forth against the mounting strength of the tide, skimming by inches between the hundred little boats. After a couple of hours of this, which was fun, I came up into the wind and asked a portly old gentleman who was standing on the dock about hauling out. He welcomed me. In fact, he practically gave me the place. Mr. Rosenberger was another old-time canvas man. *Princess* must have been quite a belle in her time. There were an awful lot of her old lovers still around.

It snowed. I came out during the winter and built a fire in the little stove. I dreamed while Mr. Kretzer down the street bent some more frames for my baby.

In the spring she was stiffened up right past her bridge deck. I put a decent floor under her engine and drew her underbody up into shape. I had company. Some boys were adding freeboard to a long racing shell, making it look like an oversize model of a Hog Island freighter.

There was a spill on the ways, which is about as sad a thing to see as a gull getting caught in a rattrap. They lifted the poor yawl back on her feet gently and did the best they could to mend her side. It has happened in the best of yards. But never to *Princess*. She never gets into the best of yards. I have seen her shimmy and shake, wobble and sway on the car all the way down the track until the agony was relieved by the gentle bed of water that rose around her belly. She always kept her footing like a good girl. She must be part mountain goat—and she could kick, too.

It happened just as I warped the last top plank of new oak around her shapely side and clamped it. I had turned and bent over to pick up a tool when she let me have it. The clamp let go and the plant hit me like a hoof. I landed in the dirt with the painful realization that the old girl wanted out. She'd had enough renovating for one spring, so I launched her.

It had been a sad winter and a mournful spring for me. Sonny Boy of the indomitable courage had an Achilles' heel. Beneath his foreboding exterior he was practically all Achilles' heel. Sonny Boy loved. He could stand no harsh words from those to whom he gave the full measure of his capacity for affection. The tiniest reprimand or a pointed tone in the voice would send him scurrying under the bed, where he would cower in abject penance for hours. Enemies he devoured with a shrug. For friends the thick hide was a thin membrane, painful to the touch, the massive skull an eggshell.

There was a fire in the landlady's apartment when I was away. She screamed at the dog in terror for his life. Somehow to Sonny Boy it must have sounded like an awful chastisement. He hunched his shoulders and crept sadly under the bed. I found him when the smoke cleared, asleep for good.

There wasn't much to come home to now. My studio seemed like a great glass vault, facing out on a panorama of nothing. I began to understand why my colleagues were painting weird forms and amorphic shapes. The cold, hard angularity of the city, the square corners, and the rigid architectural formality made these lalapaloozas they were painting a fast pitch for nature. Some of them weren't even bothering to paint them. They would just go and find goofy wooden drift children out on a lonely expanse of beach and drag them back on the IRT during the rush hour. They looked good on the wall. They looked better on the beach.

If they weren't busy doing that, they were hornswoggling a bit of good farmland from some limpid-eyed ex-pioneer and setting up, at the end of nowhere, a bit of frigid architecture inspired by a zoning law, complete with everything but a window for the cashier.

Princess made more sense to me. She was a home with personality. At times her personality was a bit obstreperous, even demanding, but she had mobility in her disposition and a capacity for contentment. I gave the keys to my studio back to the Indians. They gave me my deposit back. I added three more quarters to it and parlayed it for a silver dollar, which went into the slot in the mast step before I shipped the newly varnished mast.

I had a brand-new set of sails. The mainsail was a beauty —it set like a wing of a plane. The genoa and the spinnaker were recut from some Egyptian cotton sails off an English racing schooner that had foundered. The storm trysail was so tightly woven that it had to be beaten into submission to be stowed when wet. The old girl was a dream in her new cotton. We were a gay couple as we waltzed out of City Island and I pointed her graceful bowsprit toward the east.

Princess was dry. I had caulked her meticulously and plugged every old nail hole I could find. There wasn't a spot of water on the inside of her planking as she gurgled along. She was well provisioned, too. I had stacked cans of food between the frames from the garboard all the way up to the turn of the bilge. When one was used, the rest would roll down into position like a dispensing machine.

As dry as she was, the labels had a tendency to peel off, so that getting a meal became a kind of gastronomical lottery. When I thought I might be opening a can of soup, it would turn out to be pineapple juice. So I had pineapple juice. Facing up to a can of cold condensed vegetable soup instead of orange juice first thing in the morning was awful.

The little black stove that bore the legend "MARINE HOUSE-HOLD" had come in for its share of rebuilding. The firebricks with which it was lined and which gave the oven a steady heat were largely cracked and had powdered away. A telephone survey in quest of firebricks had brought one hopeful answer from the Lower East Side.

The shop, when I finally found it, looked as if it had been there since the days of the clipper ships. It was down on the Bowery, and it lay below the level of the street under the shadow of the elevated train. The proprietor, an old man with a full-rigged beard, knew all about the stove. It had been made at least sixty years ago. The company that made it was long out of business. I began to revise upward the probable age of *Princess*. Yes, he might have bricks to fit it, but there hadn't been a call for them in forty years. He searched for hardly more than a minute among the millions of bricks of every conceivable shape and size and then he came up with them. They were stamped with the words "MARINE HOUSEHOLD." I was amazed. He handed them to me casually, as if they were delivered to him fresh every day. For clay that old, they were dirt-cheap.

It was July and hot—too hot for any serious cooking. The stove, which had imparted a living temperature to *Princess* in the cold days of the previous autumn, now gave her a high fever. I jettisoned all the coal from the bin under the stove and substituted thin strips of kindling. A quick, hot fire with the top off the stove enabled me to heat up a pot of soup or fry a fish without the dubious advantage of having to eat it in a Turkish bath.

A gentle south wind and a couple of fair tides drew the boat down toward the end of the Island. I had bypassed all the immediate harbors in search of far places. My first port of call was to be Sag Harbor. *Princess*, built in the last hours of the old whaling days, was going into territory she knew.

When I left City Island, I couldn't resist the challenge of beating out around the south end against a strong tide and a head wind. I couldn't resort to power. Old Mr. Rosenberger was watching me from the bridge. The stories he told me about the days when little boats like mine were as common as cars were still in my ears. "And they could handle them, too, like you can."

So it was late, almost dark, when I got out of that bight and turned to catch the fair south wind. I sailed all night. Early the next morning I dropped the hook in the shadow of the lighthouse at Old Field Point, and while *Princess* played tag with the heavy yellow pine skiff she was dragging, I slept.

I got underway around noon. The wind was coming in a bit toward the east, and in the late afternoon a fog shut down. I broke out the horn and pursued my course in the direction of Plum Gut. I thought I heard singing.

It was actually the most magnificent music I had ever heard—a great chorus of voices in flawless harmony, floating out across the water. I began to wonder whether I had been touched by this small-boat business. Crazy or not, the chorus of voices swelled to majestic proportions. It was strange music. Island music, jungle music. I altered my course.

As I slowly came out of the fog, I could see the outline of a great fishing trawler. Alongside it were two long-boats forming a triangle with the side of the mother ship. More than twenty men, black men from the islands, were jubilantly hauling a tremendous catch of dancing, golden fish out of that triangle of water. They must have been working on shares. No wonder they were happy.

I hung around listening for an hour. When I drifted in close, they threw me a fat fish and two more for luck. Then they cut away into the fog, leaving only the intermittent sound of the hoarse foghorn. I went back on my course.

Night came on, and the way was obscured by the double blanket of mist and darkness. The time I had lost drifting around listening to the music made it impossible for *Princess* to reach Plum Gut by nightfall. The concert had been a treat. I was going to have to pay for it.

I groped my way through obscurity, propelled by a cold, wet wind and retarded by the flooding tide. It must have been midnight when I got too tired to care and decided to let *Princess* take over. I lowered her sails, hung a bright lantern on her forestay, rigged a bell so it would ring as she rolled, and paid out the anchor cable. When I came to the end of the cable, the anchor was still aweigh. I bent on another forty-foot length. Still no bottom.

This was all the heavy line she carried, so I borrowed the mainsheet, doubled it up, and fed it into the sea.

Now the anchor rested on the bottom with no scope and no holding power. She would certainly drag, but according to the chart I was in the deepest water in that area. Right in the shipping lane, too. If she dragged she was bound to drift into shoal water, or she would hold as the slack increased.

As I slept I dreamed that a great steamship bore down on me and *Princess* pitched and rolled with her wash. The bell was tolling wildly when I leaped up on deck. I saw the stern light of the steamer as it was swallowed by the fog. It was no dream.

There is a repetitive quality about the sea. One wave follows another, the tides are never-ending. Troubles run in packs like wolves and lightning can strike the same spot as many times as it has a mind to. I began to haul at the hook, but it wouldn't budge.

The weight of all that cable plus fifty pounds of steel sunk into a soft bottom was beyond my strength. I rigged the mainsail hoist to the cable, and as the little ship rolled she broke it free. The brief nap I had managed to get in exchange for a terrible scare and a backbreaking struggle is the kind of a bargain you can generally strike with the sea.

The wind died to puffs, and I ran under power till dawn, sounding my way toward Plum Gut through the drifting haze. Whatever bad water there was lay close to land; my eyes were raw from peering into gloom.

Around ten in the morning I grounded off the engine and went below for a bite. When I came back on deck, I stood gaping. The horizon had shifted ninety degrees; it ran clear around up over my head and down under the boat. It was as if *Princess* were suspended between two luminous halves of darkness and light. I grabbed for a shroud and hung on. The boat was still in the water, but the whole world was standing on its ear.

Then, as the cloud bank rolled away, the world explained itself. I had come upon a thing that rarely happens. I never expect to see it again. The straight, hard edge of the fog cloud, cut as if

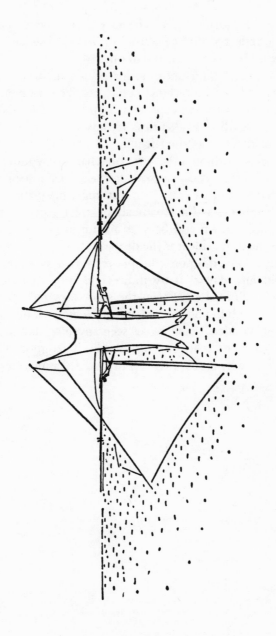

with a knife, had drifted over the face of the water and lent its image to the reflected surface of the sea. In the absence of any visible horizon, it created the illusion of one.

Picture a Mediterranean sailor of ancient times coming on such a thing. Here if anything could be the reason for a quick switch from the shaky concept of a round world to a safe platter of earth. The sea breeds skeptics. Its lessons are too often tricks done with mirrors to fool the faithful.

There is nothing in a city one half so wonderful as the things you see when you get away from it. I have seen the Indian Ocean turned to molten copper in a strange, prismatic accident of light. The copper seas one reads about are no poetic fancy; the water is reddish brown and fiery as a caldron as you look toward the sun. On the other side it is the deepest blue.

I have looked upon phosphorescent seas so bright they turned night into day as if by indirect lighting. Standing on the nearby Jersey shore, I have seen the sun's rays, split by the Palisades, turn every building in the City of New York into pure gold. But for sheer wonder, I have never seen anything like the way that fog bank turned the world up on its side. It's a good thing somebody was there when it happened. I'm glad it was me.

6

The lazy wind failed me on the passage through Plum Gut. *Princess* bobbed and weaved against that current for hours. The Race, on its way to meet the myriad appointments of a tide, forced part of its enormous bulk through the Gut. It was too much for the sturdy engine that had come to nest under the bridge neck.

Straining at the anchor cable, yawing and tossing her bowsprit at the oncoming sea, my boat had waited while I slept. When the tide turned I awoke. I always do when a change of course or any new set of conditions affects the roll of a ship. The wonderful mechanism in the ear that keeps a fellow on an even keel became part of the organic structure of the boat. I threw it in when I gave her my heart. *Princess*, a prissy little Down East schoolmarm with a wicked temper, had a happy faculty for indulgence when the chips were down.

Gardiner's Bay, whereinto *Princess* was poured by the effusive tide that swept her through Plum Gut, was green. I had never seen salt·water like it in this latitude; maybe it was the dust-free sky that lent it snap and clarity. *Princess*, her flank to the new north wind, raced across it like a wild mare in fresh clover. They say the grass is greener on the other side of the fence. The water is. I am no authority on grass.

Standing in the shadow of the lighthouse, an old man waved from Cedar Island as we cut past the point. A white cloud flew by along with a bird. I watched them, dreaming. The whaling ships lay ahead, huddled in the old Long Island harbor, their bowsprits casting wrinkled shadows on the cobbled streets. Barrels of whale oil hoisted from the holds were piled high on the quay. A horse's hoof struck sparks on the stone that had once been sailing ship ballast as the loaded wagons rumbled down the street. There were men up in the idle ships, moving in the wilderness of rigging, bending on clean canvas and tarring down the shrouds. The place hummed with the heat of work. Crowds of the curious, family, friends, sweethearts, pressed forward as a newly returned whaler was warped alongside the dock. Willing hands tugged at her lines. Now the din from the foundry was quiet; the grogshop down the street was deserted; sailmakers, still clad in their little canvas aprons, left their stools and milled around the dock as anxious eyes curried the gray ship for familiar faces. Coopers, shipwrights, caulkers, joiners, roustabouts, and riffraff rounded out the crowd and lent their voices to the babble. The town was deserted. Up on the cupola of a great white house on the hill a man in a fancy waistcoat unlimbered a long glass and focused it down on the ship. A woman with her face upturned clutched a shawl about her head and waited on his words. Four years is a long time to be away. Half-grown children who could hardly remember their fathers honeycombed the crowd. . . .

Princess slipped unnoticed into the little harbor just as the scene evaporated into the deceptive sky. The place was as clean as a whistle. Not a drop of whale oil, not a rotted spar or a rusty fastening to show for the days of her grandeur. A couple of tourists walked along the close-shaven lawn; a Snipe and a cruiser idled at their moorings. The dock was a white catwalk that led to a storybook yacht club, and a juke box sang "Why don't you fall in love" in the candy store down the street.

The water in the harbor was as warm as the breath of a whale. The heat absorbed from the sun in the great shoal areas of the Peconics was caught in this cove during the ebb of the tide. I went over the side and floated around in it like a straw in new milk. It had been too cold to swim in the Sound. Then, as I slept, the cold water coming back gurgled next to my ear. The sea at least would always be the same, and the sturdy spars of the whaling ships made abstract patterns above me in the sky.

The town of Sag Harbor had retained some of the flavor of the old days; great trees lined the streets, and the fine old houses still showed the knowing touch of the shipbuilder. I got into line with the tourists and saw the whaleboat in the front yard of the local museum and spent most of the morning pressing my nose against glass cases.

Princess was all alone in Sag Harbor now. The Snipe was out carousing in the bay, and the cruiser was gone. She was champing at her cable; I lifted her anchor, booked it over her starboard knighthead, and took her around into the warm Peconics.

Somewhere south of the Tropic of Capricorn foreign ships armed with converted cannon where busy blasting hell out of a race of whales with TNT. Back in Sag Harbor they were selling souvenir models of whaleboats for a living. A motor launch crowded with anglers was lying helpless in the bay. "Have you any gas?" they shrieked.

"Where do you want to go?" They pointed down wind to the dock about a mile away. "Pull up your hook."

After a great bobbing of heads as they talked it over, the anchor came up, and I watched as the launch drifted with a fair wind directly to the dock. I swung around and lit out for Block Island. I had illusions to take care of.

That evening a great gun-metal, spiral-shaped cloud rolled across from the mainland, and a gigantic flash of lightning like an inverted bare branch of a tree threw an instantaneous hot web across the sky. The flat hand of the wind struck *Princess*. The way she lay over and ducked under it gave me a wild laugh. Then she stood right up with her fine bow pointing right into the teeth of it and shook like a wet animal. I dropped her canvas in a hurry, and it poured.

For a few minutes it seemed as if the sea were tumbling from the sky. I was soaked. A cruiser loomed through the heavy rain, and a man called to me. I guess he had seen *Princess* lay over in the first explosion of wind, and when I doused the sails so fast, she had seemed to disappear.

He went on his merry way wrapped in plywood and plate glass replete with windshield wipers and an electric heater, no doubt, to toast his toes. The rain poured through the leaky deck of *Princess*, and most of my clothes and bedding were wringing wet. A fishing trawler heading home passed by. Men were squatting under her boat deck, nice and dry, drinking coffee. To be heard above the metallic rumble of the engines they shouted at one another. One man pointed at *Princess*. I heard him say, "That's the life!"

It wasn't so bad. The Montauk Point light, flashing every ten seconds steady as a star, was abeam at nine o'clock. The wind, still out of the east, was firm, and *Princess* cut a straight furrow with her tiller lashed. The big lighthouse on the southern end of Block Island was flashing its green light to come ahead. I went below and made a fire in the stove. It was cheerful. The warmth of the little stove drew the dampness out of my clothing, and a hot can of beans, a hamburger, and a cup of coffee tightened the turn-buckle between body and soul. I liked sailing at night. I knew where I was.

Daylight along an unfamiliar shore is full of all the distractions and duplications in the world. One lighthouse looks like another. Every bight, every point of land is a dead ringer for either the next one or the one you just passed. It is like reading a book full of endless annotation, references, and appendages. It becomes a soul-searching argument, and the sea always has the last word.

It is different at night. There is nothing to go by but faith. The chart is spread out before you, and every light that stabs through the gloom has its own message. There are no ifs, ands, and buts. Either you believe and guide yourself accordingly or you go down. That is how faith is practiced at night along a treacherous coast. Skepticism starts far out of sight of land where the abundance of sea room gives scope to the doubts of man.

Once a ship rounds over the edge of the horizon and picks up a light, all argument must cease, and the authority of the chart becomes the holy word. A landfall during the hours of daylight in the absence of local knowledge is full of trepidation, backtracking, and palaver. Give me the night!

After a couple of hours the wind veered to the southeast, grew violent, and came to blows with the emptying flow of the tide. The bell was hammering like a lunatic on the red buoy at Southwest Ledge; six miles to go. It was rough. Despite the twenty-five feet of water that covered it, an occasional comber raked across. I gave it a wide berth.

Princess was closehauled with her heavy canvas staysail taking the strain. I would have liked to get the headsail down, but it was too wild out there to fool around. When a hard gust came, I slacked it off, spilled some of the wind, and hung on. There is a factor of safety in speed, and the old girl was sure pouring it on.

Midnight came. I saw lights high up and heard the roar of a scenic railway coming from the island. As the little vessel pounded through the sharp high sea, all life was impossible down below. The bell, the lantern, any and all loose gear became unshipped and went rolling into the bilge.

At last I had the big Block Island light a point abaft the port beam. I turned and ran before the wind. She flew down alongside the island to the little old harbor like a chicken going places in a gale, with her feet barely touching the sea. She wanted to get in as badly as I did. The chart was reduced to pulp from the spray that tore across the deck. I rescued the precious piece that showed the great stone jetty, plastered it down to the bridge deck, and took a good last look with a flashlight. Then I took another look and, for all I know, another. Hard over went the tiller, jammed between the coaming and my heel, and we came about. She made it, with the assist of a slant of wind from off the hills, which drove *Princess* along the great granite rocks of the jetty, right into the inner harbor with all sail set. I unclenched my teeth.

The cozy little harbor was alive with fishing vessels tied up four deep against the dock. They were holed up, out of the storm. There was no roller coaster on the hill—that was the thunder of surf I had heard piling way up on the rocks. A group of old fishermen was sitting on a bench in the shelter of the icehouse. They saw me come in. I was their boy.

My little boat lay in the lee of a great trawler for days while the sea spent her spleen against the cliffs of Block Island. *Princess* made friends. Fishermen crawled all over her and explained in minute detail the function of such a boat. Some said she was a lobster boat. She could twist around in half her length to pick up a marker. Others swore that she was a boon to the handline fisherman. To still others she had been just the thing to drag a seine. The old gal had been all things to all men. Some even wished they had her now—war clouds loomed; gas might be short.

I lay on the beach in the sun and looked at the sky. Most of the time I gorged myself on lobster. Old Harold Dunn showed me where I could catch them and all the fish I could eat. I like that kind of fishing, right out of the well of his trawler. When I was done on both sides, I put the sun away on top of an old straw hat and climbed the hills. Once my appetite was whetted, it took only one look at the unbelievable majesty of those cliffs and back to town I went, hired a bicycle, and joined the scenery stiffs from the mainland.

I went to sea when I was still a kid. Most of what I have seen all over the world has been the sea and the edge of the land, and that's all right, too. Once in a while, when I could give the bos'n the slip, I got ashore and rubbernecked around. I have never seen the hills of Scotland or the Lake country. Except for Gibraltar and a good look through the glass at a coastal town, all that I know of Spain is *Toledo in a Storm* by El Greco. I have seen a lot of the West and Mexico, and I have looked down from that high crazy road to Caracas back on La Guaira and the swirl of the Caribbean. I am related, through *Princess*, to every pebble on this Eastern Coast. But to go the gamut, make mine Block Island.

The poetry of the place, the hills, the sudden break down to a pattern of beach, the lake in its bosom, the intrusion of the sea, and the gnarled fingers of land are too much. It has everything. Besides, I came upon it in the night.

It was still blowing when I left the old harbor. The fishermen saw me leave, and many a bushy eyebrow was raised. A channel had been cut into the island on the northwestern side, and the island now was largely harbor. I wanted to see more of it from the water, so I went clear around. It took longer than I had figured.

It was evening and blowing hard when I dropped the hook in Great Salt Pond. I noticed some of the vessels in the place had bridled out two anchors. I followed suit. The bottom was sandy, and evidently its holding qualities were subject to question.

The tempo of the wind picked up; 1939, not to be outdone by the holocaust of the previous year, was doing its level best. It did all right, too. The booming seas from the northeast climbed right over the beach and started things going inside. How a saucer of sea water could whip up to such proportions is something. It wasn't my cup of tea.

Princess rocked all night like a hobbyhorse. I could lie in my bunk deep in the vessel and look right into the dinghy dangling behind as if it was being hauled aloft by its stern. I got soaked crawling forward in the darkness every couple of hours to bind the cables with chaffing gear. This went on for hours, then days.

Three lovely little vessels dragged their anchors and ended up broken into misery on the beach. I had a fifty-pound kedge and a seventy-five-pound old-fashioned folding anchor bridled out with eighty feet of line on each. There was no more than fifteen feet of water under the boat. I kept the engine tuned up ready to go the minute I started dragging. I figured out a set of ranges to warn me if she dragged. It was quite simple. I sat on the port bunk and sighted a flagpole through one port and a steeple through the other. I sat up and checked every fifteen minutes all night and all day to see if they were still there. They got out of line the second night, and I idled the engine for hours to relieve the strain on the lines.

During all this I kept belaboring myself for having left the security of the old harbor with its soft, thick mud that held a hook like glue and the leeward shelter of the great trawlers. At least I had enough to eat. It was futile to even think about getting ashore, and to top it all, a nice homey little leak had come to live in our bilge. One of those don't-look-now jobs.

The third day it was still going strong, but *Princess* seemed to have stopped dragging her anchors. I was dead for sleep, having read everything on board, including the labels on my shirts, in the struggle to keep awake. I hadn't spoken to a soul in days. I might just as well have been making a heroic singlehanded voyage across the ocean instead of rocking ignominiously in this boiling puddle.

With half a mind to retrieve my anchors and storm out into the open sea, come what may, I stood up suddenly in the companion-way. The hatch cover slid over and hit me in the nose. Obediently I returned to the never-ending business of binding up the fraying anchor lines and the monotony of staring at those poles through the ports. I was tired of getting soaked every time I struggled forward, and bored with endless drying, so I left my clothes in the cabin and attended to the lines without them. Dressing and undressing became a kind of equinoctial striptease, and the storm went on.

Finally I heard the vibrations of a motor. It was a Coast Guard boat. They were heading toward me. They had left the sinecure of their station more than a hundred yards away, and they were braving this teapot tempest.

As they came around the counter of *Princess* a man with a megaphone shouted from the bridge, "You're all right! Your anchor is caught on the Western Union cable! You're all right!" There was a pause. As the boat slipped into gear he lifted the megaphone and added, "War has been declared!"

7

The sun shone in a blue sky. A gentle wind tousled the hills of Block Island. England had declared war on Germany, and both anchors of *Princess* were caught on the Western Union cable. The blow of '39 had abated, and if I could get those anchors off, I'd be back in business. War was something I could take care of later. Come to think of it, I owed Western Union a debt. I would have to remind myself to send a telegram if the draft board didn't beat me to it.

The Coast Guard came back and intimated that they would like to help me get those anchors up. I acted vague and they went away. I also got an unsolicited estimate from a local fisherman, but I decided to have a go at it myself.

The standard procedure for getting an anchor unhooked

from a submerged object is to pass the eye at the end of another line down along the anchor cable and pull alternately on the anchor cable and the line from two directions. This will generally jiggle it loose, but it takes two boats and two people.

There is another method which takes one boat and one man with a genius for running in circles. I buoyed one cable off to the rowboat and concentrated on the other one. I concentrated by starting up the engine and running in concentric circles. The anchor cable acted like a twisted rubber band and spun the hook loose. I did it again with the other cable. I felt dizzy, but rich.

Under a sky cloud-broken like a jogged jigsaw, my little boat slowly slipped away from the island. Aided by a north wind and abetted by the tide, with little white surf mice bubbling along her water line, *Princess* reached forward, homeward. There was sunlight astern dappled across the hills and the wet gleam of boulders on the beach.

Princess took over the helm. I toyed with a brass lily acquired from a fisherman at the old harbor and daydreamed about ironing a swordfish. Great tales were told about harpooning these fish; there was big money in it. It was all there was left to the sons of whale fishermen. It was better than carving little whaleboats and selling them, hat in hand, to oil-company employees on vacation. There was danger, too. I saw the jagged, broken business end of a sword rammed up through two inches of planking in the bilge of a trawler.

I had a couple hundred feet of light line coiled in a bucket, a steel shaft inserted in the handle of the boat hook, and a life preserver wrapped up in a bright red sweater in place of a keg. I climbed up the mast rings, got a leg over the crosstree, and conned for sights of a fish.

Down I jumped, unlashed the tiller, and changed the course of *Princess* to chase every tin can, empty bottle, anything and everything that showed its nose above the surface. I was getting nowhere as I spurned the hand of a tide that was going my way. It was time to put away childish things if I didn't want to spend the night bucking my head against a wall of water that was sure to turn on me. I was stowing the sharp spearhead and the long line, and the life preserver was shedding its silly red sweater.

Two sharp black fins, the forward one curving aft, flicked idly in the sunlight. Not one like a shark, but two. The fins were at least seven feet apart, maybe more. She would be worth a hatful of money on the dock. I unfroze like lead and ran all over the place. Down came the sails. Up started the engine. Out came all the gear. Back went the life preserver into the red sweater.

Princess had come into her birthright; here were the days when whales were plentiful, so plentiful that men answering the cry raced through the streets of coastal towns and plunged their boats through the surf to do battle. She seemed to sense the moment. She lay poised, knowing, her clean lines sweeping forward to the long bowsprit, expectant, ready to support a man with a quick and sure harpoon. There was only one rub: She had a green crew.

The fish was fretful, suspicious. I stalked it like a hunter, slowly moving forward. My hand was gripped on the combination boat hook and harpoon, and my foot was on the tiller. I would come up on the fish, drive the lily into the firm, resilient flesh, and as she sounded pay out the line and let the red float go too. Then, if the first strike had not hit the spine and been fatal, I would follow the life preserver that was fast on the end of the line till the fish was exhausted, and tend it from the skiff. All I had to do was strike.

It was going to be tricky getting forward into position with that awkward rig and no one at the tiller. We were getting closer, closer, only another twenty feet. I started forward when my poor little boat betrayed me. The shadow of her mast reaching out before us on the water tipped off the fish. It went down. I flung the homemade rig at the laughing sea. A porpoise snorted somewhere. *Princess* yawned. I had approached the fish from the sunny side. It was a mistake. I had a hatful of muscle.

We weren't speaking for a while, *Princess* and I. The unemotional little engine took over and shook the bile out of both of us all the way down past Fishers Island. The northerly freshened and I raised the staysail. It pulled and gave the engine a thank-you-ma'am.

Skirting the north shore of the island down toward the west, I lost sight of the mainland behind the hill of the horizon. Into the valley of the Sound, which is cupped by the ends of Long Island, plunges the enormous gush of tide. Past the shrinking stop-water of islands, this daily doublebucking solid earth makes the stubborn land seem more miraculous than all the persuasive sea. It's a cockeyed wonder a man can find a place to hang his hat.

Tolerated as she was in the very navel of this trouble for over fifty years, *Princess* had a reasonable expectancy so long as she never got caught between these babies.

Now she was making fair time toward the west, dragging the slothful skiff, which followed like an unwilling dog grinding the leash in its stubborn jaws and with all paws braced. This ghastly consort to *Princess* was earmarked for disposal. Not yet, though. There were still plenty of weak spots in my sailboat that were going to be rebuilt. It was comforting to have another vessel around that floated. Why it had to be a sappy pine barge with a massive affinity for the earth was no wonder. It had been judged by heft and purchased to compensate for the weakness of its running mate.

It was warm. My right foot went over the side and dragged in the cool water that washed over the lee scuppers. I was kicking spray when an ugly black fin streaked by next to my toes. It might have been a shark; maybe it was a porpoise. It could even have been that swordfish come back to have some fun. My foot went back on board.

It was not long before the tide met itself going out and the wind from the north breathed slow. *Princess* slatted around, rolling in the slick sea, while I got out and got under the deck. The engine spat its rusty chaw and went to work. The book went down off Goldsmith Inlet some fifteen miles west of Plum Gut. There were some people on the beach sunning themselves in the flat light of the late afternoon.

Three kids came swimming out with an old man hard after them. It was a long swim, and by the time the kids were safely on board it looked as if the old man might fill and sink. *Princess* upped her hook and went for him. We hauled him on deck by his arms and one leg. The smallest kid hauled on his beard.

When he recovered his voice, the old man had a lot to tell us about my boat. There had been hundreds of them fishing out around Montauk in the old days. One of them had been his, and she had never let him down.

I threaded a weary bit of bait with a hook and lowered it over the side while he talked. I had a couple of nibbles, nothing definite, mostly the leave-your-worm-and-we'll-let-you-know kind, when all of a sudden I found myself employed pulling a fat flounder up on deck. I got three of them with the rest of the bait, and we all went ashore in the lumbering skiff with the fish still flopping at our feet.

It was a contract job for a marine railway to drag that barge up the incline near the inlet, so I made it secure with a long line to the broken backbone of a bark that lay on the crest of the beach. After dark we pried loose some pieces of the old keel with an oar and built a fire. The old man fried the fish and some clams, and we had what might accurately be described as a shore dinner.

The kids took a late dip in the Sound and ran over the hill to their cottage with their teeth chattering. I sat with the old man near the fire until midnight. Mounted on the tide, the skiff had climbed up near the fire. Urged by a new wind from the southwest, it was poking at the wet sand near our feet. It would have made good kindling.

I had a rough night rolling around in the surf of the open Sound. The kids were standing on the wreckage of a sailing vessel when I left. The old keel, studded with driftpins, looked like the boomerang of a war god, blood-red with rust in the morning light.

Princess made good time down past Mattituck, where with a local chart I might have entered the night before and had a decent night's sleep in the quiet shelter of the harbor. A good chart is the cheapest insurance. I often let it lapse. It's the same silly mechanism of economy that will make a knowing navigator submit to the agony of a night in the open sea when the price of a flop in the

Mills Hotel might have assured him the full rest of a safe anchorage.

As I passed the inlet the clouds converged into a dark blue lump and broke like an egg overhead. When the sun burst through after the rain, the sky reneged on the fair northerly of the morning and dealt out a wind of gathering intensity from the west. I mean, it blew.

I had thirty miles to go before I could duck into Port Jefferson, all of it on a close port tack with hardly enough sea room to turn around. Within an hour's time the dry gale brushed every fleck of cloud out of the sky. *Princess* was in close, clawing her way along the North Shore as the tide turned against her. I was driving her hard with no reef in the mainsail, and the new genoa pulling the sheet line like a steam windlass.

The sea began to act crazy. Towering sharp pinnacles of green water traveling in pairs began to gang up. One wave, steep as a wall, would roll *Princess* way down, and the next heap of brine would pile all over her. The cockpit filled with sea water, most of which sloshed out when the boat rolled before the self-bailer could handle it. The hatch cover was battened down, and I pumped when I could.

The heavy skiff I was dragging swamped with the first wave and became the next best thing to a sea anchor, reducing the speed of the vessel to the pace of a sick snail. I was working under considerable difficulty and a perpetual ton of sea water. The weather sheet line of the big jib, which would have enabled me to come about if I was of a mind to try, whipped out of my hand and snapped at the raging shore.

The wind blew in fifty-mile-an-hour gusts. To snap the boom across in a jibe and run for the open water would have dismasted the vessel for sure. If I tried to turn and come about, the tremendous spread of the genny would snarl on the rigging. Cupped that way, the wind would have laid her down flat. Held back as she was by the swamped skiff, I doubted whether we had the speed to come about. The very idea of going forward to clear the sheet was dismissed as suicide.

Tons of water roared across the deck. The entire vessel seemed to be buried at every second wave, and the big Egyptian cotton jib caught a tremendous slice of it and dumped it back on deck. Why that sail didn't burst is something I mean to take up with a likely Egyptian someday.

I was drifting in closer every moment, and, just to make things interesting, I was out of gas. As the sea battered away at me all sorts of wild plans and alternatives surged through my head. I thought of cutting loose that coffin I was dragging. Then what if I struck the rocks submerged nearby that were marked on the chart? I was right over Roanoke Point Shoal, far inside the safe three-fathom line. If *Princess* sank, the skiff offered a way of reaching shore. One thing was sure, it was solid.

During the last hours of daylight, with my neck encased in a Turkish towel that I squeezed dry between blows and used to mop my eyes, I had worked out a way to strike the waves and to use the God-given moment between that crushing one-two punch to edge out toward deep water. After dark I followed the same pattern. It was not easy. Every pull on the tiller seemed like the last one I could manage. Wet clean through for hours and aching beyond belief, I knew that I had been written off, so I fought. That's all there was left, an endless no-decision, knockdown, drag-out brawl.

There was a bottle of brandy that I treasured, old as *Princess*, stowed in the forepeak for emergency use or a celebration. I didn't touch it. I didn't dare. This was far beyond a measure of emergency. It was sure as hell no celebration. We were well on our way to disaster. A little after sundown I wondered if there wasn't a way to relieve the awful continuation of the struggle. Drop most of the sail, perhaps, and run before the wind toward the northwest. When I cleared my eyes, I could see by the chart that a great underwater cliff, which rose a hundred feet from the floor of the Sound and shelved off in a mile of shoal water, created this contorted seaway. *Princess* was on the very edge of that shelf.

I couldn't get all that sail down without dropping it over into the sea. The drag of the sail in the water would immobilize the vessel, and before I could get it on board we would be dashed on the lee. For all I knew, *Princess* might have been grazing the rocks that very moment. I gave up wondering about another way, tightened the tension of the mainsail, and hauled that indestructible headsail in flat. We were all set, and we started slugging.

Jerking the swamped scow along, *Princess* leaped forward. Now she lay over and tore into the massive height of green water. When she broke through, I knew that we were no longer losing ground. In the lull of the trough, trembling in the gale, she inched her miserable burden toward the open sea.

It got dark and I could see the lights off Port Jeff. I could hear the surf scratching on the rocks, and I was scared. Between the overwhelming inundation of those malicious twin seas, I reached into the cabin for the big flashlight and called for help.

I don't want to remember every moment of pain, of fear, of desperation. I would just as soon forget a few pleasant things if I can forget those too. I was swamped over and over again. I prayed. I cursed. I mixed a tear or two with the sea. I can truthfully remember only one of those awful waves—there were thousands. There's no use going on and on about it. I was so low that the icy water that toppled over me felt like a warm bath, and I welcomed it. From the beach, the beam of my flashlight, more frantic than ever, must have lost its meaning and seemed a kind of obituary capsuled in code.

There was no help from that quarter. It was the sea herself that saved me. The tide turned. *Princess* did her part, held her ground hour after hour. She even gained a little, too, and would have brought me in if I could have stuck it out. I don't know how she ever coped with the deadly drag of that skiff full of water. Swamped that way, *Princess* would have gone to the bottom, but the skiff still floated.

Now the happy tide coming home picked up the entire sorry flotilla that I commanded and cheerfully nudged it over the violent protest of Mount Misery Shoals right to the door of Port Jefferson. It was four o'clock in the morning.

One of the less noticeable differences between a man and a

fish is the way the former attributes to some omniscient brain the simple acts of Nature. When the *Princess* reached for the healing grace of the harbor, one last thwarted wave lashed out and in an instant joggled all but a spongeful of water out of the skiff. She followed us in, swinging coyly on her painter, as innocent as a lamb and almost bone-dry. I am dead sure this would never have bothered a fish.

What might have bothered a fish was the terrible anticlimax of losing the rudder in the treacherous tidal rip at the mouth of the harbor. That would have been like losing its tail.

I swung the tiller handle back and forth without effect. In that full gale, running wing and wing with the enormous expanse of mainsail and genoa jib, *Princess* was flying into a string of sand barges that blocked her way a hundred feet ahead. This was the end.

I staggered up forward somehow and dropped all sail. It fell across the deck and overboard like the wings of a bird hit with lead shot. The boat slowed down with the drag of the canvas in the water.

Back at the tiller, unbelieving, I tried it again. Now she turned; the rudder was still there. You live these things over and over again. The tenth time, days later, I realized that the wind had been driving *Princess* at the exact speed of the tide pouring into the harbor. With no relative difference in speeds, the rudder was as ineffective as it was when the vessel was tied up alongside the dock.

Princess ran to the south end of the harbor under a bare pole, dragging canvas strewn all around her like the train of a bedraggled gown. I dropped the hook and crawled into the bunk. I slept till noon with the bilge full of water slopping across me as she rolled.

8

There were blood-red stains on the canvas of *Princess* where the sail had rubbed against the tacky, copper bottom paint that protected her hull from the infestation of worms and the grasp of marine life. Folded wings of sail lay half submerged, like a bloated white corpse beneath the green surface of the clear water. I hauled them on deck as I would a netful of fish, and the salt water poured out of the pockets of the canvas.

The water in the bilge was up to the level of the bunks. I had slept eight hours with that inner sea breaking life surf across me, dead to the world after the ordeal off Mount Misery.

I sat in an endless posture of supplication on the coaming under the noon sun and pumped with my face toward the east. I felt all right, no cold, no sore throat, no runny nose.

As the long, white column of water poured out of the pump and curled over the side, I began to know why. Every inch of *Princess*, every fiber of wood, every thread of cloth, grain of metal, and strand of line had been bathed, impregnated, saturated with a sterilizing solution of salt. There just weren't any germs on board. I went ashore to get some.

I felt half pickled, too, when I climbed up on the dock. I was that shaky after waltzing around with the old girl for twenty-four hours without food or future. The wharf felt warm and solid as I lay in the sun, and the heavy skiff bumped at the end of her painter and staggered around in the shadows among the pilings. It was good to be there. I leaned back against an oar locker on the dock and drank a bottle of milk.

I was almost asleep on the sunny leeward side of the locker. The topside of *Princess*, sheering up fore and aft, smiled at me from the center of the harbor. We were ringed about by high, green hills broken by the sagging white sand bluffs and the undershot jaw of the entrance. I heard men talking.

A deep voice said, "There she is." A disembodied hand reached over my head across the locker and pointed at *Princess*. It was a strong hand, etched deep by the sun and the acid sea. I waited.

The voice of another man said, "Sure we saw her." There was a long pause.

The deep voice answered the unasked question. "It was his skin or ours."

There was no use butting in. I squeezed the still dock and listened. I was right under their noses, out of sight behind the locker. They leaned on it as over a bar, and they spoke as men speak across a bar.

"I've yet to see anything in the world that gets as bad as old Mount Misery."

"I've lost kin out there." There was a word or two more, and the voices went away. *Princess* still smiled from across the water, with bits of the sun speckled all around her like chicken feed as she bobbed.

When I first acquired *Princess*, there was another Friend-ship sloop in the yard. She was a big girl with no engine, and she belonged to a writing man with a full-rigged beard and an English accent that slipped into neutral when he let go. "I'll be blowed," he blazed, "if I'll share my ship with a filthy, stinking engine. She was built to sail, and by God I'll sail her!"

These were noble words; I was impressed. Here was some-one who had it worse than I did. An engine does take a lot of space. It's impossible to catch in a drip pan all the oil and grease that keep it from grinding itself into junk. As for the smell, the es-sence of petroleum is no perfume. Enviously I had thought of all the fancy changes I could make in the interior of *Princess* if the engine wasn't in the way. I too could have a broad double bunk like his and sleep catty-cornered like a tycoon.

It was the spirit of the man that filled me with awe. His vessel was twice the size of *Princess*, and she had a tremendous beam. Alongside each other they looked like mother cat and kit-ten. Her boom was longer than my boat from bowsprit to stern. She carried an expanse of canvas that was too much for one man to handle.

"What do you do in a head tide when the wind dies?" I asked.

"I've got a good hook and more time than money."

Now his Friendship sloop was piled up on the beach at Port Jefferson with a gaping hole in her starboard side. She had come to grief on the teeth of the stone jetty. A man with a pot of tar and a piece of canvas was helping him put a temporary patch on the broken hull. The poor thing must have taken a terrible beating. The planking on her injured side was all scuffed up. It looked very much as if my friend the writing man now had more time than boat. They had evidently been heaved on the rocks by the deadly current at the mouth of the harbor.

I stood, still rocking from the effects of the latest legs of my wanderings, and stared at the headlines on the Sunday editions spread out on the newspaper stand at the foot of the dock.

I had fallen into the habit of buying an occasional newspaper, as a debutante buys a hat. If it looked good, I bought. Otherwise, no deal. I couldn't quite make up my mind whether the headline was worth it when out of nowhere a water beetle wearing a yacht captain's hat streaked across my bow and snatched every paper off the stand. "Now Germany will rule the world!" That's what it said, the voice of the beetle.

It was time to shove off. *Princess*, her motor beating like a steady heart, breasted the tide that rode into the harbor. Once beyond the inward pull, I lifted her sails, and the stream of explosions that propelled her yielded to the soft hiss of the sea along her stakes. She took the tiller away from me, and, canting before the steady pressure of the north wind, she made good time toward Oyster Bay.

I was having breakfast down below when *Princess* wallowed in the wake of a vessel passing too close for comfort. The hot coffee slapped around in the cup. I might have known: It was the fancy yacht with all the newspapers on board. Old rule-the-world was at it again.

The tide was good to me, and the cool wind fair. *Princess* made the jaunt from point to point across the open bight of Smithtown Bay running along closehauled with a Gloucester schooner. Its great black hull and giant sails loomed out of the east and overtook her in the afternoon.

I dropped the hook off Cooper Bluff, where a great wall of

hill rose out of the bay, interrupted by a narrow pebbly beach. Up this hill, bolting right up it, went Teddy Roosevelt on horseback. That's what they say. After that, his famous charge at San Juan must have been a breeze. In the shadow of Cooper Bluff, I dug clams in the mud.

I monkeyed around Oyster Bay for days. Out beyond Rocky Point to the west the winter lay in wait. Summer was all but spent, and the sea, like an open artery, grew slowly cold with the first frost that dusted across the earth. I didn't want to think about hauling *Princess*. I busied myself fixing her up as if the chill in the air was the dregs of winter snagged on the heels of spring. I worked over my little boat as if another summer lay directly ahead, as if all this business about winter was just a lot of newspaper talk. There were a lot of things to do.

For one thing, the wire shrouds that braced the mast had been nibbled by the sea till the rusty strands of steel jutted like barbed wire and ripped my hands when I held on to go forward. I bought a length of plow-steel cable, studied the old splice awhile and went to work. . . .

There was a shipmate I had known, an old squarehead who managed to get drunk in every port and stay that way long after the sobering influence of no more money squared the crew away.

He had a taste for native liquor, a white innocent-looking milk that must have been distilled from a mash of wormwood and spiked with gall. It was cheap as dirt. He went about with a sly, bleary smile and offered it with prodigal generosity and no takers. This went on even after the ship had left port.

The deference afforded him by the mate and bos'n was due to the hard fact that he alone of all the members of the crew could make a decent wire splice.

A good wire cable is twisted with the tension of a steel spring. It will unravel into uselessness if the cut end is left unseized for a split second. It was as tricky as tying a bowline with a live cobra, but on the dock at Oyster Bay the secret was at last revealed to me. Now all I had to do was learn to like that monkey juice.

One day early in October the leak in the bilge back by the sternpost suddenly stopped like a tap turned off. Once a fishing vessel in daily use swells up tight, it remains that way for the span of its life. *Princess* had been converted some years before from a work boat to a yacht. As a summer sailer, her planks were sapped of moisture by the long period of drying from the late fall to spring. At last the cells of the wood planking, blown up like microscopic bladders, had drunk their fill, and just as fire fights fire, the water itself held the sea at bay.

It seemed a shame to haul her out and then go through the whole operation all over again. I had more than half a mind to run down through Hell Gate and on out; leave New York, the winter, and the whole works. Just to think of it made my heart misfire and race. Somewhere there must be some unimproved property insulated by the sea, a forgotten dot on the chart furnished with a couple of trees and a navigable cove for *Princess* that we could have for a song.

There was a moment of decision and then a song in the shining rigging when *Princess* drove down toward Hell Gate. The decision came in the center of the Sound as we headed back toward Long Island after spending a night at Cos Cob on the Connecticut shore.

A ribbon of road that snakes along the Island swings across the Sound at Whitestone. In the shadow of the bridge the waters part and the torrents that horse down through Hell Gate are the dregs of the Sound that disdain the long sweep of tide pulsing eastward toward The Race. *Princess* jockeyed uneasily in the rip of this separation, but the north wind struck by her side as she swung, wallowing, through the indecision of the sea.

After threading her way under full sail down around the little islands that clutter the East River, she caught hold of a piling at Port Morris which juts like the sow's ear of a sack off the lower right-hand corner of the Bronx. It was dark, and giant scoops, suspended by cables from trolleys which ran along a great proscenium of steel girders, were biting coal a ton at a time from the sluggish wooden barges that groaned as they rubbed against the wharf.

Cinders from the belching stacks that towered in the darkness crunched underfoot on the deck as we waited for the tide to turn.

Beyond the busy East River and the great harbor lay the open sea. *Princess* held on for dear life in the awful current alongside the grimy wharf under a baptism of ashes and waited for that propitious moment at the slack of the tide to slip through the jaws of Hell Gate.

A blinding disk of light wheeled along the edge of the dock and came to rest on my vessel. There was a clang of a bell in an engine room and a voice boomed, "Watch that little boat down there!" Two mammoth tugs were warping a great old hulk of a barge alongside the wharf. There was a roaring gush of white water as one tug backed her engine with the clang of a bell. A voice somewhere on the dock yelled, "You'll crush her like an eggshell!"

I jumped on the wharf and jerked the bowline off the piling. The tide racing by carried *Princess* down clear of the barge to the end of the wharf, and the momentum of her weight, the whole precious five tons of it, began to pull me off the dock as I fought to check it. I was hanging onto a piling with one arm, and the line burned through my hand as she slowly tried to wrest herself free. Inch by inch the fibers of the rope tore through my frantic grasp. I could see the end of the line snaking toward me across the dock.

I was about to jump into the black ink of the East River and take the chance of hauling myself hand over hand out of the swirling water onto her deck when an old hand came out of the darkness and snubbed the bitter end of the line. "I've got her, boy."

I could hardly believe my eyes. Two gnarled, old hands with almost a century of know-how had bent the last ten inches of rope across the top inside corner of the cap log and stopped the wild little vessel in her tracks. It was easy now for both of us to haul her back and make her secure to the piling. The old man ignored my thanks. "Where you heading, boy?"

I smiled and caught my breath. The great barge shook the wharf as it kissed. There was a strange grace in the huge hull. In the checkered shadow of the steel girders her weathered wood transom swept around and under into the flowing line of her body.

"She was a sailing bark," the old man said. "They cut her masts at the trucks after she loosened up rounding the Horn." His eyes traced great imaginary masts in the empty sky. "Drove a cargo of wedges in her to stiffen her up, ran coastwise after that. I was mate on her once."

Men crawled ashore with her dusty lines and made her fast to the dock. The heavy scoop dropped with a thud into the coal that filled her, and came up with a dripping mouthful that fell like black hail on the rough floor of the dock.

"They whittled her down bit by bit," the old man went on, "sold her masts for the derrick on a lighter and snapped her bowsprit. There she lays with a bellyful of coal, dirtier than the devil."

The sky filled with clean canvas, and the decks below the neatly painted trim were burnished white with salt and stone. A sailing bark in the trades heeled gently before the wind. A diagram of lines, light gold in the sunshine, crossed and recrossed the sparkling surface of her beauty. To have come to this! The old man closed his eyes standing there. "Where you heading, boy?"

"How about some coffee?" I said.

"Okay," said the old man.

We sat opposite each other on the bunks in the warm bosom of *Princess* as the coffee heated, and we talked. The old man's eye appraised all the new framing in the flickering light of the oil lamp that swung on gimbals from the after bulkhead of the cabin. "Did it yourself?" he asked, running his hand across the frames like a kid walking along a picket fence.

"Sure did," I said. *Princess* chafed with a scratching sound against the pilings of the dock.

"Where you heading, boy?" said the old man, and reached for the coffeepot. I asked him about Hell Gate.

"It's bad," he said. "They tried to fix it up, slow it up, make it safer, around the time they built the bridge. Blasted and dug and fooled around, ended up making it worse than it was before. Damn tricky business to bring a sailing vessel through there now."

The old man spoke as if the whole dredging operation was a diabolical scheme to ruin the waterway for canvas.

The tide was beginning to slacken. The drumming gurgle under the hull diminished to a barely audible swish as the coffee began to bubble on the stove. I broke out a can from the stock of provisions which had been willed to me by a hotel man. His cruiser was headed for hauling, so he dumped the entire contents of his galley aboard *Princess*. It was fancy stuff—kumquat jam, caviar, and what not. "Do you like caviar?"

"If it's anything like salt horse," he said, "I can stand it."

We had a bite and a drink, and before he handed me the bowline from the wharf, all made up ready to stow, the old man put his hand on the new shrouds of *Princess* and nodded. "Sweet little vessel."

The wind from the north curved the straining sail, and we parted from the coal dock. I started the engine and kept her idling just in case. *Princess* putted down the brimming river straight for Hell Gate.

There is humor in the awkward, clumsy might of heavy water trying to dance with the wind. Bouncing it like a baby on its knee, the boisterous sea can tickle the risabilities of any craft. The old and the infirm expire with laughter.

Years before, I had made an ill-considered midnight passage through Hell Gate with a Snipe sailboat and an outboard kicker. I was catapulted along with the angry tide, spinning like a bottle. To top it all, a great liner passed me under the bridge. It was straining full ahead against the torrent, and the way its wash rebounded from the opposing walls of the banks and then snapped together ten feet into the air when they collided was a thing to etch a crease on the brain.

This time the calculated passage of *Princess* through the treacherous waters of Hell Gate was like a ride on a rowboat across the lake in Central Park. I caught the devil farther down.

The wind swept through the great chasms of the buildings, whirled around among the stacked-up lights, backed and blew in sudden bursts as it does at the corner of a street. Over on Park Avenue a man's hat blew off his head, spun down the block, and settled at last like a tired top in the leeward calm of the gutter. Down in the blue Caribbean an island edged like the facets of a cut stone gleamed in the sunlight.

The ebbing tide was fast reaching the peak of its force, and the East River ran like a rapid. *Princess* swung and jibed, and the current kicked her along. I doused the sails and ran under power with the throttle wide open.

The crazy river was alive with traffic. Blackwells Island, which cuts it into two long strips of wriggling water, lay dead ahead. To the right I could see a Christmas tree of red and green lights, the riding lights of oncoming tugs and barges, and above it two fast-rising companion stars, the masthead lights of a great, looming ship.

I made a fast tardy turn to port and headed for the channel on the left of the island. The determined little engine, dead game, was no match for the rip. The tide, spreading its fury down along the river, elbowed *Princess* within inches of the gulping rocks.

I jerked wildly on the halyard of the big genoa jib, and a sudden gust of wind bulged her out. The violent tug on the canvas zipped my little boat like a yo-yo off the hard nose of the island.

Princess yawed and bucked and practically braced all four feet against the tumbling persuasion of the tide. There was no mistake, she wanted no part of the open sea.

I leaned on the slides of the hatch, resting. My eye checked the oil pulsing in the little glass gauge on the head of the motor. In the flickering light of the lamp, swinging wildly on its gimbals, I stared aghast at the gray gleam of the floorboards floating around at the level of the bunks. The leak that made history had climbed back on board.

9

My little boat was sinking. Right in the middle of the East River, halfway down along the island of Manhattan, practically in the bosom of my home town, *Princess* was letting me down.

A couple of wet steps off the east end of Forty-second Street the old girl became possessed with a sudden fierce thirst for salt water. She staggered and careened with half a load, as if neither direction nor the very plane upon which she had her being meant a damn thing, and I pumped.

The engine had been throttled way down to reduce the vibration that had shaken loose whatever bit of caulking or flotsam plugged the careless gap in her bottom. Down below, the floorboards floated alongside the edge of the bunks in the nervous light like barges being warped to a dock in a hurricane.

My eyes, as they came up with each frantic jerk at the pump handle, saw a million spare stars piled up along the shore as if waiting for a vacancy in the overcrowded heaven. *Princess* rocked on down under the high bridges that flowed across the sky and wallowed heavily in the spiral of the tide. With one hand for the tiller and the other for the pump, I pulled deep and full and fast. I gained on the salty little lake that lay below the level of the sea and was scrounging a ride in the bilge of *Princess*.

As my boat was funneled down past the point of Manhattan, the rate of leak slowed with the pace of the engine, and it was easier pumping to keep her dry. That wonderful wet wheeze, a cross between a gargle and a gasping snore, that announces the triumphant moment when the pump sucks dry sounded like the official anthem of the state of nirvana.

I cut across the point of Manhattan, dodging between two patient ferryboats, and the other island, the dream one, was all but lost in the dark sea that lay beyond The Narrows. All that I wanted now was two railroad tracks with a taste for salt water and a simple, unpretentious car fitted with outlandish crutches for the kind of cripple only a boat can be when it goes ashore.

Such a thing had vanished with the years from the shore line of Manhattan. In the old days when the eager bowsprits of great sailing vessels were thrust row upon row across the dusty water front, their taut stays humming to the tune of lumbering cart wheels, there were places here to haul a vessel. Once the ring of a caulking iron sounded in the hollow along Canal Street, and tall, bare sticks of a bark on the ways rose strange and straight above the foliage. A clear stream that still slips unnoticed into a sewer under the hard-trodden shell of Spring Street once wandered down and joined a tidal inroad that was jammed with boats.

Now the deepwater docks and express highways have won complete command of the water's edge. But for the possibility of being plucked bodily out of the water by the great crane of a lighter, there was no way here for *Princess* to escape the pressure that had found her leak.

The tide running down the Hudson River more than

matched the force of the East River. I slipped into the yawning stillness of a great ship's berth, tied up, and waited for slack water. With the engine quiet, the leak let up to a point where I could lay off the pump for minutes at a clip without having to break my back to get her dry again.

I stood at the head of the pier and watched the tide go out without me. A bird passed by with feet awash, riding an empty wooden crate. That bird and the fellow with the seaplane had the right idea. If it's an island that you want dipped out of the sparkle of the tropics, learn to fly. In the chill of a gray dawn, on the point of one island teeming with life, I leaned on a piling and thought about an empty one.

What is an island? A body of land surrounded by a state of mind? A lap of land that appeared out of nowhere when the crinkled crust of the earth collapsed and sat down in the sea? What could a sailor with a passion for sea room want with an island, a place with barely enough land room to turn around?

In the brown gloom of a joint on South Street, over a chipped mug of hot coffee and a cigarette, I wondered how the hell I could come by these same two urgent commodities on a deserted island in the Caribbean.

There would surely be other things to smoke. Some kind of weed like the fur of cat-o'-nine-tails or goldenrod, which we used to roll up in newspaper when we were kids, a puff of which would dissolve a Pittsburgh stogie, band and all. There must be some kind of beanlike berries to boil that had the lift of a cup of coffee—something to help a fellow get underway in the morning or, better yet, with the kick of a mule that would put him back to sleep till noon.

There are better boats, too, nice sound ones, but I was attached to *Princess*, now quietly sinking at the dock, just as I was attached to my habits, good and bad. I raced back. She was still afloat.

Seeing her there nosing the black, oily pilings with her clean, white sprit, I began to suspect she was the type of babe that decides to end it all when she is damn sure there is someone around to save her. Returning to the pump, sleepless, I could discern in myself a halfhearted hope that the old gal would try it just once when nobody was near enough to haul her back by the handle of the pump.

It was morning, and the shops along South Street began to open. As the pump sucked dry, I looked up. There was a man on the dock in business suit. His hands were thrust into the pockets of his pants, and there was a smile on his face. It was Eddie Samara.

Eddie owned one of the old buildings on South Street. It was jammed full of every conceivable type of gear that was ever carried on a boat. There was literally nothing a boat needed that you couldn't find in his place. The trick was to find it.

Neither Eddie, his man Willie, who sulked around the place with a soft grin, nor any living soul had any idea of the infinite assortment of marine hardware that was scrambled up and down those five musty floors. In all fairness to Mr. Samara the businessman, he knew where the things were that sold day after day. But the special part—a fitting from a half-forgotten era, the spare limb of an antiquated rig—was lost in the limbo of metal heaped to the ancient rafters.

When you were hot on the trail of a long-lost part, Eddie would smile that same quizzical smile I saw in the early sunlight and, with his hands in his pockets, nod toward the long trail that started at the stairwell. "You're welcome to look for it."

I had prospected the Samara lofts for years. When I found what I wanted, which actually happened now and then, and crawled down from the dusty maze with my find, Eddie was as surprised as anyone. Money was never an issue. Eddie loved boats. He belonged to the Godforsaken brotherhood of boat rebuilders, and even he, armed with bins of fastenings and unlimited access to stores of fittings, equipment, and gear, finally gave up with a simple statement of fact: "I can't afford a boat.

"It wasn't so much the cost or the effort. She was a tidy little vessel, a sweet sailor with real nice lines. Willie and I worked over her for several years. We rebuilt her from stem to stern, trucks to keelson. We fastened her with bronze and plundered the shop for fittings. When it looked like it would never end, I gave up, sold her to the first buyer who came along for a tiny fraction of her cost. The man was tickled to get the boat. I was glad to see him happy. But do you suppose that was the end of it?

"Nothing of the sort," Eddie went on, with that smile of his. "The new owner came around the very next day with a cop. He claimed that I had failed to furnish the dinghy with oarlocks. I gave him oarlocks," said Eddie Samara.

It was comforting to see him there on the pier. Maybe this man, this provider of things to men burdened with boats, would help me. I was too tired to think.

"Get out in the tide and take her up the Hudson to Edgewater," said Eddie. "You can haul her there."

His hands were still thrust in his pants' pockets, and that smile was on his face when I cleared the dock. I have no recollection of the trip up the Hudson from the Battery to Edgewater. There is a point of fatigue where the mind closes like a kicked clam and the things that happen slip unrecorded off the hard, protective shell of the brain.

All I can remember is that the wind was fair out of some quarter of the south. Running across it under sail, I was about to jibe the big mainsheet across to catch the wind full. I was too tired to come about. As I turned and prepared to ease the sheet, a shrill series of short blasts piped from a ferryboat that was heading out away from *Princess*. I hesitated. A hand appeared out of the after window of the pilot house. I could see a single digit in the sunlight wagging, "No! No! No!" I came about properly and followed the ferry upstream.

In the shadows of the Palisades *Princess* was drawn out of her element while I slept. The last thing that I heard as I drifted off was the creak of the car wheels and the steady drip of water that fell out of her leaky bottom as she came to rest.

Edgewater lies beveled in the corner of the perpendicular rock hills of the New Jersey Palisades and the horizontal mud flats of the silty Hudson. It is well named. So is the Undercliff Boat Works, where *Princess* was hauled out. A short skirt of land that permitted no more than a shore road and a thin row of houses rose without any nonsense to a height that made the loftiest spars seem like toothpicks stuck in toy boats. From the top of the hill in the morning I watched the reflection of the rising sun sink under the houseboats and the scows crowded in along the shore.

A good part of Edgewater is made up of old railroad barges slugged into the mud flats, whose handy tracks are extended off into navigable water. It was on one of these condemned lighters, shot full of auger holes to pacify the willful tide, that *Princess* was hauled out. She was among friends. The fluent passage of brackish water in and out of those barges is a language she had come to understand in her old age.

I left her safe if not sound, perched on a mother barge that leaked by proxy down below, and I took the ferry to the island of Manhattan—for money.

Money, they tell me, is at the bottom of everything. Some of it is at the bottom of the sea. Pirate gold, shiny pieces of eight lying on the sandy floor of the ocean, blink at the smiling sun as it wheels neutrally across the sky.

Wandering in the wilderness of sand dunes below Hatteras, a man stubbed his toe on the lid of a great chest of gold and ran all the way home, forgetting in his excitement to mark the dune. When he got back, dragging a shovel and a gunny sack, the stupid wind had dusted the sand across his discovery. He dug and dug and finally dug himself into the boneyard, where he lies today, peaceful as pirate's gold. A few years later another man suddenly blossomed forth with a brand-new, five-hundred-ton fishing boat and a fertilizer factory to go with the stink.

The sign of the dollar is a figure S like the sweet curve of the bottom of *Princess*. It is crossed by a bar or two to keep the double curve from opening up after it has left the bending form. That winter the good Mr. Kretzer, snowbound in City Island, bent thirty dollar signs, for as many dollars, out of sour oak and crossed them with strips against the time when I could seat them in the shaky, leaky aftersection of my little vessel.

73

The friendship of Red Gillyard was sorely tried in transporting this humiliating cargo—thirty nine-foot dollar signs—in his Model A roadster all the way from City Island down across New York and out by ferry to Edgewater. This time there was going to be money at the bottom of *Princess*.

Spring came early, all sunny and warm. I just about abandoned my diggings in New York. Unfinished paintings littered my studio. I unloaded a raft of them among the initiates. A rising interest in modern art began to provide a market for unfinished pictures. The more unfinished they were, the better they liked them, and the better I liked it, too. Outside of the esoteric considerations of art, it gave me more time to finish my boat.

This time I was playing for keeps. *Princess* was either going to float like a lady or sink like a tramp. I was burned out on the installment plan of rehabilitation, the heartbreaking business of trying to save her rotten old soul like a visionary bucking a confirmed and cynical bum.

First I had to get the mast out. Jack Carlow, the yard manager, was very pleasant, very cooperative. He turned me over to Ozzie, his partner, a rangy fellow from Down East who spent a lot of time petting a brown dog that pointed all over the barge. "It'll cost you thirty dollars," said Ozzie.

After listening to a long explanation about rigging a huge derrick, I walked out of the office muttering to myself about this thirty-dollar conspiracy that seemed to prevail in every bight and corner of the boat business. Fifteen minutes later the heavy mast was lying alongside *Princess* on the deck of the barge and, what was more wonderful, I was still alive.

In the amusement park up on top of the Palisades, some monkey with more brass than brain would dive off a tower into a drum of water at the stroke of midnight to keep the crowd from going home early.

The act was widely advertised, and the preparations were elaborate. Standing poised in space in his spotless skin-tights, attended by two adoring maidens also in skin-tights, he would hold a finger up to test the wind and ripple his highly cultivated muscles in the white spotlight. When the suspense became unbearable, what with a rising roll of the drums and a flourish from the band, down he came in his dramatic plunge.

My unheralded performance at the Undercliff Boat Works at 10:22 in the morning without changing from my business suit was for the sole amusement of the yard manager, his partner, and that unapologetic pointer.

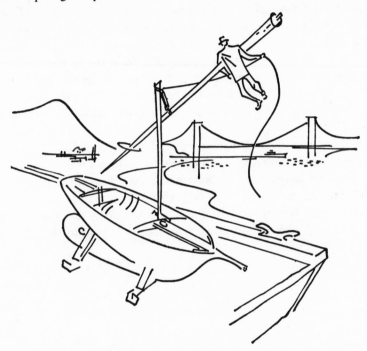

I found a pole lying around, jammed it into a crack in the barge, and clamped it between the chain plates of my boat. From the top of the pole, which extended halfway up the mast to a point on the mast a few feet above the deck, I rigged pulleys and started hauling, and the mast began to come up and out.

Everything was fine till the foot of the mast cleared the deck. I had neglected to provide a line to check it. With gathering momentum the bottom of the mast lit out into space like the short end of a seesaw. The long end swung down wildly and was sure to crash through the deck of the boat. I hung on to the foot of the mast with one arm and clutched the hauling part of the line with my free hand. The only way to save the boat was to lend all my weight to the short end of the mast and help equalize it. My weight was not enough.

Up I went, ten, twenty feet into the air while the top of the mast, counterbalanced by my weight, came down with diminishing force and bounced, harmless as the business end of a drumstick, on the deck.

Fine, but there I was suspended at least thirty feet up over the oozing mud flats, hanging on with one arm. Down the mast I slid, paying out line as I came, and pretended as I hit the deck and lowered the mast away that it was all a very well-calculated procedure.

That was enough for one day. I tipped my hat to a small but appreciative audience, polished my fingernails on my lapel, and started off the barge back to New York. As I passed the office the dog pointed at me as if I were Superman or something. Jack Carlow, who was leaning out of the office window, made it unanimous. He said, "We could use a man like you around this place."

10

Down through the long fairway of experience, from the unrecollected headwaters of time, the preponderant direction of man has been toward the land. From the first glimmerings of life deep in the belly of the sea, his struggle through eons against untold forces has brought him at last to his place in an easy chair in front of a television set with a highball at his elbow.

Somewhere in this saga of life, death, and transfiguration, one man, having achieved the collective objective of land and having learned to have his being thereon, saw a bug sailing on a leaf across a puddle.

Some years, when the boys at Edgewater are lucky, a million dollars' worth of shad fish, driven by the same instinct for a quiet place to hang around and reproduce, storm up the Hudson

77

River all at once. Some—those that are not hamstrung by the gills in their eagerness, and escape the fence of nets strung on locust-wood stakes along the Jersey flats—return when their mission is accomplished. These are called backrunners.

There are men who backrun, like the man who got the idea from a bug sailing a leaf, but unlike the sated shad, who wander aimlessly out to sea, the men who go back are supposed to be cagey. The trick is to be a little aloof—to be on the sea, not of it. The fate of a seaman depends on the kind of condition of the vessel he sets foot on when he decides to do a little back-running. . . .

Princess's type did not constitute a problem. She was de-signed to take just about anything the puddle had to offer. Her condition was another matter. Like a chain whose weakest link can let you down just as nicely as if it were all weak, the sound, new structure of her bow and midsection was sure to share what-ever fate lay in store for her wobbly tail. As for the leaky deck, that was a constant, gnawing disorder that no boatman worth his salt would tolerate for a fraction of the time that I put up with it.

I resolved to rip away at the old girl till every vestige of rot, leak, and weakness was removed. Then, if I had a notion to dò any backrunning, I would be all set.

A weakness is not always a disadvantage. A shipmate of mine got his arm broken one night in a small war he engineered at a place where they serve drinks. He went back the very next night, fortified himself with a couple of boilermakers, and pro-ceeded to hammer the place into shambles and hospitalize the oc-cupants. A plaster cast is a terrible truncheon.

His tactics were commendable, but the flaw in his strategy was that he never dared to go back after the cast was removed. The same situation would have existed if I had cared to follow the jaded advice of a few tired, old boatbuilders and put *Princess* in a plaster cast. Her weakness could be corrected, they claimed, by tossing a load of Portland cement into her bilge. It would stiffen her up all right and stop the leak for a spell, but it would complicate out of reason any hope of really putting her into shape.

The miraculous cure I had up my sleeve was a miracle of monotony. I was going to keep on pulling her apart piecemeal and graft on new wood till the old girl became as sound as she was able.

Up on top of the hill at Edgewater I found a lumberyard and a steam sawmill that seemed to be trying to bury itself in a mountain of sawdust. Their specialty was oak—fine, first-growth white oak.

The head sawyer was sitting on a tremendous log in the spring sunlight, filing a handful of teeth detached from the big circular blade in the mill. "Any of this wood seasoned?" I asked.

"Birds were singing in it day before yesterday," said the head sawyer.

I dragged some long strips of green oak all the way down the hill. The part that wasn't worn away by the friction on the cobblestones I figured to use as stringers and clamps. They would bend nicely and season underway. Then I went to work.

It was wonderful to whale away at that miserable, leaky deck with a pry bar. In the reassuring warmth of a perfect spring day I lashed and tore away in retaliation for all the wet nights, the clammy bedding, and the sopping clothes it had treated me to.

The cabin came off in one piece. The deck planking came off next. It was spongy, and so stale that I could almost kick it away, but the skill with which it had been laid down had kept it in place for more than half a century, long after the fastenings had been burned away by salt water. The way each narrow strip of planking was notched into the king plank forward and faced into the fashion piece aft was like the finest of inlay work.

When I got to the beams, I almost hated to tear them out in spite of all the annoyance they had caused with their everlasting dry droppings. I just stood there and marveled. All down and around the curvature of her stern each piece was fitted to the next with the accuracy of machined steel. It fell apart like wet cereal when I tackled it. Off came the entire deck. She was now as wide

79

open as that big yellow pine skiff of mine that glowered at me from her mooring in the mud.

Now the frames that were bent during the winter were fitted in place and fastened one by one. Each day the sun climbed a little higher in the sky. When at last it sat on the shelf of the vernal equinox, every rib of *Princess* had been renewed.

I came out every day now from my studio in the cliffs of New York to the cliffs of Edgewater. I could see my little vessel from the moment the ferry left her berth at 125th Street. She was perched on the old railroad barge, and her reflection danced in the water when the tide was up.

When the ferry docked, I was the first ashore. I trotted up River Road and bounced along the shaky catwalk to get to her. I worked hard. Bit by bit she was reassembled. My girl got herself a new corset in the way of a stout bilge clamp and a stringer for her chine. Now that she had a foundation like that, I could hardly wait to dress her up with paint. Once her shape was in shape, if you know what I mean, I advanced to the work on her deck. This time the topside was going to shed water.

I worked late. One evening, when the tide that washed in and out across the slippery surface of the mud flats was on the rise, I heard a running gurgle along the barge that went up the auditory scale like the mouse that ran up the clock. It was created by the wash of a passing vessel rolling ashore at a time when the tide lay an inch below the great rub strake of the barge.

Those little waves curled along under the rub strake like screaming meemies and were clapped down with a slap as they hit the blunt face of another jutting barge. It was the most comical sound I had ever heard. I got to hanging around and waiting for it after it became too dark to work.

Sometimes, when the tide was right, there would be no vessel passing to supply the right kind of undulation. At other times a wind would come out of the east at the propitious moment and drown out my silly symphony with a rough chop. When I was too busy to bother about it, I would suddenly become aware of that hilarious noise while I was working on the inside of *Princess*. I don't know what the neighbors thought, but I laughed like hell every time I heard it

One of my neighbors was a tall guy with a grin. He was supposed to be over at the university across the river studying for a doctorate in chemical engineering. He divided his time with scientific impartiality between a centrifuge in the department of physics at the university and the rotten stem of a motorboat hauled up out of the mud at Edgewater. Archie was just a little too hard of hearing to appreciate the foolish music the waves played against the sounding board of the barge. He was not only deaf to my unaccountable laughter but too amused with his own idiotic extracurricular enterprise to be concerned with mine.

Archie's nemesis was an eighteen-foot relic that had received a belated grant of power, a disproportionate amount of topsides, and a scrap of deck, and was thereby elevated to the status of motorboat.

The very first time I saw him, Archie was sitting crosslegged like a long bird in a great nest of excelsior at the end of the barge. Alongside lay a big, broken packing crate. For a moment I saw a glittering Christmas tree towering above him, and I heard the sound of bare little feet running, hesitating, and then jumping down a staircase. Spread out and gleaming in the sun was a semicircle of new tools—chisels, gouges, a couple of planes, a brace and bits, shiny new saws, a hammer, and just about everything else money could buy in the way of hand tools.

But this was July, not December, and this bird was older than myself, and I was thirty-one. He looked down the river where a tug was toying with a scow in the summer haze. "My uncle died and left me a hundred dollars," said Archie. "I always wanted tools."

Then there were all the sidewalk superintendents like Sam Somebody, the man who brought me the sheets of waterproof plywood and helped me carry them from the truck on River Road over the catwalk to the barge. He wouldn't accept a tip. All he wanted was to sit on the transom way up over the water as I tacked the plywood to the new deck beams and ask questions.

"What are you going to do when you finish her?"

"Shove off," I said.

"Where to?"

"Away somewhere." That seemed good enough for Mr. Somebody, and what was good enough for Mr. Somebody was good enough for me. While he hung around, his eyes big with envy, I worked faster. There is nothing that rewards the spirit so much as tacking panels of plywood in place. The sense of accomplishment increases by squares as the smooth surface expands.

Now that things were going right with my little boat, just about everything else in the world was going wrong. Europe was boiling over, and the art business had crawled under a stone. It looked like a good time to break away.

A lot of stuff had accumulated in my studio. I had to get rid of it before I could leave. Sometimes I wondered who had title to what and what had title to whom. Little by little these things were sloughed off or went by the board. Some were lost, some strayed, and the rest were stolen.

A chair went next door to hold up a lady and never came back. Some furuncle borrowed a lamp and went looking for an honest man. Books were borrowed and used as nucleuses to found small personal libraries. The drift was in my favor.

Finally I was down to a bed and a huge plaster cast of an old-time actor by the name of Gordon. I couldn't get rid of that statue. I went to the trouble of leaving the door unlocked, even ajar. Still no luck.

The reason for that odd piece of sculpture went way back. When I was a kid, the man who carved the original from which that bust was cast gave me my first set of paints. He wandered in and out of our house for years. We lived out in the wilds at the end of nowhere, and he dropped in for protracted visits with always the same unnecessary excuse: "I was just passing by. . . ."

Where he was going when he passed by except to visit us, we never knew. We loved the old guy. His name was Jules Butensky. Jules always said that when he was introduced to Teddy Roosevelt, the future President of the United States said, "Butt-in-sky, that's what they call me!"

My friend had carved portraits of half the crowned heads of Europe. His own head was like that of a lion with a shock of gray hair and a deep scar of a saber slash on his left cheek. The man who had crossed him was dead. I listened to the story of his life, and he taught me to draw.

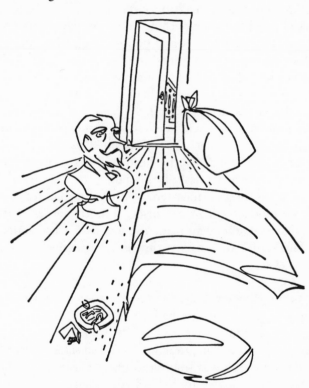

Success yielded to him again in the last years of his life. He was commissioned to do a series of busts for the Hall of Fame at New York University. When the money came, he went back to Paris and the Old World, the world he still lived in. I saw him off.

He was shaking with excitement like a kid with a new toy, or a paint set. It was all very sudden. He left the things he owned scattered all over the lot. I was left holding the bust.

It had no material value. I couldn't sell it, even if I had a mind to try. It was made of a kind of cement like the bilges of a lot of old boats I know. It was big and heavy and a terrible responsibility. What value it had was hard to say. The subject was of little interest to museums or collectors. It was just one of many copies cast from the original bronze statue.

A portrait is a strange thing. You can pay thousands of dollars for one, but try to sell it and you will be offered next to nothing, unless it has a certain something known as "art." Take a picture of yourself. The only one who will buy it is someone who loves you (unless, of course, you have curves and you forgot to get dressed before the shutter clicked).

It looked as if I was stuck with this big, fierce likeness. I could just fancy it as a figurehead on *Princess:* two hundred pounds of plaster down by the head with its beard in the drink.

Suddenly I had a flash. I called up a theatrical union and offered it reluctantly as a donation. Within ten minutes, four members of the union were in my place. The tenderness with which they carried that job away made me feel that it had found a good home. The vanity of actors is timeless, impersonal, and all-inclusive. I was free.

As for *Princess*, there was a hardware store way out of the shipping lane that somehow had come into possession of a gallon can of green antifouling racing bottom paint. I asked no questions, slapped down two dollars, took it away, and slapped it on the bottom of *Princess*. She was smooth as glass. I had sanded her down with a borrowed power tool. I was dead sure she would be dry this time. I was willing to bet on it.

"Bet she leaks," said Ozzie, the yardman.

"A bottle of whiskey she doesn't."

We launched her. *Princess* was dry as a bone. I mean, dry. The rain came down, and the cabin leaked. Ozzie reneged on the bottle of whiskey. I went up the hill and bought a can of gray roofing compound, smeared it along the break of the deck, and hoped for the best.

For better or worse, one little matter was pending that had to be resolved before I could even think of shoving off. It concerned that big yellow pine dog of a skiff that hung like dead weight to the apron string of my girl. It had to go.

Unbelievably, I actually found someone who was willing to pay money for it. There was really nothing wrong with the boat. It was as sound as a rock, and had about the same specific gravity. The deal was consummated in an atmosphere of utmost solemnity. Once the money was in my pocket, I did cartwheels all the way up to the office, and bought a lightweight plywood pram.

All bright and shiny, *Princess* snuggled coyly against a flat floating dock at Edgewater. The little houseboats with their tidy trim and gold tugboat eagles were gay in the summer sunlight. The tiny gardens, squared off with picket fences dead ahead of them, were singing with flowers. The fragrance of lilac along a country road is nothing compared to the heady nose wine of lilac and salt water. Lazy flies buzzed around the old-fashioned store across the road, where the smiling, plump wife of the little butcher assembled huge sandwiches and sold them for peanuts. It was a pleasant place.

I went back to New York to pack my things and caught the phone in the act of ringing its bells off. Now that I wanted to get away, I was in demand. Suddenly everybody had to have an artist, just as if the city wasn't crawling with them. I responded to every ring, drooling like Pavlov's dog, but it didn't prove a damn thing. A week went by. I seemed on the road to success at last, while out in Edgewater *Princess* rose and fell with the life of the tide.

It was near midnight around the middle of July, hot and humid, and the air was full of the sickening apprehension of war. The tide was going out. All at once I knew it was now or never. This was the hour of departure. I didn't have enough bed sheets to reach all the way down to the street, so I paid the rent and ran.

II

My sea bags went leaping over the subway turnstile like smart-alecky school kids during the rush hour. I dragged them into the car and sat on top of them in the middle of the homebound theater crowd. A suitcase plastered with labels will never draw the interest of people the way a sea bag being toted by a man in a business suit does.

I felt more at home on the ferry, and when I was at last in the darkness of the long barge leading to *Princess*, whispering in the easy flush of the tide, my heart beat like hell. There was no time to lose. Every second of that tidal current was worth its weight in BTUs. But the foot-pounds of efforts that had gone into that dream lying there at the dock called for a moment of dedication.

I stood with my fists clenched around the necks of two fat sea bags and stared down the ramp at her. The lights from the amusement park up on the Palisades blinked off and on, and so did the blurred white topsides of *Princess* in reflection.

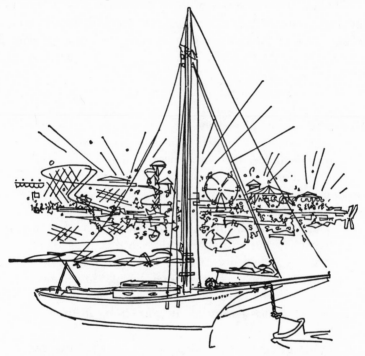

The hatch cover was shoved forward, and the sea bags went down to sleep like portly pigs on the port bunk. I lit the running light, hooked them on the port and starboard shrouds, and cast off her lines. She drifted out clear of the dock and picked up the urge of a west wind in her staysail without a sound or a sigh. We were underway.

The sea, going back to itself, spurred by the fresh flow of summer rain, began to drain the long tentacle of its tide from the deep river. The ferry, recrossing at midnight, its illuminated gullet tilted upstream, passed the bowsprit of my boat. The gaff of *Princess* climbed into the night sky. The boom crutch kicked like a chorine and threw its burden to the wind. We picked up speed.

There was a sailing that night at the foot of Fifty-seventh Street. A great liner, all lit up and alive with people, was building up steam at her berth. The rat guards were off her lines and stowed back aboard. Steam was hissing in her wildcat and in the windlass on the afterdeck. Strings of confetti hung down her dockside. The red and white pilot flag took steps to go aloft. The warning blasts of the ship's whistle shook the guests loose and piped them ashore.

Princess headed across into the fast flow of the channel and slid past the towering fantail of the crowded ship. Caught in the spread of the mainsail and the jib, the west wind pulled us down toward the open sea. My little boat passed close astern of the liner, trying maybe to feel the warm breath of those farewells. Down past the darkened docks, empty and fragrant with the dust of a million cargoes, I timed our speed by the lengthening wet stain of water on the piles.

This was the dream. This was the target of all my years, the end that lay buried in the endless prosecution of the means. My boat was standing out to sea. I had to believe it. There was a pile of evidence. The deck was certainly solid under my feet. The shifty wind was hard to pin down, but caught in the tightly woven net of canvas its testimony was strong in the pinch of the sheet lines.

For a guy with no debts except a vague due bill from a local draft board not yet established, I had shoved off in one hell of a hurry. All the things left undone were represented by members of lumber at large under the bridge deck. The struggle to square a ship away before the sea cancels the credit advanced by a fair tide is an old story.

There had been other departures and other ships, half remembered: all hands on deck before the watches were set, too busy to feel the excitement of sailing; booms dropped thundering into place; heavy hatch boards slid and slammed to fit; tarpaulins soggy with tar dragged across the hatch to seal the holds; the ship's carpenter dogging the crew and locking the steel batten strips with a sack full of oak wedges and a walloping maul; fat steel booms jerking at their stays as the ship lurched past the sea buoy; the calligraphy of steel cable on a steel deck. Only the silent tankers that slink out of port with the turn of a valve get away without this prelude to passage. . . .

We were sticking our chin out. *Princess* was hardly made ready for sea. The boards were still loose on the cockpit floor, and the self-bailer was disconnected. The wide new bridge deck served to cut down the size of the cockpit and the possibility of being swamped. Kicking around down below was a panel of plywood ready as a jury hatch to batten down that vulnerable opening if it got to playing rough out there. Mooring and anchor lines were loose on deck, and down below food, gear, keepsakes, and sake were scrambled around. It looked like a boudoir after a bullfight.

There was no time to stop and get organized. The tide was almost halfway out by the time *Princess* passed the captive constellation of the city. The current was bossy, and the tiller of my little vessel held me by the hand all down the dark, inconstant river.

The current was all in her favor going out. It is only at the rise of the tide that the surface flow of the Hudson River runs in one direction while the great mass of its water heads the other way. I had seen deep-water vessels moored in that river without a breath of wind to blame it on breast the incoming tide while a nondescript navy of debris went charging downriver right in the face of it.

Leaning on a locust-wood pole that was soon to stand the pressure of frantic fish compounding the heavy undertow, a shad fisherman up at Edgewater had pointed with a spoke shave to the fresh water that slid like a sheet of ice down over the opposing bulk of the heavy salt sea. There wasn't a thing my eye could see except when the last of the fresh water yielded to the brine. Then, if the wind blew, a cat's fur of a different texture than that made by the salt water drew a line along the retreating front of fresh.

"We ran up and down the river by latching onto the layer of current that favored us with the centerboard of a sailboat," said the fisherman. "Now we've got gas." He looked at me as if it was my fault and went back to stripping the bark and burrs from the fish stake.

When the *Half Moon* first thrust her curious nose into this continent, the strange, uncertain tide and the sharp cut of the Palisades could easily have made this river seem like a great divide that promised a passage to the East.

Steady as she goes, and very offhand about it, *Princess* sailed away from Manhattan and swung under the arm that carried a torch on Bedloe's Island. Down toward The Narrows in the exuberance of the tide, the torch rose over the truck, was eclipsed by its own hand, and fell. The lights of the city drew together in the arithmetic of perspective. We were on our own.

The wind grew fresh and veered to the northwest. *Princess* tore down toward the open sea, as moon-struck as the tide. The lights on the lump of Staten Island got mixed up with the stars, and the lowlands of Brooklyn off the port bow were topped with a layer of glow. A steamer, bucking the current in the hourglass waist of the harbor, moved toward us. I lashed the tiller to go forward and check the running lights.

I was still dressed in my good suit. My pet Stetson was on my head, and my feet were freshly shod in heavy leather. In the excitement of shoving off I had neglected to change my clothes. I was dressed for an appointment. The only concession I had made to the new life was to loosen my tie and collar.

Those new shoes were clumsy. Up forward the lights were bright. I started back over the top of the cabin as my little boat heeled in a sharp gust. The lines that were stretched along the cabin top rolled like conveyer cylinders under my feet.

I fell. My feet went out and my spine struck the corner of the cabin top. I slid twisting into the sea. I felt the cold wet grab, and the current sluicing along the lee strakes folded over me.

Princess, hog-wild to go to sea, slobbered over the bone in her teeth and plunged ahead. I have as witness, instrumental in this writing, the thumb and index finger of my right hand. With all the adrenalin that fright produces punched through my system, these two members froze on the rigging in a mad stab. I hung onto the lee turnbuckle with the grip of a C clamp.

The cold-running sea clutched and dragged at my clothes, and the slip of the vessel pressed me against her chine. The chill of the wash eased the pain in my back, and I got hold of the toe rail with my left hand. Flopping around out there like a forgotten cork fender, I inched forward and shifted my grip. Now I had the turnbuckle in both hands, but still the pain and the pull of the sea put that deck beyond my wildest hopes.

Immediately astern, yawing and bucking against the distant tangle of lights, the new plywood dinghy pursued us at the end of her painter. Hanging by the shroud, I could see her climb and coast down the furrow of our wake, swinging wide for an apprehensive peek at me around the corner of the transom. Somebody cared.

Princess ploughed ahead. I wondered if the tiny bulwark would hold me. Was it worth the chance to go hand over hand around the two-inch toe rail that was edge-nailed to the deck? I might snag the painter with my right hand, burn along the wet line, duck under, and wrestle up into the dinghy. But not at that point—not with a steamer bearing down on me—not the way I felt.

Just a little time, a little luck, one good heave, and I'd be on board. Get a knee on that deck, and the rest would be easy. The insistent sea swarmed over me and bubbled through my clothes. Was it the cold or that blow that numbed my legs? Would it get better or worse? All my strength was in my hands. I hung on.

The dinghy, in another silly gesture of empathy, poked her nose around for another look to see if I was all right. What a way to go to sea! She swung her head slowly in the negative and scudded away for another look at the dark, converging edge of Staten Island. The steamer off the starboard bow drew closer. We were bound to meet in the vortex of The Narrows.

I caught a glimpse of the ship, looming bigger and bigger every time my boat lifted the hem of her genny. Suddenly it towered over me abeam. Something had to happen. It did.

The ship passed me by.

The common stock of life appreciates in value with the years. It is unnegotiable, nontransferable. In trust for you unconditionally, it requires only that you honor it. I was careless, and I was gone—dressed for an appointment.

For whatever it's worth, the rest of the story might have been compiled by a ghost from scraps of paper that glutted the limbers of *Princess* and would be pressed out with an old flatiron in a clam-digger's shack somewhere on Sandy Hook or the Azores, wherever *Princess* finally fumed ashore.

With the kind permission of the sea, it was written by the same two fingers that hooked on the aforementioned turnbuckle. Acknowledgment is made to the anonymous freighter that passed *Princess* going through The Narrows in that fateful hour. My girl must have known, too. She held firm to her side of the channel, steady. When at last the wash of that passing freighter reached her, it rolled me up over her topside, onto her deck.

It was no more than any friend will do, seeing a thread on your coat or a forgotten fender dangling in your wake. Dripping, I reached for the hatch runner and crawled back into the cockpit. My hat was gone. One shoe was missing. I tore the lashing off the tiller, and *Princess*, interrupted in her flight, came up into the wind, flapping her leech and tossing with impatience.

Hove to, we bucked the tide while the water oozed out of my clothes and zigzagged in little rivers across the deck. I spotted the hat. It was sailing down nicely on its own, the brim trimmed like a lugger, and making fair time. It ended its little side excursion on the end of the boat hook. I searched around for the shoe. I don't rightly know how long it was before it occurred to me that a shoe might not float. I had nothing to lose in the experiment, so I launched the other one by the lace. It sank. I let it go to join its mate. New shoes, it was better to leave them together in the locker at the bottom of The Narrows.

A strange thing it was that in all the years I had been to sea and with all the goings on in small boats, I never knew that leather shoes go down. What a place to find out, and at what a time! And of what use could such knowledge be to a man determined to go native on a tropical island?

12

The red nun and black can buoys that mark the Ambrose Channel writhed at their mooring chains and leaned toward the sea. *Princess* passed between them, heading out with no sympathy and a fair wind. People in bathing suits lay on the beach of Coney Island or plodded in the hot sand. Night stole away through the cross-hatch of the roller coaster and the parachute tower, batting for the Sultan's turret, bunted a shaft of light.

My good suit, all wool but the buttons and the brine, was a soggy lump at my feet. I sat at the tiller in a pair of wet shorts and wondered what the hell I wanted with a suit in the place I was going.

My shoes were already resting at the bottom of The Narrows. The island, that nameless jewel in the Caribbean upon which my dream rotated, was a long way off. Assuming that I succeeded in completing the long voyage, how would I be received? What is the protocol connected with going native? Are you invited, coerced, or cajoled into it? Or do you just go?

I had no experience in these things. Natives have a social organization of their own comprised of stations and levels. Perhaps it would be better to come ashore decked out in store clothes and reserve for myself something of the civilization I was fed up with. If I made the right kind of entrance, who knows but what I might be crowned king or taken for a god, a casual, lounge-model, one-button god with a modified drape.

I decided to play it straight, gave *Princess* her head, and cut toward the northeast. The nosy bowsprit, a willing party to any new nonsense, took a bearing on a tailor shop hidden in the Rock-aways.

My coat and pants hung from the topping lift in the sun and sprinkled the last rinse like tropical rain across the poop. *Princess*, clinging to a mooring in Rockaway Inlet, bided her time while I slept. Late in the afternoon I took the suit to a tailor, who retraced the course of its crease with the mastery of a Magellan.

When he handed it back to me on a hanger, all pressed and perfect, I rolled it up carefully and stuffed it into a sea bag. The captain of the flatiron stared at me. His world was coming apart at the seams, but I knew what I was doing. . . .

I had made a long voyage years before on a slow vessel carrying general cargo to the Far East. She was loaded badly. Her behavior resembled the motion of a dismasted sailboat with deep ballast and no sail surface to to steady her. There were steel rails in the lower hold.

We were at sea for a couple of months, most of it rough going. My good suit was nicely stored away on a hanger in the cabin locker. It was too hot to wear the suit in India. At last we came rolling home with a cargo of jute, which is relatively light stuff. Now our ship had more topside surface exposed to the wind than a square-rigged bark, and not enough weight in the hold to keep her on her feet.

My suit never saw the light of day till the first attack of channel fever hit me on the way up the bay. I dragged it out to get ready to go ashore. I couldn't believe it was my suit. Brand-new when I left, here it was completely worn out, threadbare. The lapels were frayed, the flaps of the pockets were in shreds. It looked as if it had been dragged by land, if not by sea, all the way to India and back. It had.

The motion of the ship, swinging night and day, had worked it over like the testing laboratory of the bureau of standards. The place for a suit is in a sea bag, ready for all state occasions that do not specify shoes.

The rest of the day was whiled away ministering to the wants of my best girl. I shifted my cargo of possessions all evening, the way newlyweds move furniture about.

The tide slowly bulged beneath the boat, filling up for its run out at midnight. No one knew that I had left town. That's the way it is when you go for good. The fervent farewells are a hedge against a lonely homecoming. There was no home for me here. Home was an island, unfounded, waiting, its substance bathed in the alternating transparency and opacity of an idea. Had the tide been in our favor, I would have left without a backward glance. It's waiting that makes things go soft, that turns things to pumpkins and pillars of salt.

I hadn't gone very far. Brooklyn was just across the bay, a five-cent subway ride from Times Square. There couldn't be any harm in saying good-by. Armed with a handful of nickels and numbers, I took a short-term lease on a phone booth. Down the list I called Red Gillyard, the friend who transported that disheveled carload of frames for *Princess* all the way from City Island to Edgewater during the previous winter.

"What are you doing in Rockaway?"

"I've pulled out of the rat race, Red. You can scratch me. I'm going native."

"But nobody goes native," Red came back, in an arrangement of static that sounded as if he was eating potato chips, "in

Rockaway." Another potato chip crackled across the wire. "Even if the police are willing, what would the neighbors think?"

"This is just the first leg."

"Sounds interesting. Are there any more legs?"

"The next leg will take me down to Atlantic City."

"Good idea. Ought to be able to pick up a leg down there." The obbligato of potato chips yielded to the theme. "When are you leaving?"

"The tide goes out around midnight."

"Stay where you are till I get there. I've got a week coming to me. I'll help you with the legs."

"*Princess* sails at midnight."

"I'll be there."

This was going to be tough to explain to *Princess*. Riding at her anchor, white and lovely and suddenly young against the dart and dab of the carnival lights, she turned gently toward me in the waver of the tide as I came up on her in the dinghy. She was my bride. This was our tryst. We had embarked on a sea and a way that was just for us.

She seemed bewildered when I took her to the wharf and the tide began to seep away from under her while I waited for Red. *Princess*, with a total capacity of five gallons, fidgeted at the gas dock trying to act like a customer. I filled up a spare gallon can with gas, which didn't impress anyone. I might just as well have ordered an eyedropper of beer at the bar across the street. I tidied her up. The floor boards in the cockpit were fastened down, and the tide ticked away.

Still no Red. What was keeping that guy? We were excited enough, facing the prospect of our first taste of the open sea, without having to double up with the frustration of a tardy supercargo.

Red showed up just before the tide went down the drain, and he brought a fresh wind with him. We shoved off. He held her to the channel while I was down below trying to figure out what to do with his suitcase. It wouldn't fit under the bunks. It blocked off the forepeak completely. It was square-jawed, inflexible and defiant. I lost the argument and left it for a pillow on Red's bunk. "Don't bother about it," said Red. "Put it anywhere."

Anywhere was dead ahead when I got back on deck. There was a great swoosh of sail, a sudden jar, and *Princess* rolled her port side down. She was taking off for the hills with the silver dollar under her mast as mad money. We were running right into the shoal at Point Breeze.

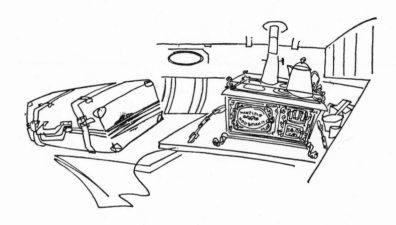

"Sorry, Red." I apologized for her, and borrowed the tiller. She came about with an unresponsive and airy kind of indifference in the concurring flow. When I got her headed straight, she lifted her skirts and flew off in the chilly northeaster.

"Saucy little devil, isn't she?" Red said it in a half whisper, like a guest witnessing a family brawl.

"She has her moments." I showed my friend the tip-off to her boiling point. I pressed the tiller hard to windward and *Princess* went off her course. On the edge of the wind, the luff of the staysail curled in a gentle threat, lay away, and waited for the provocation of imbalance. I supplied it. The staysail bent in a curtsy, lifted the baton along its foot, and with a flourish of incredible grace wheeled to the starboard with a slap.

The balloon jib lost heart and started after it. I released the drag of the rudder, and the mainsail recalled them as if for another reading, like pages of a book. "When she does that, ease your helm."

"How come?"

"Because she's getting ready to bean you with the boom."

"What has she got against me?"

"You kept her waiting at the dock."

We passed the point and headed south along the breakwater. Beyond the light the bell and the gong were swinging an off-beat rag with the bell getting the extra licks.

The wind, veering slightly, was cold and damp. The stars dissolved like bubbles in a flat drink, and my little boat began to roll and pitch as we drew across Ambrose Channel. The current, now in its maturity, blustered by, setting her to the east. As she reached, she speared the ebbing tide with her outhaul. At every gust a tiny sea hopped aboard at the clew of the mainsail and bled itself out long the boom. I handed Red the tiller. "Hold her on the light."

"Where are you going?"

"The big hook is out on the bowsprit. It's making her pitch."

"You going to get it?"

"Yeah, keep her on the light."

"You mean that iddy-bitty light out there in front? I thought that was a firefly."

"That's Sandy Hook. Keep your eye on that staysail and keep her steady."

"Yes, sir, by all means, sir."

Gillyard was a man of weight, a man of substance—any edible substance. He thought highly of chow. I went below and started a fire in the stove. It tempered the wet draft that filled the cabin, deflected off the surface of the sail. The little stove leaned back, rocked and cracked in agreement with the water that talked back an inch or so beyond the strakes.

"Red."

"Yeah."

"How about something to eat?" There was an ominous silence. I looked up. He was still there. I leaned out of the companionway. "You hungry?" No answer.

Evidently I had touched on a very delicate subject. Red's brows were knitted together so closely that they joined in a single red line. His lips were rolled in along his teeth, and the color of his face had gone up like a curtain into his hair. I knew it. I could smell it.

Princess had vented her spleen. She had taken it out on my friend. I felt a wave of guilt; I jumped and took the tiller. Slowly, imperceptibly at first, I began to feel something of his torment. I had a glimmering of it in the remembrance of my dinner.

An hour went by. We had passed the buoys of Gedney Channel, and the great light on Sandy Hook yawed to the beam in the following sea. Red lay sprawled on the afterdeck, his feet dangling in the cockpit. He clutched the toe rail and the sheet traveler, and his cheek was pressed to the cold, unfeeling deck. It began to rain. I threw an oilskin over him and listened to the moan of the man and the wind in the rigging.

The color of day, like a miscible white pigment, was poured along the edge of the eastern sky. It spread as if driven by the wind across the face of the sea. The wind was still on our side, but the alliance of the tide ended at its published time. After an hour of grace, while it gathered its strength, the current threw itself without shame at *Princess*.

One half of the crew was stricken, immobilized. If I could only get to the windward of Gillyard, perhaps I would be spared.

I didn't have the heart to move him, or the strength. It was cold. It was wet. I was tired. There had been a lot of false starts. What difference would one more make? In the life that unfolded before me, what was a day, more or less? There was only one way to get to the windward of Red. Turn the boat around—even if that meant going back. At least I would have a favorable tide. I put *Princess* about and started back.

Red Gillyard sprang to life. "Where are you going?"

"Back."

"No, no, no!"

"Are you all right?"

"Yes." Now he was.

I came about again, resumed my course, and changed seats with my friend, like we used to do as kids when we played Going to Jerusalem.

13

"Sea" is a loose term. The solution that creeps into the sounds, the inlets, the bights and bays, that charges up the mouths of rivers and assimilates the drain of the watersheds, is spoken of as sea water. I prefer ocean.

This one wasn't bad as oceans go. We took a beating with that seventy-five-pound anchor lashed to the bowsprit crossing Ambrose Channel. After it was dragged in, folded, and stowed deep in the bilge, the little boat behaved herself.

If you've ever been appointed candlestick and stood in the middle of a seesaw you can understand why. The redisposition of weight on a vessel must be doubled in the reckoning. Whether it be through accident or art, the lifting of weight from one place and setting it down in another has twice the effect of lifting it from one place and tossing it over the side. That's what makes floating property so damn tippy.

It has its advantages, too, in the quick way a vessel can be made to right itself. Gripping shovels and boxed in in the eerie light of a ship's hold, men have fought to throw back a loose cargo that shifted in a storm. Ships have been saved and crews have taken heart knowing that every shovelful thrown up the hill carried the weight of two.

It is a man's hard luck that the thundering ocean knows when her might is doubled by the nature of a ship's cargo or the way he loaded it. There is nothing more vital to a ship's long expectancy as his insight into her trim.

Ships have worked for generations of masters whose knowledge of celestial navigation was limited to latitude and backed up with the lead. One of these, an old Nova Scotia skipper I knew, called his shots "lateetudes." He had three. One was an observation of the noon sun when it was on the "shelf," and the other two sights were of the North Star when the handle of the Dipper was resting at the same altitude. That gave him two or three chances every twenty-four hours to ascertain his "lateetude."

He tracked all over the Atlantic and winged home at last along the avenue of his home port after batting around for months, paying no more attention to drift, set, or sailings than he did to the only chronometer on board, which banged around on a hook in the galley and was cranked up to the bursting point every morning by the cook, who had paid a dollar for it. This old man never had a ship break its back under his feet or founder from the punch of a loose or intolerant load.

One knowledge is gained and another goes by the board. The years go by and the price of passage stands. The lives of men, payable on demand to the sea, are swamped with public-relations releases hammered out by the steel mills and the fabricators before they ever sign on a ship. Down at the pier when corruption knocks off, ignorance shapes up. Ships are doomed at the dock. Trip hammers of heft are swung blithely aboard like time bombs, readied to be released by the first big wave.

Ask any shipmaster whether his vessel was loaded so that the center of gravity is where it should be. Like as not he'll tell you what the old man from Nova Scotia told me: "Half the ships that make port can thank the merciful sea that interpolates the intention of heaven."

Salt is the spice. Shaken into the wind out of the cellar of the sea, it peppers the eye and whets the gambler's appetite. The ocean can afford to book your bet. If she loses now, the rain will bring everything you own seeping down to her, if it takes a million years.

We sat in the cockpit of *Princess* in a very fine drizzle while the northeast wind rolled us like dice against the wall of the tide. Red Gillyard, looking glum and confused by the snarl of heavy traffic in his digestive tract, retired to the cocoon of the cabin, curled up around his infirmity and waited for wings.

We had made a start. *Princess* lay about five miles offshore with the Highlands of Navesink barely visible off the starboard quarter. The flow that gave us our start was being gulped back into the lower bay, and the wind, sweeping my boat against it in long curves, held the edge in the balance of power.

It is too much to ask of a small boat to mitigate the gloom of rain or to dance to the dirge of a foghorn. It was sufficient that I had made my departure, that my dent in the mud of Manhattan was filled by the same tide that carried me away. My friend, lusting after Atlantic City, had his enthusiasm watered down, but he did what he could to help, in the way of a couple hundred pounds of ballast on the port bunk.

The wind veered a bit to the east and buckled down. With her head steady on magnetic south I lashed the tiller of *Princess* and invited her to mind her business. It was ten o'clock in the morning. Microscopic wet lenses, suspended in mid-air, which spread the myopia of fog, were dissipating in the wind. There was nothing in sight, and we were heading a bit offshore. I had to get a wink of sleep.

Down below Red was out like a light. I went for my bunk.

It had an occupant, a thick-skinned, double-belted customer with plenty of brass. It was Red Gillyard's suitcase.

I had half a mind to give that great mass of shiny leather brazening it out on my bunk the old heave-ho. No small vessel should be put upon by a suitcase. That's what sea bags are for. Displaced from my bunk by that stiff and uncompliant dog, I sprawled in the corner next to the stove and dozed.

I woke as the veering wind swung my girl like the door of a damp closet. The mist, fugitive as the fog of breath on glass, was licked up by dry, clean air. It was noon. The wind quit, and *Princess* rose from her work as the tide slackened. As she pitched, drops of rain on the bottom of the boom traveled fore and aft chasing one another, consolidated, and splashed down on the cabin floor.

I went up on deck and rove in the slack of the sheets. We lay about five miles off Shrewsbury rocks. Now and again when we rose on the inflated crest of a glassy swell I could see the protruding end of a buoy stuck like a splinter in the flat hand of the sea. Beyond it an inverted mirage of land above the horizon bled down into the real thing when we rose, and returned, fat as ever, when we fell.

The engine under the bridge deck was waiting for a workout in the blue sea. It was years since it had exchanged its boisterous heat for the cool of the ocean water. This was warmer than the water that wove in among the rocks Down East, but it was just as clear and clean. I was hesitant about starting the engine. To subject my prone friend to its noise and fumes might set him off again. The vagaries of his malady were no fault of his. The staunchest seaman has his moments at the bulwark and will swing like a mean drunk if you want to make anything out of it.

The old-timers get surly instead of sick, and by inhaling with the upswing and breathing out with its fall, substitute their own respiratory motion for the heave and plunge of a ship. They can do it in their sleep. Down the alleyway leading to the fo'c's'le, as the ship lifts you can hear that inspirational snore.

The punctual tide bustled down to make amends for its hours of opposition. The north wind came along. *Princess* was kissed by them on the starboard side, and she reached. It rolled Red out of his bunk.

He came up with a smile. "How do you feel?" he said.

"How do I feel? I feel like setting the spinnaker."

We tacked it to the business end of the bowsprit. The boat hook, caught in the cringle at the clew, held it open. A huge lotus petal of Egyptian sailcloth blossomed from the jib halyard and filled the sky.

Princess, an old-fashioned working girl from Down East, was a stranger to this newfangled hoop skirt, but she knew how to wear clothes. She flew along wing and wing in a class of her own and with her tiller untouched.

The long swells that accrued to the easterly were cut down by the new north wind. A transitional surface texture quarreled and slapped happily under the hull. We made time.

Red was doing nicely. The excitement of our pace had him. The façade of the shore lines rose. Old summer mansions, beaten by the weather and the tide of fashion, focused their shingled deadeyes on the sea. Against the precept of their crumpled abutments and the constant warning of the surf, bright little cottages edged every which way toward the water. Dots of color, loud umbrellas, and bathing suits clustered and drifted loose along the beach. "Girls," said Red. Things were really looking up.

The mouth of Shark River seethed along the beam, its angry, white saliva spewed in the sun. The wind added a number to its force. We closed in at Sea Girt to a mile. The rock jetties of Manasquan lay dead ahead. We had another mile to go. Red held her southwest into the midafternoon sun while I jabbed the wind out of the spinnaker and tossed it below.

For nearly forty miles a facet of the New Jersey coast from Monmouth Beach to Barnegat Inlet, its straight edge lined emphatically north-northeast and south-southwest true, shelves into deep water at precisely a half a mile. The only break in this unimaginative piece of work, except for a couple of shallow slues, are the two rocky, knuckled fingers of the Manasquan Inlet that kept asking to leave the room.

The surf that snowballed down along this grade raised particular hell when it rolled against the jetties. We passed the lesser of these, tightened the mainsheet, and directed our course up the channel. The tide was pouring out. The wind held its breath for a moment to see what would happen.

Princess was lifted by a swell and lowered back by the undertow and the tide to within range of the lethal punch of the south jetty. I saw the grain of granite through the clear green, and the keel struck lightly once against the rock with an aiming tap. We rose for the blow.

The point of the boat hook, released from the turnbuckle of the shroud, whizzed overhead and caught in a lucky fissure in the ready rock. It was barely enough. We cleared with the rock flushed a foot off our port quarter. Red grabbed the pole and added his bulk against the following swell. I let go, jumped below, and gave the flywheel a violent half spin.

It wouldn't do it again without choking, but it did it that time. The engine went off with a roar. I jammed the shift lever forward, and the counter of my boat came down, teasing, an inch or so from the rock and we puffed clear.

Every man has his quota of miracles. I couldn't help wondering as we chugged up between these parallels whether I wasn't running low on mine.

It was three o'clock in the afternoon, a scant twenty-four hours since I had slept. We were safe in Brielle. A serious traveler, utilizing any one of a number of public conveyances, could have duplicated our distance in less than an hour's time and come out with a fair amount of change from a dollar bill. That Caribbean island looked impracticable at this rate.

This was the third sleepless night in a row, brought on by the demands of the adamant tide and the flurry of departure. I was hanging on the ropes, beaten by fatigue, and living on little naps in the afternoon.

My numb skull recorded a scudding white cloud against a very blue sky, a silver whip of surf along a lemon beach, and the charred prongs of the channel. There was a big white house on the hill to the left with green lawns and a flag flying. There were cool depths under the skirting trees ahead. A fancy row of deep-sea machines, stern to dock, fished for customers, using the latest swivel chairs and chrome contrivances as bait.

Tied up, we turned down the sparkle of the day, submerged into the seminight below, and slept.

A stiff breeze spanked things around in the cool of the evening. The incoming tide was drumming with impatient fingers on the hull. *Princess* wanted to skip down the inland ditch. I couldn't see any harm in it. There were still a couple of hours of daylight left, a fair wind, an agreeable tide, and nothing to upset Red's recently replenished breadbasket. We blew for the bridge and headed through the canal for Barnegat Bay.

My little boat was restrained to the channel by her draft. She shrugged off the failing tide and employed the wind. We squeezed between the wedge of Herring Island and the slender springboard of Island Beach. Another bridge broke open for us along the road to that strip of sand, strung out as if to shield the body proper of the bay from the cresting eyes of the sea.

We could hear the ocean boom and shear along the narrow wall of sand outside while the little waves in the bay licked along the bottom of the boat in endless congratulation. *Princess*, with sails outstretched, bowled down the alley of the bay without spilling a drop of wind. The channel buoys turned in their cushy berths as she passed, spelling out their white numbers in the gloaming. There was a gull perched on almost every one. I often wondered where in hell those birds would sit if it wasn't for the Hydrographic Office and the Bureau of Navigation. I have seen the pigeons lobbying for them down in Washington.

A rambling relic of a summer home appeared on a point of the mainland. A dark shadow of sail flew along, blotting out the wind ripple that continued off the surface of the water up into the trees.

Red gaped at it. "What can that be?"

"Damned if I know." I pretty near put *Princess* aground staring.

"The *Flying Dutchman?*"

"Not in Barnegat Bay." It came about and drove across the shoals, coming at us like a ghost off the filigreed veranda of the old house. It was one great mainsail. It didn't seem possible that a vessel big enough to stand such canvas could afford to monkey around in eighteen inches of water.

It shot by, crossing our bow, an elliptical shell of boat. It was all beam and no draft, with a centerboard sticking up above its hogged deck like the fin of a predatory fish. There were a girl and a boy in bathing suits plastered to its polished deck. It proceeded to run rings around us with the little waves drumming under its shovel nose.

Humiliated, *Princess* strained ahead to cover more distance and her exasperation. If she hadn't been a lady, she would have invited the boat outside. We dropped her hook in the mud at Goose Creek and hit the sack. Ten miles added to a day's run makes twenty miles; ten from the point of departure plus ten toward the port of desire.

14

A square, hot patch of sunlight, cut by the open hatch, swung from bunk to bunk as *Princess* rolled. The bright warmth licked our faces like a puppy bucking for a romp in the morning. The smoke from Red's cigarette, caught between the carlins of the cabin top, overflowed into the sky. I grubbed a light from the butt before it went spinning through the hatch, snapped by Red's fat finger. It struck the furled canvas and landed on the deck. He lumbered after it, shaky as a big bear coming out of a cave in the spring. He tried again. This time the burning butt hit with a tiny hiss. A great splash rocked the boat.

There were some bubbles and a trail of foam on the still water when I got out on deck. Red was gone. I saw him streaking for the beach. When he touched bottom, he lay there in the tepid water and dug for clams in the mud. The water was warm going in. The air was even warmer coming out. The sun searched close across the sea and the land.

Red emptied the sand from his sneaker over the side. With the corner of a towel for a potholder, I reached for the coffeepot and filled the cups on the bridge deck. Red cocked his head and pumped his ear with his pinkie. We lifted our cups in a toasting gesture to accommodate the wash of a passing cruiser. "While we're at it, here's to *Princess*," said Red. "Hope she makes it."

We drank to the proposition as the wash clapped against her freeboard. "By the way, have you any idea where she's going?"

"South, sort of," I said.

"Let's go," said Red. "The papers are piling up on my desk."

The railroad bridge at Goodluck Point was asleep with its mouth open. There were no more bridges to worry about for twenty miles. The channel was well-marked. In the manner of the lesser latter-day explorers, we ran without a local chart. We ran aground. After we kedged her off the flats, the old girl did it again and again, like the lady in the limerick. The third time the anchor gave up in the mud, and the engine would have no part of the proceedings. We made sail and waited for the wind.

I cut a new deck, and Red dealt. We swam and ate lunch, and in the afternoon it blew from the west a little. *Princess* looked real pretty. Her sails were flat and drawing, and a wisp of grass from the duckblind was in her teeth. She was all dressed up with no place to go. She was stuck in the mud.

I was stuck, too. I was down about half a dollar, trying to bluff a measly straight with deuces wild, when the offshore wind heeled *Princess* well over and blew her to some deep water. The parlor matches rolled from the bridge deck and joined the other chips in the bilge. We were off.

After that good deed, the wind died. The sun poured a hot haze over the yellow swampland. The little engine, now helped, now hindered by the tide that waded out across the shallow inlets, provided an asthmatic cloud that drifted along at our exact speed and in our general direction.

Our general direction was all wrong. We were rushing the season. Who ever heard of heading south in July? I remembered the cool reaches off Montauk and the chill and tonic of a Down East summer wind. What were we doing slugging it out in a sweltering labyrinth of eroded mud pies, backtracking in a windless blaze of swamp grass? What island paradise waiting two thousand miles away could be worth this trial by fire?

The sails of *Princess*, like an unruffled banner, advanced through the inferno of reeds. A black fly crawled up along the lock stitching of the mainsail to meet a friend. We swatted a quorum and were rewarded by polka dots before our eyes. In the space of an hour, the sails were covered by a plague of black flies that obscured every inch of canvas.

Unmindful of the indignity, *Princess* drew her skirts up and sloshed through the muddy backwaters of Atlantic City with the weight of my friend cooling his feet off her transom and her bow held high.

We met a shark in Brigantine Channel. I like to think it was a shark. It may have been a porpoise. It had one big, black fin that cut across the bow like the protruding tip of a knife, severing the narrow channel. There was none of the playfulness of a porpoise in that businesslike blade of fin. It cut straight along as if it knew all about the distance between two points. We turned, opened her up, and went after it, brandishing boat hooks, table knives and bared teeth. A lot of good it did. The fin stayed just out of reach and sounded after a while for reasons of its own which had nothing to do with our display of ferocity. We turned, and the black flies were gone to wherever sharks and black flies go in the summertime.

We came into Atlantic City by the back door. *Princess* must have been ashamed of us. We looked like a couple of bums. *Princess* nosed alongside, and as I laid out her lines, Red was hacking away at his fiery stubble with a safety razor and a saucepan of hot suds. There were girls on the dock at Atlantic City.

For a solid week Atlantic City was a great place—if you like rain. The grip of the heat wave, loosened by the wet east wind, clenched its soggy fist on the Eastern Seaboard. The pressure burst in a raging, purple storm that dripped for days while we waited for the healing northwest wind. The girls went back to their typewriters, and Red Gillyard went to the post office.

"Got any identification I can show to pick up your mail?"

I looked in my wallet. "Here's my social security card. I don't expect to need it where I'm going." He took the card, and he also took me at my word: He never returned it. There was no mail, anyway, and it rained some more.

My friend became fretful. I watched with unconcealed anticipation as his suitcase gulped up his gear. The leather accordion pleats opened up, and it grew bigger and bigger as he fed his laundry into it. I helped by sitting on top, and the clasps clicked. The belts that girdled it were drawn and buckled, and out of the hatch it went, leaving a long-awaited vacuum. Down the dock we stowed it in a cab. The captain of the hack had no feelings about that bag, but mine were mixed when Red Gillyard shoved off.

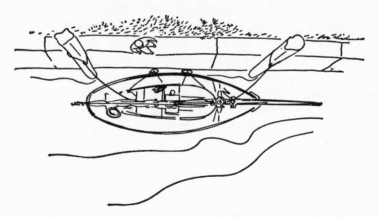

Princess, huddled in low water beside the wharf, inclined her smooth, round spar toward me as I held to her stays coming down. Her cabin was warm, and toward night the rain fell from the familiar clouds. A tiny bomb of water forming under the edge of the cabin house made practice runs over my head and splattered on the bunk. I hung some tin cans at strategic intervals and placed a skillet on the bunk to catch the overflow. I fell asleep with my bones draped around it, listening to the weather drumming on the deck.

The sun poured all over me in the morning. A little girl and a little boy were sitting on the bridge deck giggling. I had to go along with them. The ways of the sea are strange. It isn't every day you see a man sleeping with a frying pan of fresh water.

I blew myself to breakfast on the boardwalk and studied the sea over the second cup of coffee. The gruff surface, beaten by a week of rain, gave rise to a modest surf that lapped the long un-printed sheet of sand. The boardwalk, wide enough for forty peo-ple to walk abreast, stretched clear out of sight to the south. It must have taken a forest of trees to build that grandstand. There seemed little room for doubt that the sea itself was the biggest show on earth. In the smallest possible way, I owned a piece of that show. Like a theatrical angel, I took a proprietary interest in the size of the box office so early Monday morning.

The audience strolled along, sat on the benches, or leaned on the railing and stared at the moody expanse. The tide was run-ning out of Absecon Inlet. The red nun buoys which clung to the bar that lay parallel to the beach were nodding to the south. Forty miles down the coast lay the harbor of Cape May. It was time to run down along the beach before the audience got bored and went home.

Princess was in favor of it. Her sails went up right at the dock, and she surged and trembled with expectancy. A full com-plement of kids climbed all over her and reluctantly handed me the lines from off the shore bitts as she undocked. They scrambled after us out along the jagged granite rocks of the pier, ran and wriggled through the crowds on the boardwalk watching *Princess* round the bend.

My little boat passed close aboard a big schooner, tied up with her foresail set and tugging, that waited on the pleasure of passengers. This shapely old lumber coaster had lost her mainmast somewhere down the line and went out looking for it twice a day with a fresh load of wide-eyed tourists paying to help.

Jostled in the eye of the stream, my girl filled her clean canvas with the new wind that poured off the washed land. She turned to the right at the bend of the channel, rose proud with each roller, and swept down along the beach. Passing just out of surf-casting range of the Steel Pier, I waved, as I could well afford to do, in response to the waving arms that reached out of that cage after us.

We sailed southwest. Frisky and independent, *Princess* let go of my hand and, guiding herself, she sliced the morning sea without leaving a crumb of froth. By noon we had lost the tall buildings along the beach that were boxed in gold by the sun. I lowered a lure over the side. A new ball of line jumped around the cockpit floor and diminished as it invested itself in the blue water.

The mooring lines were made up and stowed, the bedding aired, and I dried the laundry, washed before I left. Breaking out some odd pieces of wood stowed under the afterdeck, I built a rack for a pale-blue water cooler bottle picked up in Atlantic City. The bottle was imprinted with the words "PROPERTY OF GREAT BEAR." I felt like a rumrunner. I built a swivel rack for it and put a noose around its neck so it could bow down as it poured and atone for the capital offense of running away from the office.

Princess seemed happy. We were well on our way, and, for reasons that a man will never understand, she was steady and yielding now that she had me all to herself. I went about hauling the main and trimming the jib sheet for whatever advantage, real or imaginary, that might accrue. She pushed through the pleasant sea with no perceptible change in her rate of speed, indulging me in my theories of efficiency. Now and again she tossed me and rose with a slight shudder, feeling apprehensively for my feet. All the afternoon, as *Princess* minded her course through the gentle summer sea, I dozed on the bridge deck and thought about the great singlehanded voyagers and the knotty problem of the lifeline. . . .

An unbreakable link between a man and a boat has its

drawbacks. In the stress of a seaway the very line upon which your life depends can do the work of an evil hand or strangle like a looped umbilical cord. Dragged through the sea, a man is more likely to drown at the end of a lifeline than to pull himself back on board. There was Captain Blackburn, Down East, who solved the problem one terrible night by letting his hands freeze solid to the oars. His dory lost the mother ship while out tending the nets in a sudden, violent blizzard off the Banks. With his hands frozen, lifeless as the ash-wood oars to which they were stuck, he pulled himself four hundred miles into port with the bodies of two men slumped at his feet, dead of exposure. Not long after, he sailed alone in a little boat across the Atlantic to England and back, with iron hooks for hands.

Singlehanded sailing is just about as near to being free of the ties of earth as a man can get without going overboard about it. It can also be one hell of a lot of work. When the wind is of an even disposition, the course appropriate, and the boat right, there is nothing like it. The drag of the rudder through the resilient water, balanced against the draw of the canvas, determines the mean of the course. I tightened the sheets a bit, eased the tiller a degree, and it was steady as you go. Now I could do as I pleased, and there lay the danger.

The wheels of ships and the tillers, endlessly polished by the palms of men, reflect the tedium of the long watch. From the day when the wind was first employed to drive a vessel, the mind of man has hankered for the answer to the variables of wind and water that might relieve the drudgery of the helm. This search was more immediate to a helmsman than the quest for new land beyond the limb of the sky. The answer came, in part, not at sea but in the shipyards. The man from Friendship, Maine, who grew old along with *Princess* once showed me her secret in the flat cheeks of the bottom just forward of the sternpost. The boys with the slide rules have other ideas, and since sailing has become largely a sporting matter, what if the sleek new racers work you half to death? At least it keeps you hanging on the wheel, where you can't fall overboard.

For all her years, *Princess* was a smart little vessel, and ours was a very modern arrangement. We were free: no ties, no apron strings, no lifeline. My baby had been around. She was no clinging vine. I wasn't so sure I liked her that way. Not way out there.

The ocean was empty except for one little boat to the east, far out of hailing distance, that kept ducking below the choppy edge of the long swell. *Princess* brushed aside the waves that presumed before her bow and hurried on. She had no time for me. The thin line of land to the west was parted at every bight and inlet. The wind grew stronger, and I put on a life jacket, mostly to keep warm. *Princess* didn't seem to mind. This was no time to fall, roll, or stroll over the side. It would be a long haul to the beach.

I went below, and while rummaging in the fineness of her forepeak as it bored rumbling through the sea, I found a thirty-foot length of three-eighths-inch Manila and snaked it up on deck. I tied one end to my belt and the other to *Princess*. It didn't make much sense. We were clipping along at nearly seven knots. It's fine to get spliced, but what kind of marriage can it be with thirty feet between a man and his boat and a seven-knot current if I went overboard?

The wind, veering heavily to the north, scraped together enough gray clouds to form a thunderhead. The sky, after its long week of weeping, broke in an afterthought and emptied the rest of the bucket all at once. The little vessel that lay to the east drove past us full tilt with a cargo of wet and bedraggled anglers pining for a change. *Princess* took it without a murmur and tore through the darkened seas. The northerly went to pot with the cloudburst and came back gentle and relieved from the southeast. I changed the course of *Princess* and, gathering way, she drove west toward the harbor of Cape May.

Scattered pieces of the storm, driven in above the land, burned briefly in the last, staggered rays of the sun and turned the color of ash. I was still fooling around with that thirty-foot length of line, watching the tiller drawn to the weather side, straining to match the milling tend of the wind on the snubbed gate of the sail, when suddenly I hit on it. I had the answer.

One end of the thirty-foot line was made fast to *Princess*. I lashed the tiller with the first few feet of that line, using a lady's knot. The other end, the hauling part that would slip the knot and release the tiller, was married to my belt. Now if I should take a sudden notion to go by the board, my weight, pulling on the line, would slip the knot and release the tiller, and the old girl would luff. She would have to hang around till I got back on board, whether she liked it or not.

I went forward, dragging the lifeline. It was a nuisance. It snagged on every bolt, bar, and button. It got wound up on the Charlie Noble and fouled under the fantail. But when I pulled on it, the tiller came free and *Princess* swung right up into the wind, paused, and luffed with a great flapping and commotion. I had to reassure her, but I loved it. I got her out of irons and back on the course, lashed the tiller with the slipknot, and did it again. It really worked. I was tickled pink. The lady loved me.

It was nice at night. There were stars, and the long Atlantic, trained by the recent northeaster, its swell topped by curling waves that were turned in the stiff southeast wind, spent itself on the deep and shoaling coast. The loom of the Cape May Point Light, making up its mind to flash every thirty seconds, cast a slow, admonitory glow out over the nervous little lights that blinked down along the beach.

Princess acted silly about going in. Lurching before the solicitation of the wind and the sea, she tossed and yawed and demanded attention. I took her tiller in my hand and poked her nose at the polemic of red, white, and green lights that argued according to their individual notions of time at the end of the jetty.

The direction of the channel lay close to the axis of the earth. I had the word of the North Star, and we moved southwest until its image smiled on the flower of the compass. Then we turned and ran in between the lines of rocks.

It was dark in the harbor of Cape May, and quiet after the drumming of the ocean on the hull. The wind that worked up the open sea left this pocket of water unmoved. A deep-draft vessel alongside the wharf unburdened itself in a glare of light before a hollow warehouse. *Princess* lay over and ran close-hauled to the western limit of the lonely, mile-long harbor. I swung her into the wind and dropped her hook in the soft bottom. The southeast wind rustled her canvas as she drifted back with loose sheet lines and fetched up at the end of the cable.

There were music and people and the paintpot brightness of neon lights on the shore. I made *Princess* comfortable, hung a lantern on her forestay, and took the dinghy ashore for a nightcap.

The place was jammed and all lit up. It was a summer place, with rough beams and untrimmed rafters crawling with electric cable. The bar was beautiful. Mahogany, rich and red, it lay in state in the center of the room and sprang to life with foaming heads of beer. I found a hole between guard and tackle and plunged through to intercept a lateral pass for my first down. The lady on my left looked me over and said, "Where did you come from?"

It was a hard question to answer. I was still rocking from the long day at sea, all the blue, the unexpected storm, and the evanescence of the day's end. The beer was good, and as I considered the tang of hop blossoms turned loose on my tongue, I spoke briefly of these things.

The lady's eyes grew big and soft and came down suddenly till they looked like little rips in straining canvas. "You certainly have your nerve with you," she said, "talking so romantic to a stranger!"

The guard on my right skipped a stanza in the middle of a ballad to run interference for me. "Cut it out, Lizzie!" Then to me, "That's m'wife, flirts with everybody, pay her no mind."

I paid for the beer and walked across the low hill to the curve of sand that caught the brunt of the sea. Down through the swift channel of Delaware Bay a ship bore to the east, its red riding light yielding at a point abaft its beam. I watched the masthead light pass between the stars, and I looked for the lights on the opposite edge of land that led to Norfolk.

There were two ways to go. One was directly down the coast. The other was up the Delaware and down Chesapeake Bay.

This was the end of July, and the wind when it came off the land was like a wall of fire. Beyond that wall lay the cool trade winds and the tropics. To break through meant taking *Princess* way outside. After taking either route, I could then go out around Hatteras and down through one of the eight passages through the Banks into the Caribbean. I thought of the sternpost, which was prone to dribble in a busy sea, while I cut across into town, bought a bottle of milk and a bottle of brandy, and went back to my baby.

In the morning, leaning on the hatch runners, I blinked at the shining sands of Cape May Inlet. The water was deep and clear, and there was room for a hundred ships instead of the single one that was still disgorging its cargo at the western end.

It takes more than deep, protected water to make a busy port. It takes people and crossroads. This clean nose of land with its deep harbor is passed up by ships in favor of the mouth of the Delaware and the gullet of the crowded river that twists into Philadelphia. The harbor at its western end was furnished with a fisherman's wharf that carried a single spur of track and a channel that turned past an old-fashioned saltwater garage into the sparse little summer town.

I threw some shavings and a match into the stove. While it was urging the coffee to boil, I stared at the cleat on the starboard combing. The long fishing line that had hopefully gone over the side at Atlantic City was still trailing off the stern of my vessel. I pulled it in, all thirty fathoms of it, and the lure flashed in the sunlight and clanked into the cockpit. *Princess* had dragged that phony through forty miles of open sea, into the harbor in the dead of night, tangled and untangled it with the tides. I was certainly one red-hot fisherman. I rowed into town for a pound of chopped meat.

There was a Friendship sloop up on the ways. She was waiting for ribs, and she was being picked clean in the process. It happens to houses left untenanted, and it happens to boats. It shouldn't. A man's house is his castle; his boat is certainly no less.

The moat that surrounds it, protects it, is the sea itself, and that can be as wide as a boat's ability to venture.

Every mile of deep that comes between the land and a vessel is a mile of assurance added to its sovereignty. Up on the ways, a boat is as helpless as an open city. Strange eyes rake it over, and strange hands finger its fittings. Strange heads are poked without shame into every section of its house and hull.

On the beach a boat is like a museum without guards. The connoisseurs will carry away everything that is not bolted or riveted down. Some of the more persistent art lovers will bring their lunch wrapped up with wrenches and cold chisels. Hope lies in the possibility of reaching the sanctuary of the open sea.

There once was a man who spurned the fittings and stole the whole boat. He wanted to go to France. He was not a tourist; he was a Frenchman. He had no money, but he had taste. It was a Friendship sloop that he took in the dark of the night. It offered him, broke and desperate, a way to go home. With a gale in full pursuit he sailed clear across the Atlantic. Just as the tumultuous coast of France rose above the bow, he found a place to bury his loot and a wet grave for himself among the bitter reefs of Brittany. There was no ground tackle on board. Retribution came to him through the agency of an earlier and less ambitious thief who had merely stolen the anchor.

I left the Friendship to the mercy of her admirers, picked my anchor up out of the mud, and cleared out of Cape May. I heard gunfire above the roar of the engine as I ran out through the channel. The rap of bullets tearing through the barrel of a machine gun echoed along the jetty. I climbed up on the cabin and peeked between the granite rocks that towered above the fallen tide.

It was a machine gun, sure as hell, and a fellow in uniform was squatting on his hams in the sand, rattling away. I ducked at the next burst and headed for the open sea. I had no idea what was going on. I should have bought a newspaper. If this was war, they were wasting it on me. I needed information. I looked at the calendar. It said July 1940. All the clock dangling on the galley bulkhead had to offer was 11:30 A.M. The tide table was vague on world affairs. The southeast wind whispered about an island some-where, and I was inclined to listen.

Princess pounded out past the sea buoy and picked her way through Prissy Wicks Shoal with the staysail holding her steady through the surf. The soldier with the machine gun was still cutting himself a slice of target as we passed out of sight beyond the point. I broke out the spinnaker and killed the engine. The tide and a fair wind eased us up the Delaware. The sky was clear, the wind was steady, and the boat, crowded with canvas, ran true with her big rudder unfettered and acting as a gentle drogue. Hour after lazy hour the light air and the fair current worked her up into the narrowing bay. Up along the receiving line of gaudy lighthouses that looked like vain little ladies vying with one another in the way of lace curtains and fancy trim, I lost track of time. It was evening as *Princess* reached for Ship John Light and the tide turned.

Then I knew that the wind had done little more than hold her head on the course all day. We had come this far with tide. The torrent that turned and tumbled down toward the sea made a huge joke of the southeast wind that stood against it. *Princess*, edging up a little further by every means, found a place for her hook in nine feet of water to the windward of Ship John Light.

In the shadow of that squat lighthouse with its hoopla cupola, I wallowed around down below and managed to clamp a couple of slices of bread around a slab of store cheese without an incidental amputation. The coffeepot warmed up while skating around the top of the stove. I drank from the spout, turned in, and tried to sleep. It was no dice. The wind from the southeast came out fighting as if the pummeling tide were forcing it out of a corner.

Grabbed by the tide and slugged by the wind, *Princess* ran up on her anchor looking for a weapon to protect herself. Reassured by some lesser current flowing past the granite rocks piled fore and aft that gave the lighthouse the appearance of a ship, *Princess* backed broadside into the channel, defied the whip of the wind, and acted much worse than the company.

I got dressed and went on deck to watch the fun. The old girl tried to duck behind the breakwater of the lighthouse. Then the tide would drag her out by the keel, and the wind would lay her over. Back and forth it went, half the night, with my baby being batted around at the end of her cable. At last the tide came to terms with the wind. It was midnight, and I drifted off in my bunk with the whine of the wind in accord with the booming slurp of the water, counting to six each time the great light above her ghosted through the open hatch of *Princess*.

Before the break of day I was up, remembering the onslaught of the down-running tide. In the scant hour that remained in her favor, my little boat, free of her clutch on the bottom, drifted upriver and came to head on her course as the great spread of mainsail was drawn creaking up against the canvas color of the sky. I had slept no more than three hours. I searched the chart for a brief haven. There was a wrinkle on the chart, a tiny tributary of the Delaware called Smyrna River seven miles above Ship John Light, that might offer a comfortable anchorage before the wind and the tide started throwing things again. Three hours' sleep seemed worse than none at all, and my ears were ringing from the tom-tom played by the sea against topsides. I began to look forward to a vacation from the strain of trying to get away from it all.

The chart showed an old tower to the left of the mouth of the Smyrna River. Through the early morning haze I saw a looming shape along the shore. *Princess* swung in toward the flashing green light at the end of a wooden jetty. The looming shape turned out to be a broken pine tree, and the tower referred to on the chart was an old farmhouse chimney that had been carried away brick by brick to build other chimneys.

As I turned in the sharp bend at the mouth of the river, ominous gray-blue clouds gathered in the southern sky, and a fork of lightning shot across it like an illuminated system of veins. Tall reeds, stretching their slender, light-green stems ten and fifteen feet up against the gunmetal sky, crowded the bluff mud banks of the tiny, meandering river. There was not a breath of air.

Princess, edging slowly up the channel with the last of the tidal flow, swung around and around like a bit of flotsam nudging the soft earth bank alternately with her bowsprit and her boom. To be transported so suddenly from the hammering violence of the Delaware to this silence and this beauty made me wonder for a moment if I was alive.

To find this deep river, to be folded in the silence of this tall grass, to move without wind or sound and without grounding through the majesty of these towering, golden-green reeds when the mind is tired and the body starved for sleep is an accident. As I held to the mast and saw the peaceful pastures, the motionless low hills, the quiet farmland between the top, thinning blades of the reeds, I knew I was dead or crazy.

Heedless of the rudder, *Princess* drifted on. Beyond another bend in the river a thing happened that took away the slightest doubt that I was gone. A skiff came toward my boat, rowed by a very old man with a white beard. In the stern of the boat sat a very old woman wearing an old-fashioned hooded bonnet. They came to *Princess* without a word. The old man took the anchor line, made it fast to a thwart, and rowed off in absolute silence till my vessel was drawn to a dock alongside a farmhouse close by a turning bridge. The old man made *Princess* fast to a piling, tied up his skiff, and helped the old lady onto the dock. Together they went into their house. I lowered the mainsail and the jib, furled them, and ducked below quickly and went to sleep.

The sun was past its zenith when I got up. I sat on deck and saw the old man spading up potatoes in a shady patch alongside his house.

"I want to thank you," I said, and waited. The old man straightened up and spoke.

"There hasn't been a boat come in here for nigh on a year. Government pays us fifteen dollars every month to tend the bridge. Saw your sail above the grass and went out to get you. Runs mighty fast under the bridge. Fellow with a sailboat got in trouble once." The old man spat on his hands and went back to work.

"Well, thank you anyway."

"Nothing to thank me for. Saved us opening the bridge. Takes two of us. Wife's kind of lame."

I left and walked out onto the bridge. The tide, which was slowly running out, was accelerated into cold fury for a distance of a hundred feet by the narrow sluiceway that ran between the bridgeheads. The fellow with the sailboat must have had a hell of a time.

I looked across at *Princess*, tied up at the dock, and saw for the first time that she had a friend. And what a friend it was! Bridled between the end of the dock and a tree there was a craft. In its way it was a sailboat; that is, it had a mast or bean pole or fish stake poking up through the top of its house. Its lines took the general shape of a boat, and yet there was something about her that made one think of little children building boats with blocks or forming them out of chairs and sofa pillows on a rainy afternoon.

I ran over to look at her. She had everything—a hull, a rudder, a wheel, deck, and a house. Every bit of it was carved as if with a broadax. She was put together with such love and such ignorance of proportion as to stagger the imagination. She seemed to have been designed and built by someone who had never seen so much as a picture of a boat, someone who had heard about boats through a friend of a fellow who knew somebody who swore he had seen one. She was about twenty-eight feet over-all, and she drew about eighteen inches of water. She had at least six feet of topsides, and a house six feet above that. She had no engine, a bilge full of field stones, and not a trace of paint anywhere. I spent the balance of the day going over her like an archeologist with a discovery of the first importance. Then I bought a chicken from the pilot-bridgetender-farmer for a quarter, stuffed it with bread, put it in the oven, and awaited developments.

I didn't have long to wait. I was gnawing on the second drumstick for the lack of a better form of entertainment when *Princess* rolled her starboard side down with the weight of an incredibly heavy foot. A big, round, red face beamed in the hatchway, and a massive hand was thrust toward me with a "Howdy!"

We sat in the cabin passing the pint bottle back and forth, and Big Randy, who drove a truck for a living, told me a story. The story concerned that boat, which lay bridled between the dock and a tree, as if it weren't quite sure enough to give up its last tie to the forest that produced it.

"Two brothers built her," said Big Randy. "They live up in the hills about twenty miles back in the woods. They had an old man, awful strict, worked them night and day, wouldn't let them get away, not even to go to school, taught them himself. The old man was a schoolteacher once.

"About the time they were twenty, the boys broke down, both of them, started talking about an ocean liner that was coming right up to their farm. The old man was too hard on them. Thanks, I'll have another." Big Randy gulped. "Nice liquor, what's it called?"

"Brandy."

"They began to dig a canal," Big Randy went on. "Twenty miles up in the hills, dug by daylight and dug all night by the light of lanterns. People around here knew about it, tried to get them to a doctor, but they wouldn't leave off. 'Big steamship coming up to the farm, got to hurry, dig the canal.' "

Big Randy sat with the flask in his right hand pointing with its neck out the hatch across the flatlands to the hills, where the sun spiraled down among the trees. "It was a bad thing. The old man was too strict. Where do you hail from?"

"New York," I said.

"Big city," said Randy. "Drove up there one time with a load of tomatoes."

"What happened with the brothers?"

"Oh, the brothers, yeah, I got them out of there. Went up one night with the truck. 'Come on and dig,' they said, handing me a shovel and pointing to a great big hole in the field. 'Steamboat coming in from the ocean, got to get the canal dug.'

"This is great canal country," said Big Randy, "and it's the finest farmland in the world. Hundreds of sailing vessels used to run between these meadows hauling stuff to market. Trucking did away with all that." Randy had the last drink, and the bottle went out of the hatch and plopped into the Smyrna River. I waited.

"I went up there one hot summer night," said Randy. "I dug for a while, and then I said to them, 'Look, boys, it's no use sweating this way, we need men, lots of men to help us dig this canal. We've got twenty miles to go. We need men, lots of men.' 'Yeah,' the brothers said. 'We need men, lots of men.' I said, 'Let's take the truck and go get some men.'

"The brothers got in the truck sayin', 'Let's go get men.' I took them down to the hospital."

"How are they now?" I asked.

"Fine," said Randy. "Things changed. The old man died and the boys snapped out of it. They went back to the farm and built that boat between crops, rolled it all the way down on old tractor wheels, twenty miles, it was a hell of a job. Had to chop their way out of the woods. I went up and helped them with the truck."

15

The talking machine in the darkened parlor of the farmhouse pleaded "Please don't take my sunshine away" while the sun glazed the air outside and put a torch to the plant tops in the soggy fields. I sprawled in the shade of a matronly elm and held my fire till I could see the red in the eye of a persistent horsefly. A torn sheet of newsprint, scorched by the sun to the color of earth, flopped loose-footed across the grass and snagged on the hard scabs of bark. I peeled it off and studied the black words. There was war, and there were rumors of more war. A white cloud slipped between the tree and the sky, passed, and it was hot again. I got up off my back, slipped the lines of *Princess*, and ran out of Smyrna River with the southwest wind and the edge of the tide.

The wind, caught in the throat of the mainsail, swept my

vessel down between the bowing reeds. I got to thinking about this grass in the fall when it was dry, about roaring prairie fires and the crumbled old chimney on the point. I could picture it, after a hundred years spent containing a little fire, standing at last in a pyre of flame fed by a farmhouse.

Between the moving curtain of high grass I saw three grazing cows hove to on the low hills, and a plow on a reach cutting a sure furrow in the warm earth for a second harvest. Down by the delta of the river the reeds were thinned out by the shears of salt that clipped the edges of the fertile soil. *Princess* turned to the right at the last bend and, gathering the unobstructed wind in her mainsail, stepped out along the protective arm of the breakwater into the torso of the tide.

The deep channel turns north to the western end of the Chesapeake and Delaware Canal. The wind from the southwest was fair on the port beam and steady. I aimed the bowsprit of my boat at a flashing red buoy known as 8-L, which marked the edge of the dredged channel, lashed the tiller, and went below to finish off the roast chicken before it spoiled for lack of ice.

The buoy was no less than three miles away. There was no traffic in the bay and nothing to worry about, but I took the compass down with me to make sure that I was on my course. I didn't figure on the current.

When it happened, it threw me on my ear with a bang that sounded something like the end. The conscientious old girl joined hands with the tide, ran right up true, and smacked 8-L right on the kisser with her port chine plank. It was hard to believe, but there was the crack in the plank and there was old 8-L blinking in broad daylight and red as a beet. We left it wagging its head and spinning in bewilderment while *Princess* bustled off to save as much of the tide as she could for the Delaware side of the canal. I took the chicken up on deck.

The crack in the plank was not serious. It was a small break in the center of the wood, forward and far above the water line. While I nibbled away at that chicken carcass and held my foot on the tiller I wondered what kind of wood it was that could take such a blow, and hold the stringy toughness of its sinews long after the oak ribs of the boat had folded up. According to the old-timers, that planking was Maine pine. After more than half a century in salt water there is no smell, no taste, no grain or perceptible fiber characteristics. There is nothing but sog and salt water to it. I have seen the experts smell it, chew it, peel it, and peer at it in every light and from every angle, and always the verdict was: "Maine pine." The lumberyards don't carry it.

There is a special type of tropical hardwood that is erroneously known in this country as *madera*. Down where this stuff grows, *madera* is the Spanish word for lumber. Ask for *madera* when you have a boat built down there, and you will get a very pleasant smile and any lumber that's handy. Ask for Maine pine up here, and you'll get the same routine.

It took me ten years to find out just what kind of wood Maine pine really was and what happened to it. One old man with a little more patience than the others explained it this way. "Maine pine is spruce."

"Sitka spruce?"

"No. Sitka spruce comes from Alaska or northwestern Canada. Maine pine used to grow in the state of Maine."

"What happened to it?"

"Most of it went out to sea, one way or another. It went out as ships, or they cut it down so fast that the log jams broke in the rivers and it went out with the bark on."

"Doesn't it grow again?"

"Got to plant it. Spruce is fussy."

Men suspended mid-air on scaffoldings are fussy too. The interlocking rings of growth that tie the spruce tree together make it the only wood acceptable where a man's life is at stake. A New Bedford whaleboat fast to a straining line, pounding in the wake of an angry whale, smoke strung back from the stem bit, is part of the story of the silent spruce. A Yankee clipper logging twenty knots in a full gale, stiff-masted, cargo balanced against the lightness of its masts and bulkheads, whispering the secret of its speed to the skeptical sea. A fishing vessel, broached and pounding on a beach, halyard blocks swinging crazy, torn cotton waving ghostly arms, tossed high and dry before she could fill and sink because her hull was spruce.

There is spruce, and there is spruce. A tree, like any other plant, is subject to breeding, and the story of its evolution is as deep and mysterious as the forest itself. The pollen that sweeps wind-driven through the woods can create as much havoc as fire.

I remember the man squinting against the sky at the long check in the mast of *Princess*. "You could put your arm clear to the shoulder in the cracks of the old ships' masts and never fear for them in a hurricane."

Even spruce can take just so much. I gave the iron channel markers that rose from the river bed a wide berth. We passed them one by one as *Princess* neared the back alley to the Chesapeake. The towers of the high-lifting bridge at Reedy Point were bitten into the sky, and a long line of black dolphins stood sentry duty on the right bank of the canal.

There was a man in uniform with a clipboard of paper and a pencil standing by as I caught hold of a piling to wait for the bridge. I heard his voice through the advancing dusk. "Name of vessel?"

"*Princess.*"

"Number?"

"Ten-D-seven-oh-five."

"Owner?"

"Joe Richards."

"Port of registry?"

"New York."

"Destination?" I hesitated. This was no casual acquaintance shuffling reminiscences. This was the Government of the United States.

"Destination?"

What could I say? There was no sense being coy. There was certainly no call to be flippant, but there I was, not knowing for sure and wanting to know myself where I was headed. How could I say what lay beyond the spume and fog that rose from the distant face of the sea? What the hell did the Army Engineers want with my dream?

The man lifted his eyes from the sheaf of paper that curled over his writing hand in the evening breeze. He looked first at me and then at my little boat, which waited, heading back into the wind. This time the voice was louder and the word rang like a command. "Destination?"

The dream broke and the pieces fell into the sea, arranging themselves like the tiny islands of an archipelago. "Caribbean," I said, and I saw the pencil move across the board.

The man's face came up, and there was a smile under the shining emblem of his hat. "Lucky dog," he said.

The bridge went up without asking and then came down a bit so that the bridgetender could see my girl better from his booth as she passed in the failing light. We moved by sail, and a voice from the catwalk behind us called, "Want a passenger?"

The wind backed into the south and freshened. *Princess*, closehauled, glided in the moonlit path of green and white flashing lights. I yielded to a tall tug that nosed a skittish barge down against the current and passed beneath the high bridge at St. Georges. Under the black railroad bridge that was all but lost in the night sky we slowed perceptibly.

The fair current offered by the Delaware gave over to the tidal habit of the Chesapeake, which threw its bulk against my boat. We gave up at Chesapeake City in the dark hours of the morning, still under sail and with twelve of the sixteen miles of canal behind us. I lowered the hook in the basin, rowed ashore in the dink, and had dinner in the diner up on the highway with the other night travelers.

Chesapeake City lies at the navigable head of a little river called Back Creek that runs into Elk River, which in turn dissolves into the bay when it passes the lighthouse high on the knoll at Turkey Point. Of all the many twisting threads of water that creep back into the countryside, the headwater called Back Creek comes closest to the Delaware and points to the great cities of the Northeast.

Years before the wall of earth that separates the Delaware and Chesapeake was cut, Chesapeake City was a key port where people and cargo took leave of the vessel that had carried them from Norfolk or Richmond or Washington to board a stagecoach or wagon for the journey north. That which the uncompromising surge of time and the railroads failed to do to Chesapeake City, the canal and highway finished. There she lies with a few of her old stone houses still standing after a hundred and fifty years, empty of the crinoline crowds, the sideburns and silk hats, her wharves bare of the bales of cotton, while the ships pass her docks and the cars careen across the bridge above.

I circled the basin and saw *Princess* reflected in the same still water that duplicated the old stone tavern, all of which was set against the mechanistic backdrop of a lift bridge and a honking stream of vehicular traffic. I walked back to the dink, which was tied to an ancient ringbolt in the old stone quay, and joined *Princess*.

We waited till noon for the tide to take us down into the Chesapeake. The temperature, trying for days to shove the mercury clear out of the top of the glass, reached a crescendo. The newly dug earth on the banks of the canal was baked to brick by the sun. The heat, compounded in the windless depths of the chasm, poured out along Back Creek.

Once the groceries were aboard, my boat moved out under sail against the relinquishing current. The deck blistered to the touch, and the sun, caught between the reflecting angles of hot clay banks, seemed to come at us from every direction. Sweating, I ran my fingers through my hair. I looked at my hand. I had a handful of hair. It was burning the mop right off the top of my noggin. That was enough. I dove over the side and, hanging by the footrail, I steered *Princess* by kicking her rudder with my foot all the way to hell and gone out of Back Creek.

Coming abeam of Courthouse Point, I deemed it wise to get back aboard. There was a giant tanker coming up the channel. Hand over hand I reached for the low point on the leeward beam to haul myself on deck. Something tickled my toes. I felt again.

Whatever hair I had lost from the top of my head was amply compensated for by the beard of marine growth that had taken root and was luxuriating downward from the bottom of *Princess*. That bargain in bottom paint purchased back in New Jersey that gave her a slick finish and a fast start had come a cropper. I was going to have to haul the old girl or shave her.

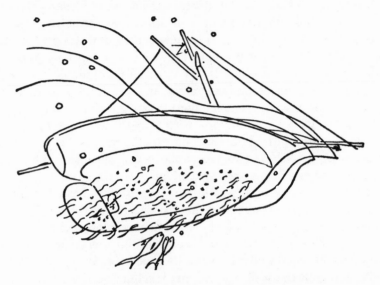

The channel expanded and the wind from the southeast evened out. After the wake of the tanker broke along the edge of Town Point Neck I went over the side with a razor. It was the little coal shovel borrowed from the stove and tied to my wrist with a lanyard. The backwaters of the Chesapeake provided the lather.

With a once over lightly and hand over hand around, we left a fair part of the green beard floating in our wake. What I couldn't reach with the shovel I scratched off with my toenails. The old girl showed her appreciation by picking up a little of the speed that she had gradually lost with the accumulation of grass.

The high, dark-green hills at the head of Turkey Point gobbled up the sun in the late afternoon, and the deck, sprinkled with spray in the rising wind, grew cool in the shaded water. A schooner loaded with freight came from the sunny side of the point, joined *Princess* and we headed down together into the sunglanced, wind-spanked bay.

Handicapped by the goatee of green grass that still grew all around her keel, my boat was soon forced to follow the schooner, whose heavy-gauge canvas and massive sticks took the strong wind blowing out of the Sassafras River in their stride. Heeling slightly, the sailing ship stood right up and drew away from us. *Princess* was a bit on the tender side. The new equation of weight between her original ballast and the light plywood deck not only kept her dry and fast out at sea but also gave her an indisputable advantage in the swamps. She could heel over in any wind and by that reduction in her draft walk off a reef like a long-legged bird.

But my baby would go over just so far and no farther. The fat tumble home of her belly took care of that. When the wind got too fresh, she liked to wheel about and talk back. The wind was fresh enough rounding Grove Neck, and the schooner, its sails shining like kettle sides, was lost in the dusk off Howell Point. I doused the genny, slacked off the mainsheet, and held the tiller to the wind with my foot. The lights of Betterton opened apart as we closed in. The anchor caught bottom in nine feet of water in the lee of the excursion boat rock, and I ended the day rocking in the open bay with the wail of a clarinet reaching out over the dissonant water.

16

The wind blew out of the Sassafras River all night long. At sunup the tide turned, and the dinghy kicked up a big ruckus back aft, butting the fantail of *Princess* with her little oaken nose. The old girl, yawing indecisively between the moods of the morning, complied at last to the demands of the prodding pram and got underway before breakfast.

It had become August overnight, and the sun, going south, drew a thousand gleaming sabers of light and laid them on the table of the bay. *Princess* cut across them toward Annapolis and the source of the tide. Cloud cotton, ginned white, absorbed the sharpness of the sun, and the cool wind came to us, smelling of sweet hay.

Spread on the bridge deck and pinned by the coffeepot, the

chart spoke of a bell on Howell Point that sounded during the winter months. Five miles to the south a light on Worton Point flashed every ten seconds during the season of ice. It was slow going. Laboring down against the current, I heard no bell at Howell Point, and, coming abreast of Worton Point after two solid hours of hard sailing, I saw no light blink. At least we had covered that piddling distance all in the same season. Here the bay opened up, and the tide, distracted by the thirsty recesses of Gunpowder and Bush rivers, no longer concentrated its force to oppose us.

By midmorning our part of the Chesapeake was alive with outboards and runabouts that skipped for short distances at great speeds like flies hopped up by the sunlight. They had something. On the chart the blue, shaded lace of shoal area forbidden to our draft hung like a fancy fringe all down along the endless indentations of the bay. There was reason enough for the planing bottoms and the violent speed of these small boats. There could be no other way in the span of a lifetime to see all the turns and half the wonders of this expansive lung of the sea.

The leisurely pace of *Princess*, plying somberly down the deep center of the Chesapeake, permitted no more than a sidelong glance at the parted mouths of the rivers that ran back into the rolling hills. Down past the towering lighthouse on Pooles Island, with the breakfast dishes carefully chocked in a bucket and the wind freshening out of the south, we cut across the broad entrance of Baltimore Harbor. The smoky line of horizon trailed into sea and sky, and on the chart I traced the backwaters of the bay. I could see men in punts, sounding with a knotted line, men lugging transits through the silent bush, feeling the morning wind, smelling the spice of low tide, hearing the sudden arguments of molested birds along the lonely angles of the shore.

The tide and the wind changed at one time as if in accordance with the terms of an ancient contract. While we drifted in the sultry air of midafternoon I swam and *Princess*, hobbled by a loose tiller, practiced coming about from port and starboard like a girl dancing alone and dreaming. As I floated in the water I saw the rough rash of wind as it clipped the surface of the bay to the north. I was barely aboard when *Princess* picked it up, breezed down past the yellow edge of Gibson Island, and headed for Sandy Point.

A breathless usher of wind whipped down out of the north and led us, reaching, toward the feelers of steel that thrust their tall antennae into the sky at Greenbury Point. Taut with the excitement of it, we rushed hungry-eyed toward the port of Annapolis. This was a long way from Friendship, Maine, where *Princess* came into being, and a long time. She was of the stuff of which naval history was made. Fashioned by the same hands, she was kin to the clipper ships and the men-of-war. Now, nearly three quarters of a century since she was built, she was not only afloat but heading full tilt under her own canvas toward the home of the United States Naval Academy. Her little American eagle was wall-eyed with wonder as it cut the following sea. In sight of the Severn the outhaul parted.

The straining mainsail, reaching out on the port side, was gathered up by the insistent wind that whipped the clew of the sail against the sagging boom. Caught in the sea, the boom staggered drunkenly from the crest of one wave to the next. The mast slipped out of the jaws of the boom, and the canvas thrashed away in billowing folds like the family wash on the back line. It was a mess.

This was no way to enter Annapolis. Poor old *Princess*, dragged along by the tide and driven by half a gale, rocked dolefully at the idea of making this port, of all places, in such preposterous condition.

I went forward and dropped the mainsail. The sea, delighted by the opportunity, crawled all over it. I went aft and dragged the mainsail onto the deck, while the jib, taking the wind on by itself, heeled us over. I went forward again and doused all sail.

The outhaul of the mainsail that had parted was rove through a hole in the bitter end of the boom, way out of reach beyond the stern. The bay was rough and getting rougher. I fetched the dinghy up close and jumped in with a new length of line to replace the broken outhaul. The wild little pram, possessed by the goings-on, heaved up and pounded *Princess* to get moving. The trick was to stand in that skittish plywood pram and reeve a three-eighths-inch line with a fuzzy end through a hole not much larger out in the overhanging end of the boom.

There is a painting by Rembrandt. It is a very great picture. It is serene. It shows a woman sitting quietly in half-shadow, bending gently forward in the soft light of afternoon. On her face are the marks of age, of suffering, of acceptance, and of peace. I thought of it as I hung on by my teeth and struggled in the middle of the Chesapeake, trying to poke the burred end of that stiff and subborn hunk of hemp through the deadeye in the end of the boom while the dinghy skittered, slid, and slammed around under my feet.

I chewed the line into some sort of beard and twisted it with the lay, pushed, caught hold of a tip and pulled it through. A big wave sloshed into the dink.

Back aboard *Princess* I hauled the wrinkles out of her wet cloth and raised it slapping and spitting brine up into the wind. There were two towering white sails off our port bow as we rounded Hackett's Point. The big racing yawls of the Naval Academy were coming in, all spit and polish and crewed up to the ears. *Princess* looked nice, too. Her genny was set and her mainsail, smooth and tight, turned her by the big, red bell and up against the tide in the river.

There were people watching in Eastport, and others, all dressed up, on the green lawn and the stone bulwark that lay alongside the school. The naval yawls overtook us in the channel and taxed away most of the wind and all the attention. *Princess* trailed after them, ranging close to see the midshipmen, precise as in drill, latch to their mooring, lower sail, and furl. It was a great sight. The sun set. The cannon boomed. The colors were struck. *Princess* went quietly to the corner of Eastport and dropped her hook in the mud near the bridge.

While she rocked in the harbor, flirting with the fancy boats that lay all about her, I wandered in the peaceful shade of the tall trees that stand on the green lawns of Annapolis. The old buildings, armored with ivy, were empty for the summer months and cool in the noon sun. I had heard about Commander Weems, and went looking for him. I walked under a low stone arch and found him in his study, next to an empty classroom.

Weems was tall, balding, and sparse. He was a man with an idea, a Don Quixote of the sea, tilting with the windmills of tradition. He had, it seemed, worked out a method of navigation that bothered the old-line mathematicians. It was too simple. It was a graphic method worked out by computation but, in effect, not unlike the rule-of-thumb calculus practiced by the old shipbuilders. On his charts the plotted curves that denoted the paths of the stars were beautiful. This was the kind of mathematics that Wilbur A. Morse must have used to arrive at the lovely lines of *Princess*. It worked, too. He offered to teach it to me—so much per lesson.

I begged the issue, being low on cash and content for the purposes of my journey with what I knew of coast piloting. I couldn't afford to buy a sextant even if I had the money for the course. So I listened.

He sat in his leather easy chair in the low-ceilinged, oak-paneled study. The halation of sun on the high arc of his forehead made me think of Euclid, da Vinci, Archimedes, of men defiant and unorthodox. He was brilliant. There was no telling how far a man like that could go if he didn't go about upsetting applecarts and textbooks.

I didn't know enough at the time to get the full gist of his theory, but I was sure that here was Nathaniel Bowditch all over again, teaching the bos'n and the cook to navigate, letting the boys in on the secret of celestial navigation, firing a barrage of knowledge broadside to cut the mental fog of caste by which men hold dominion over men.

While he spoke the sun passed its crest and on its way down inched columns of shade across the close-shaven turf. I rose to go. Commander Weems laid the transparent, lined protractor on the blotter of his desk and showed me to the door. I was proud to shake his hand.

There were rowboats clustered around *Princess* when I got back to the yacht club that has a corner on the bridge. My girl, competing for attention with all the historical landmarks of Annapolis, was doing pretty good for a start. I went out in the dink and barked for the crowd till I was hoarse, and then moved on to Eastport to arrange to have her hauled. We were getting nowhere with the barnacles that clung to her historical bottom. The man who owned the marine railway worked over at the academy during the day, but according to his wife and a dozen kids who played around the yard, he would haul *Princess* any evening after work. I agreed to the following evening, when the tide would be right, and rowed away.

I was just about back on board my boat when I spotted a familiar-looking little motorboat turning into the harbor with a tall guy at the wheel and a girl. It could be nobody else but Archie. Archie the scientist, Archie the philosopher, Archie the boat doctor with his little black bag of hand tools, his black iron bolts, and his impeccable boatside manner. He had pulled her through, brought that somewhat bedecked skiff all the way from Edgewater, New Jersey.

"Hey, Archie!" The sixteen-footer, heading tentatively here and there like a stranger coming out of the dark into the bright light of a room, spun around, raced over, and kissed *Princess*. With the two tied up together, Archie's wife cooked dinner for all hands while Archie and I drank immoderate quantities of store beer and discussed the trivia of our separate trips.

Archie, Dr. Archie now that he had his Ph.D., was bound for Richmond and a cushy job on some hush-hush chemical project. They left in the morning for the James River. Tall, skinny, and standing motionless amidships, he looked as if he might do for a spar, something to carry a scrap of canvas to steady that tub in a blow. His wife waved prettily, and they were gone around the bend.

I waited for evening, when *Princess* would rise up out of the water. No sight in the world is so interesting to the man who owns a boat as the sight of her bottom at the moment it comes up on the ways after a long voyage or a season of sailing. Sunsets are nothing. Niagara Falls and the Grand Canyon pale beside the luminous vision of the curves of her shining hull and the pathology of flora and fauna that come up with it.

I lost patience around noon and went looking at other hulls hauled out. There was one in the yard carved out of a solid log, a big one, over a hundred years old and in almost perfect condition. It was one of the few remaining Chesapeake dugouts, or sharpies, used for dredging oysters and speeding them to market. The tree from which that boat was shaped must have taken root at the time Columbus stumbled on this continent. I wondered what the man who carved that twenty-odd feet of hull with a hand adz would have thought of the engine that snuggled in its bilge. Except for a couple of long checks caused by lying dry in the sun, the beamy old craft was as good as the day she was whittled.

Wandering down toward Horn Point, I saw the one I must have been looking for. She was set up under the spread of an apple tree. Her planking was quite dry, and the caulking hung out of her open seams like something half eaten. She was a thirty-foot yawl of conventional design, and there was nothing special about her except the sorrow, the smell of apples rotting on her deck, and the leaves piled high and dry, molding in her cockpit. I took the liberty of climbing aboard and clearing them from her scuppers. The doors of the cabin were open, and the cabin, shaded by the tree that leaned over her, was strewn with bedding and running gear. This baby had not known the feel of salt water for years.

I sat on the edge of a torn old mattress, remembering the day I found *Princess*, and my hand touched the frayed leather cover of a book stuffed in against the ceiling. It was the log of that boat. I began to read. Here, if ever, was the power of understatement. To those who have known the restless sea, called her turns, and come back, there are no understatements more powerful or more worthy of elaboration than the entries in the log of an abandoned vessel.

Simple as can be, the first entry read, "April 26, 1935, launched boat 11:00—pumped."

"April 27—pumped all night." Then came terse inkings of engine trouble, parted stays, rotten canvas, and the leak. There was brief mention of family, a few friends, less money, and the pump. On June 3, all provisioned and with the family aboard, she set out, still pumping.

"June 6—02:00—aground Horseshoe Point—blowing hard NE." Nothing about the kids screaming in the dark, the frantic wife, the seas piling all over and the leak. Nothing; just "Aground—blowing hard NE."

By four o'clock the vessel was hard and fast, lying way over, the kids were clinging to their parents on the sloping deck, and the turning tide was seven hours away. It must have been awful. Think of it, aground in two feet of water. The vessel drew close to seven, hammered by an onshore wind howling down out of the northeast. The logbook lay heavy in my hands. I read on. The returning sea, lifting and pounding, slid between the top strakes faster than the pump could handle it.

"09:00—afloat." But the engine had been dunked. Before they could get out of there, the wind veered and tossed them back for another round of cold and wet and misery. They tried kedging her off, but the windlass wouldn't work lying way over, and soon it was too late.

The understatements reached a climax, and there was suddenly a whole world of blank paper, some of it stained with salt water. I sat there and listened. The summer breeze rattled the rusty blocks that clung like petrified fruit to the trucks. Lines of light glared in her open seams. I laid the log of the vessel reverently on the dusty galley table and closed the doors of the cabin behind me.

Over under the shed I found a mechanic drawing a flat file between the tight ends of a piston ring held in a vise.

"Know anything about that yawl?"

"Yep. They got in all right. Man never was the same." The mechanic looked up from the piston ring, drew the file all the way through, lifted it and tapped his temple twice with the blunt end. "We're waiting to see how he gets on. It's been five years now."

I left that yard and went back to *Princess*, waiting for evening and my chance to beard her on the ways.

17

The one-lung engine at the head of the marine railway backfired, coughed, and buckled down. The steel cable lying loose between the tracks drew taut, and up came *Princess* out of the still waters with a fat haul of inedible marine life clinging to her flawless curves. I went after her with a farmer's hoe, a street cleaner's brush, and a fireman's hose.

She was scaled, scrubbed with sand, and washed clean. Her bottom was anointed with red copper suspended in oil, and back she slid into the harbor of Annapolis. Shorn and unresisting, she drifted out to a mooring and lay in a formation of pleasure vessels that swung in unison to the tide or faced about with the wind.

Under the influence of either wind or tide, the vessels in the anchorage maintained a respectful distance from one another.

If the tide was the dominant factor, they turned to face it; if the wind was boss, they met the wind as one—all but *Princess*. I caught her a couple of times cozying up to other boats. I didn't like it. She would do it when I wasn't around. You know how people talk.

It was about this time that I began to notice a tendency on the part of *Princess* to react to anything on my part that might be construed as neglect. God knows, I lavished twice the time on her that I might have on a mate, whose claim on me had a legal basis. Not that there weren't papers on board that established a connection between us, but that sort of thing is outdated. Nowadays a woman wants to be something more than a man's property.

It could have been my fault. Maybe the old girl had me figured for a bum. I decided to get a job and go to work. The captain of a great white bugeye which was being fitted for a winter in the Caribbean hired me. For the lordly sum of five dollars he commissioned me to paint an elaborate scroll trailing back from the fierce American-eagle figurehead.

Suspended out on a bobstay under the long, octagonal sprit, I let the golden flourishes flow off the end of my brush. With a pot of gold in one hand and a pint of bourbon in the other, the old man rode the bowsprit like a bronc. I worked with the fury of a Michelangelo spurred on by the backbreaking scaffold and a running commentary that could have been inspired by the Sistine Chapel roof. The old man might have gone completely overboard if it hadn't been for the counterpoise of two white handlebars which swept out to port and starboard from his upper lip.

When I got back from work, I found *Princess* making up to a big black bugeye from the eastern shore that belonged to a preacher. It didn't set so well. I knew what was on her mind. So did the preacher. So did his wife, his pretty daughter, and three young sons, to say nothing of a little white dog called Snooky. Snooky was some dog. I have never seen or heard of a dog like her. I know children who suck their thumbs, men who habitually chew the dead stub of a cigar, and cows that chew their cuds, but this I believe was the only dog in the world that sat in an attitude of penitence, endlessly sucking her left hind paw.

I took up some slack in the mooring cable to help *Princess* keep her distance. After dinner I sat in the companionway and watched the sun go down. The preacher's pretty daughter came by rowing a dinghy with Snooky along for the ride. We talked in a guarded way about boats, mine and theirs, the weather, mine and theirs, and New York, mine. She said, "Do you go to the Stork Club every night?"

I didn't want to let her down. I couldn't let on that *Princess* and I were not really in the swim. "Oh yes," I said. The stars came out. She had a load of them in her eyes when she rowed back to her father's boat.

I had it out with *Princess* before I went looking for work the next morning. I broke out the folding anchor and bridled her fore and aft just to make sure she'd behave. As I rowed away in my plywood pram I had the uncomfortable feeling that Princess wasn't entirely to blame. These things take two, nowadays.

With the bow of the bugeye as proof, I got myself a job working for the captain of an eighty-five-foot cruiser. I painted topsides, white on white, while I dreamed in broad daylight about color. The captain fancied himself a deep-water man, a Don Juan, a pirate. I had lunch at the captain's table. We ate chicken, each in proportion to his mass, and I found that it was the regret of this man's life that his teeth were not strong enough to grind it up bones and all. I could see that there was no future in my job. Bristling toward all hands and surly even toward the owner, the captain's unbounded girth turned to putty in the presence of the cook, who pattered around tight-lipped at his elbow.

"You've got to be nice to cooks," he told me in the strictest confidence, "or they'll spit in your stew."

I looked at him. Suddenly I had an overwhelming appetite for the island that was on my mind.

The west wind which swept through the dark campus and dusted the city dock trundled my plywood pram out to *Princess* just as she turned away from the big black bugeye. She sighed uneasily in the ebbing tide as her friend, sheet-blocks creaking, flattened sail to round the point. The last thing we saw was Snooky teething at the taffrail. The days went by, and one vessel after another peeled off, leaving scope and idle mooring cans in the anchorage.

One night it rained, and the wind came out of the east at dawn. I picked up charts, a mess of groceries, and two fathoms of line that were lying loose under the abandoned vessel and the apple tree. I shouldn't have taken it. I did.

It was just what I needed for a new painter for my pram. *Princess* took me away in the morning. I left Annapolis, the big family in Eastport, and the children who had crowded the cabin of my vessel like a nest of young birds. I could hear the ring of kids' voices halfway to Horn Point. "Come back and go huntin' wiffus in the fall?"

One port tack, and the venerable buildings of Annapolis retreated among the trees. *Princess* ran the channel, showed her slippery heels to the big bell, and, turning at Tolly Point, reached for the south. Finding new life in her clean lines, my baby swung ahead, whipping the prattling pram along by its frayed and chewed-up leash.

After heading down toward Bloody Point with the lighthouse at Thomas Point drawing abeam, I went below for the little piece of line I shouldn't have taken at Eastport. I fried an egg down there and ate it sunny side up. I sipped coffee, and spliced an eye in my loot and a Turk's-head tassel on the bitter end of it. Now that I was out of town, I could bend it on the pram. The diaphone spoke from the starboard quarter, and I went on deck.

A half-hour had gone by. The lighthouse had begun to recede below the busy crown of the bay. I saw the parted end of the old painter unraveling astern and trailing in the wake. The plywood pram was gone.

I looked back. My eyes searched the wilderness of white-caps for a sign of the little boat. It was nowhere. I tore the lashing from the tiller, put *Princess* up into the wind, and went forward, still clutching that guilty length of line. I was jinxed.

Backing and filling, *Princess* plunged into her own wake and gored the steel sea like a unicorn, and the sparks of spray that showered over us ran like tears down my face. Salt-blind and confused, I scrambled up the mast hoops and got one leg over the oval crosstree and the other locked behind the mast. I looked. Darting from crest to crest in a sea that swarmed with the ghosts of little boats, my eyes contended with the eccentricity of the point of view. An hour went by. No boat.

It began to rain, and the wind reached near gale force. Hove to with her tiller unattended, *Princess* stormed into the violent eye of the wind. Surging back against the breaking sea, she dove, tossed, filled her canvas and swung up, struggling to keep the lighthouse in view. Shaken and soaked, I hung to the truck. Hours went by. No boat.

The best part of the day was spent. I came down at last, and *Princess*, easing her motion in the rain-dampened sea, took me to her bosom. She turned slowly, her long sprit scanning the dark water for the last time in search of her little one. In the gathering gloom we reached for Bloody Point. Now we were really alone, for better or for worse.

It wasn't quite the same without the hearty slap and banter of the pram. My baby plummeted down the bay, doing her best to forget. The western edge of the red sector glared from the high lighthouse on Bloody Point Bar. First red and then white, it dilated like an astonished eye over my shoulder. I tossed the ill-gotten length of line with its eye splice and Turk's-head down below, turned the head of *Princess* east, and made for the outlying shoals of Sharps Island.

The tide had turned. The mass of water that squeezed between Cove Point and the flat face of the eastern shore swiped half the contribution of the fair wind. Sharps Island Light came slowly at us in ten-second flashes over a sea that crawled hissing across the shoals. Blinded by long peering and whipped by the pendulum of my perch, I saw shifting shadows of land and an overpowering stray light off Cook's Point.

I headed for the light. It ran away with a roar. It was a fisherman's gas lantern. I dropped the hook in twenty feet of water hard by a red light that rang a bell, and when the sails were down I dove for the bunk.

A great white beam of light burst in my eyes. I came up out of the hatch. The rain striking my face cleared my head. A voice in the light roared, "Can't anchor here. 'T ain't safe. Might have a bad nor'easter."

Groggy, I crawled forward and hauled the big hook up out of the sticky bottom. Back aft I kicked over the engine and followed the fisherman. It was past midnight. My eyes swam with fatigue. I followed the fishing boat for about an hour, cut the engine in the lee of a hump of land, and dropped the hook. Shivering and wet, I went for the wool blankets.

I was out cold when back came the persistent Samaritan with a roar of his starboard engine and a light that stabbed through the boat and me like an X ray. "Can't stay here," came the voice. "Get swamped in a nor'easter."

Too tired to pit my will against local knowledge, I staggered forward to perish at every pull on that seventy-five-pound hook. It clanked at last against the bobstay. I started up the rock crusher and followed the bright star some more. At last my guardian angel gave me the high sign and went away. I dropped the hook in faith and slept.

The tide was running out in the morning, and the short dock at Oxford seemed as scared of deep water as *Princess* was of shoal. I was going to have to thumb a ride ashore. I turned and did a double take. There, scarcely a hundred feet away, lay the big black bugeye. A little white dog on the afterdeck pulled her left hind paw out of her mouth and came sniffing to the taffrail. It was Snooky.

The kids came by in the dinghy, and I had pancakes on the bugeye with the salty preacher and his seagoing family. "There's an old, canvas-covered boat lying behind the rectory," said the sky pilot. "It will take some fixing, but you're welcome to it."

We left at noon for Cambridge with his wife and daughter crewing the big black bugeye and his three sons as pilots for *Princess*. The boat behind the rectory took some fixing. It was an old cedar-planked outboard/rowboat/runabout, whose principal defects consisted of age, a broken transom, stove-in ribs, cracked planks, and torn canvas, mostly aft. I went right to work and shaped and fitted a wide board dragged back by bicycle from the sawmill. I tacked it to the planks in the middle of the boat to stiffen her up.

With this watertight bulkhead suggesting a new stern, I decided that fourteen feet was too long for a dinghy. *Princess* would be sure to resent anything that big trailing along behind her, so I sawed off the after half. The result was the damnedest-looking boat you ever saw. It floated. Not only that, but it performed the vital function of making *Princess* look excruciatingly beautiful by contrast.

That evening a bunch of guys from Baltimore piled off a little yawl spoiling for fun. We did the town, winding up in the local Stork Club, part of which we carted away for the hell of it. I really hung one on that night. It was a beauty. When I got back in the wee hours, there was a faintly scented mash note pinned to my pillow. Not only that, but *Princess* got hung up on the dock, snapped her bobstay, and was fit to be tied.

In the morning I went to the church. The preacher spoke like an old shipmate sharing your watch. It was a good sermon. I remember the part where his eye lifted from the text, and he repeated the words, "He that loveth the danger shall perish therein."

18

Danger is where you find it, whether it be the innermost navigable creek that pales to sweet water or the bitter wells of the pounding sea.

The lifeblood of a boat is the water. You can feel its pulse and stand in it quite dry, yet half submerged. Its arteries and veins are drawn with pinpoint accuracy on the chart. Its circulatory system was known and employed long before man discovered his own. The tides and currents that clear the sea nourish the framework of a vessel and bring to its wooden skin the glow of life.

Pierce that dermal membrane, and the inward flow, like the gush of a staved artery, will spill death into a hull much the way life pours out of a stricken man. Constant as the pressure of blood against our flimsy hides is the cradle of water that supports a vessel. Never was the touch of a mother or a loved one so even, so unvarying, so sure. If there is danger at all, it must be part and parcel of the land.

Tied to the land and restless, *Princess* chafed and gouged her sides on the piling of the dock while I monkeyed around town. I brought visitors aboard, and she showed off in the bay with a weather eye peeled for emotional entanglements. It was all right for *Princess* to shine up to total strangers, but not for me.

I chafed, too, under the double standard she imposed. One night I damn near eloped, but *Princess*, at the moment of decision, showed her broken bobstay and smirked.

It was fall. The nights lengthened at both ends, and the days drew in sharp and clear. The noble arbor of elms that spread their shelter over High Street and the white Victorian houses stood half naked in the scattered tide of fallen leaves. The kids went back to school, and *Princess*, who didn't give a damn whether school kept or not, hankered for the open water.

Snug in the fishermen's slip, I watched a savage storm that struck the town of Cambridge during the night. The black trees groaned and thrashed their limbs against the blinding, cracked shell of sky. Sliced by the wind off the top of the bay, a sheet of salt spray tore across the breakwater and seasoned the driving rain. From what I had learned of the sudden violence of the Chesapeake, I was glad to sit that one out. The sun rose unobscured in the morning and smiled through the interwoven web of bare branches.

Rowing toward the center of town for a new shackle to secure the broken bobstay, I saw a man replace a plank on the bottom of a skipjack. The squat vessel with its raked mast had a strange grace for all its square corners. The yellow pine plank ran thwartships from her keel to the massive chine of her obtuse bottom. It was the simplest planking job I had ever seen. There was something odd about setting a plank so that its grain ran contrary to the direction of the vessel. It was a thing I would have hesitated to do without express permission of the tree. The drudgers have their reasons—come to think of the thousands of times such a vessel is grounded among the oyster beds, what is its main direction but up and down?

I rowed around and studied the skipjack reflected in the still water. Then I went back and got a piece of canvas and my paints. I had me an art class before long, and I learned about an old man over in the cove who had made enough money criticizing art to build himself a houseboat and retire. I went over to pay my compliments.

The homey little vessel was hauled up among the reeds. It commanded an enviable view of Hambrooks Bar and the long bridge that spanned the Choptank River to Bolingbroke. The old man had planned the houseboat himself. It had every convenience. Enfeebled by his ninety years, he seemed to manage nicely with the help of some good girl that looked in now and then.

His name was McCormick. He had been chief art critic on the staff of a large metropolitan daily. He spoke of the old days in New York, about artists, big dealers, and great collectors. While he went on and on I grumbled in silence, talking to myself about struggling painters who rarely eat enough to stay afloat till ninety, let alone having enough to come up high and dry with a houseboat. I was on the wrong end of the art business.

"When I die," said Mr. McCormick suddenly. A grim look invested his face. He saw the bright flowers in the window boxes, the shirred curtains fluttering in the autumn sunlight, the picture-less pattern of painted bulkhead trim, neat as a Vermeer. "When I die," said the art critic, "I'll burn her up."

Here again in the last months of 1940 I heard more talk of war. The draft law was passed, the factories hummed, and the preacher secured his bugeye and went off to offer of himself "that which belongs to Caesar." I picnicked with the hospitable people of Cambridge, still dreaming of an illusory isle wasting in the blue Caribbean.

It was a cold day, the day I left. Stirred by the scent of distance, *Princess* picked up the thread and drove for the mighty channel of the bay. When I went below for a jacket to break the penetrating easterly, I saw two big brown eyes peering from the lazaret. I looked again. It was Snooky, the preacher's pooch, stowed away with her left hind paw for provisions.

Turning back, I tried to get an answer from Snooky. Do dogs go for tropical islands? What lap of land in the sun-flecked sea beckoned? What call was stronger than the siren of a master's whistle? All I could get from Snooky as my boat luffed at the foot of the town dock was a very faraway look. I dropped her safe on the quay, and *Princess* fell away before the wind.

What with all the leave-taking and the stowaway, it was noon before my boat got underway and late afternoon by the time we rounded the grassy lumps of land at Castle Haven Point. I had lost the best part of the tide, but the wind veered in the early evening and the warm sun broke through the scattering clouds before it set.

Princess turned at the mid-channel lighthouse. We ran close-hauled to Oxford with a brisk mooring breeze and the flooding tide. The sudden change in the direction of the wind chopped the Tred Avon River to a rasplike surface dusted with the yellow filings of the sun. There were sails on the river. I followed them around to the little harbor, anchored, and rowed ashore in my latest acquisition.

That dinghy, cut down as it was from a family boat, excited considerable interest in this boatbuilding town. I had quite a time getting ashore. It resisted all means of propulsion. It could not be properly rowed, poled, or sculled. It twisted and ducked around as if in an everlasting search for its after half. With its new stern installed in the wide midship section of its previous contour, its only virtue was that, when hauled out and set on its transom, it could stand up like a man. The Gothic arch of its forefoot made it an excellent shelter. It was one great big generous bow, and that's all. It towed nicely, and it was as good a place to sit as any while you wave a rope end and pray for help.

Ugly as all get out, and for that reason, perhaps, amazingly tractable, the dink trailed the lovely *Princess* out of Oxford in the early morning. It blew hard again from the northeast all day, and the tide, converging in the narrow gullet between Cove Point and

Taylors Island, swallowed us through mixed with all that water from the upper bay and with the fair wind as a chaser.

It was one of those runs, wild and rough, fast and free, the promontories of land turning to look at us and the seething bell buoys rising quickly and as quickly dashing out of earshot, whining with the wind like a locomotive bell.

The sun broke through again at five o'clock, the way a good-natured snapper might, checking on what the day had done. The wind redoubled its effort. We rolled down to Drum Point and slid like the free part of a parallel rule along the sunny leeward side of the land to the shining arm of Solomons Island. *Princess* minded the red bell that hammered on the spit of sand, and we were in.

Satisfied, the sun sank below the wall of storm cloud. The

last rays of the sun seesawed to the sky. Congregated in the little harbor, which stretched every which way back into the land, were boats of every kind holed up in view of the weather. *Princess* bustled down the aisle, decked out in almost every sail she owned. Zigzagging between the cluster of cruisers and sailboats with the speed of a Yankee clipper, she spied an unoccupied mooring can, came about and made for it.

When the halyards were made loose, the wind undressed her, and her bowsprit, coming up to the mooring can, tapped it gently as we pitched, as if to say, Is this the one?

That was the one. I made her fast, furled the sails, and took a look around. We were right in the hub of a wheel of water that stretched its spokes up Mill Creek, Back Creek, around the town and out into the bay. Forgathered here with the wisdom of Solomon himself was a whole harem of little vessels riding out the storm. Moored off the high, wooded point of land with the name *Maskee* lettered in gold on its highly polished transom was a cruiser that belonged to a man with a round face and a pair of binoculars.

He was all eyes and lenses when *Princess* stormed in. Then he went back to his fishing pole, which he shared with a rangy guy who wore a grin and a yachtman's cap. The lady of the boat stood behind them, waiting for fish. It was near suppertime. I passed them, wrangling the dinghy toward the dock.

"Any luck?" All three heads swung in the negative. "What do you use for bait?"

"Worms. Want to try?" The tall fellow held out a sandworm.

I took it back to the boat and dug a spool of line and a rusty hook out of a crack in the cabin overhead. The worm was soon divided in three parts. I threaded one piece on the hook and lowered away. The spool was still paying out when I got a strike and a persistent vibrating tension. Up came a fat flounder with the bait shoved back to the eye of the hook.

The rubbery piece of bait went down a dozen times and came up with a dozen flounders. Splitting my catch with the jovial couple and their boat guest on the *Maskee*, I threw in two thirds of the leftover worm for laughs.

I was wringing out my laundry on the town dock the next day when a dinghy came ashore with the owner of the *Maskee*, his friend, and a black Scottish terrier called Jerry. The captain of the *Maskee* was a retired Marine Corps colonel, recently recalled to active duty. Fraser, the fellow who followed him like an early-morning shadow, was his aide.

"You all alone?" asked the colonel. I allowed that I was. "We thought you must have a crew of ten, the way you brought her in." Having an ear for music, I beamed. "I'd like to go aboard your little ship."

I bundled up my wash and rowed them out. The black Scotty was the first on board. The colonel looked below at the little stove and the galley table that doubled in brass for a chart table. I described the little islands of mayonnaise that rose up through the printed pulp like coral heads.

His eyes traced the halyards to the truck and came down to where Jerry was honoring the spruce mast the way dogs have honored trees since time and dogs began. "Jerry!" roared the colonel. "Say, I'm sorry."

I laughed because it was funny in a salty kind of a way. I said, "A tree is a tree."

"Is a tree," said Fraser.

19

For all her solid American virtues *Princess*, built by the God-fearing men of Maine, held a pagan symbol deep in her bosom.

Before I had any notion of shoving off, my seafaring friend Slivers had made me a present of a heathen idol. He brought it to my place wrapped in a newspaper and the kind of cotton waste you find around an engine room. He ambled in, drew it out of the clinging tangle of cotton threads, and held it up to the light. It was something to see.

It was carved out of a single piece of hard, dark wood in the shape of a man and a woman. These two little figures, while sharing the sinews of the grain, faced away to the poles of the earth. He had picked it up in Africa on a fever-wracked voyage that had taken eighteen months and the lives of two shipmates. He took it home and set it up in his parlor.

His wife threatened to throw it out. They had four young children. Besides, it didn't go with their mission furniture. It came to live with me. Lashed to the mast below deck, it had an aura that took the curse off the gloomy, unlighted recess of the forepeak. It was a functional little double-barreled god with all kinds of rough places to scratch matches on. I aimed to carry it all the way to the island and deliver it to the cousins and kin of the men who fashioned and worshiped it.

This idol, the symbol of a primitive old-time religion, was my ticket to paradise. New ideas are dangerous. Having little taste for the classic fate of a missionary, simmering in a caldron while hungry natives howl around brandishing their lunch hooks, my zeal had plenty of English on it. My knowledge of the Caribbean was sketchy and all mixed up with the South Seas.

Late one night, anchored in the lee of Solomons Island, I was lying on the port bunk studying the intricate design of the carving through the blue blur of tobacco smoke when I was startled by the thump of a heavy hand on the deck. Leaning across the transom of *Princess* with his feet supported by a punt was a descendant of the old Chesapeake oyster pirates. His long face was grained like weathered oak. "You heading south?" he asked.

"Expect so," I answered, ducking below to see if I had a spot of coffee percolating that I could offer him.

"Watch out for Wolf Trap," I heard him say, and he was gone in the darkness when I looked up. I turned in.

Maybe I was too touchy about it. But it happened again the next day. I was getting set to leave Solomons Island. The sun had come through at last, and the wind was fresh from the northwest. An old-time three-masted schooner loaded with schoolteachers was negotiating the tricky entrance with a knowledge that was foreign to classrooms. *Princess* was stomping around restlessly when some buzzard in a jumper loomed out of the country store, looked right through me, and said, "Steer clear of Wolf Trap."

I rowed out right away and dove for the chart. Wolf Trap,

sure enough, there it was—a lighthouse on a sand spit down near the mouth of the Chesapeake, no great variations and depth or peculiar bottom characteristics, just a lighthouse on a submerged bar running parallel to the tide, with a scary name. Wolf Trap—so what! I shoved off.

Princess turned at Cedar Point and beat down the bay toward Norfolk. The wind was where she liked it, just forward of the starboard beam, and steady. Poised on her port chine by her helping of the wind, she found the absolute mean of motion between the slant of the head wind and the groove of her keel in water made dense by her speed. She was an intelligent girl. I didn't always go along with her notions, nor she with mine, but in these things she knew best.

The ten-mile curve of beach to Point No Point melted in the morning haze that clung to the borders of the bay. The lighthouse came slowly out of the mist, its octagonal white house capped with a red roof that was interrupted by little dormer windows that blinked at the four winds. Set on top like a sentry box, the light itself seemed an afterthought. As we surged toward it, I saw, piled up, the great rings of steel upon which this house was neatly settled. Circular caissons, sunk far down through shifting layers of sand to solid bottom, were filled with concrete. All that work to hold a light. Resisting the flow of the sea, it stands still as death, a shining symbol of perversity, a sign for men who cross the water or a monument to those who hold a light for others who do. Here was Point No Point, but good.

We passed this timid nub of eroded land that lay between long easy bights on the western shore of the bay. From a distance it held a promissory note of shelter from wind and tide. Drawing back into the anonymous line of coast as we passed, it honored nothing but the force of the elements.

Princess headed south-southwest magnetic from the lighthouse to shave Point Lookout and ride the tide that tumbled down out of the Potomac. The sun dispersed the mist by noon and glistened on the forward facets of the dark waves. It was windy enough in the mouth of the river that goes to Washington. The odds were even money that both houses were in session. I had half a mind to run up the Potomac to the Capitol, but that would have been literally flying in the face of the wind. I figured to hear soon enough from that quarter.

Princess, calling with the luff of her staysail like a fluttering heart, pointed to the lighthouse on Smith Point, and we crossed the Potomac as if it were a deep and personal Rubicon. Minding her course in the slack of the tide, my boat sloshed through the rip and gave way before the mounting pressure of the flooding tide. She turned into the Great Wicomico River and drifted into Reedville with the faltering wind.

There were two tremendous lumber schooners anchored in the shelter of Bull Neck. On one I saw the solitary figure of an old man raising her heavy canvas with a deck engine. I had no idea what he was up to. Drying sails, I supposed, after all the wet weather. I looked back as we turned into Reedville. The schooner was passing the point at Fleeton, heading out. That schooner was all of two hundred and fifty feet from stem to stern. I had heard of men sailing such a vessel singlehanded in a pinch. It can be done, just as the *Queen Mary* can be brought to dock without tugs. It takes knowledge and it takes nerve.

Steering such a ship out in the expanse of ocean is an academic affair. Errors can be corrected. Close to the land a great ship feels like a planet coursing through space, its mass capable of dashing those concerned to oblivion. I have known such ships, and one night alone on deck, years later, I felt the burden of such a pinch.

She was a Liberty ship of the usual seven thousand tons. She had done her job. By that time the war was over. She lay in the harbor of Norfolk waiting with several of her sister ships for the last funeral passage up the James River to the bone yard. A good part of the crew had paid off. The rest were ashore, all but the second engineer, an oiler, and myself. I was on the articles as mate.

There was a storm, and her anchor dragged during the night. Swinging on her cable, the ship came closer and closer with her massive transom to the bow of another anchored Liberty ship. It was too late to pay out additional scope. In the shrieking gale her anchor, loosened by the storm, ripped along the harbor bed, and we swung to crash. The wind eased her victim to one side, but the ships touched as I sprinted forward across the wet steel deck to the bridge.

"Got any steam?"

The second engineer on the other end of the tube yelled, "Yeah."

I rang the telegraph slow ahead. I could feel the rumble of her engine, and the great ship shook with the thrust of her massive propeller. I stood in the darkness at the wheel, alone. Seven thousand tons of vessel were underway.

The anchor, of course, was still on the bottom. The ship ran up on it. I stopped the engine. The ship was yawing wildly in the full gale, and I saw from the wing of the bridge that we had just cleared the one that lay anchored astern.

Then we drifted back. I rang slow ahead and we cleared again. This went on for more than an hour. I got used to it. It was like a milk run—up on the anchor and back, up on the anchor and back, just in time to avoid the crash, and the storm raged on. In spare moments between these tethered trips I grabbed the blinker and called for the Coast Guard. I called for a pilot. I called for the commander-in-chief. No one showed up, not even the mess boy.

After several hours a Coast Guard tug came by with no crew that they could spare and no pilot. They said that they were sorry. They were, and they went away. After the Coast Guard left, I rang the engine-room telegraph full ahead. The ship shook in a frenzy of power, the pilothouse doors rattled, and she drove inexorably forward through the darkness, dragging her anchor halfway across the harbor like an underwater plow, and I steered.

I stopped the engine, put her slow astern to fetch up on the anchor cable, stopped her again, and rang finished with engine. My conscience was clear. After all, I had my girl to think of. *Princess* was fast asleep back on the number five hatch.

Unmindful of the future, my love swept cheerfully out of Reedville in the morning. The red-brick canning factory and the cluster of houses peeked after us through the shorn trees. The wind had come around to the south, and the sky was reserved for the warm sun. There was no hint of cloud except the soft haze of Indian summer that shook the outline of Tangier Island. We tacked across to the shoals of the eastern shore, came about, and sailed back to the lighthouse on Windmill Point, which clings to the submerged upper lip of the Rappahannock.

The fair tide was in there pitching for us. The tide, the ever-present movement of salt water, the silent partner of every voyage, has made liars out of most of us. Try as I may to be honest, when I say sailed, Lord only knows how much we owe to the tide, or how little.

The stigma of an opportunist is the badge of a sailor. Measured with an even hand, the tide is his portion. It is spurned only by landsmen grown silly bucking away in a herd. Drawn apart from the competitions of the shore, the seaman must accept the universal favors of wind and tide as no reflection on his vessel or himself. Only the vain will needlessly breast the tide or strive against the manifest will of the wind.

With the blessing of both, we crossed the translucent shoal of Rappahannock Spit in the early afternoon, ghosted into the Piankatank, and, turning in the lovely hollow of Hills Bay, curled around into Milford Haven.

I tied up at Callis Wharf and watched the sun go down. It grew cold. I was hungry, too hungry. I hadn't been eating enough—too busy sailing. I stood on the wharf, tired after the long day's run, and shivered in the frosty air. I walked around the dock, stretching my legs, which had been confined so long in the cockpit, and trying to remember having ever had so ravenous an appetite.

There was a shed on the wharf, and a big pile of black chunks that looked like coal clinkers covered with mud, retrieved for some strange reason from a sunken barge. "What's that stuff?" I asked a fellow on the wharf. He reached over, lifted a clump, twisted his knife into it, and popped an oyster into my mouth. It was the first raw shellfood I had ever eaten.

I have devoured steamed clams till they came out of my ears. I was gone on oyster stew, but for the life of me I couldn't abide raw shellfood till that day. It was unbelievably delicious, sweet and slightly salty with a fragrance of the sea as subtle as the faint perfume of a modest woman. It braced me like a shot. I sat on the great heap of oysters with my pocketknife and glutted myself till it was too dark to see. Then I kindled a fire in the stove and slept like the just.

There is an easy way out of Milford Haven through a break in the western shore between Gwynn Island and the mainland. With three feet of water at low tide and a stake set up by the fishermen to follow as a range from Point Breeze, it would be fine for *Princess* at high water. We could save seven miles. It led right out behind Wolf Trap. Wolf Trap—what was it I had heard back in Solomons Island about Wolf Trap? We went out at noon, retracing our steps the long way around, with a cargo of shellfood and the south wind blowing hard.

I should have spent another day staking a claim on that mountain of oysters. The wind roared straight up the bay. *Princess* tacked across and back a couple of times, running off every time we got near Wolf Trap and the tide turned against her. It became late and dark and cold. The tide, committed to fill the Chesapeake, roared in between the solid shoulders of land. The ominous light of Wolf Trap flashed every fifteen seconds a couple of miles north of *Princess* as she wallowed, tacking across in the windy night. A floating palace of a houseboat churned by, heading for Norfolk. We could have used a tow. We lost ground on the last tack, and the seas grew big and sharp.

There was no place to duck into except Horn Harbor on the western shore three miles south of Wolf Trap. I'd be damned if I'd turn back. My chart showed shoal water at the entrance to Horn Harbor, and little in the way of aids to navigation. You'd think I'd know better than to get caught out there without a large-scale chart. It must have been the oysters I ate that sent me charging out half cocked.

It was totally dark when I came about again and headed to cross the southern shoals of Wolf Trap to get a look at Horn Harbor. Maybe *Princess* would stumble on a line of buoys to show us in.

Princess stumbled, sprawled, and heaved her bow to the sky. I have never known anything like it. Take a fair-sized lake and place it in an erupting volcano, and you've got a rough idea of what goes on in the toils of Wolf Trap. Monstrous solid waves loomed up over us from every quarter without rhyme or reason. One nasty one, pinched together by the insane configuration, punched *Princess* into the air and, bouncing away, dropped her in a great mouth of trough surrounded by toppling teeth of water.

Batted, slung, shaken, and thrown with a spleenful vengeance, the tiller was unavailing and the boom jibed like a flailing arm. It went on and on till Wolf Trap tossed us out of its deadly jaws through sheer enthusiasm over our agony. We ran off in a hurry, glad to be afloat and to hell with Horn Harbor.

Heading out to the relative calm of the turbulent bay, I heard a persistent racket down below. I looked. Among other things, the heathen idol had become unshipped and was rolling around, rump over teakettle, lewd as a wayward dervish on the cabin floor.

20

With the rollicking heathen idol stashed away in the dark niche of the forepeak, we marked time. *Princess* wallowed at anchor, holding her ground in the night. The wind was square out of the south, and heavy. I tried to find a bit of lee along the eastern lining of the bay, but the wind knew all the angles. It gave the mounting tide a boost, curling it up inside Cape Charles.

I tried to sleep. It was no use. The impact of the open sea, rolling in like a cue ball hit by the south wind and banked obliquely off the hard, straight cushion of the coast, made sleep too much to ask. It was a long night.

I got the anchor up just before daybreak. I was too tired to give a damn which way we went. *Princess* tacked down with a weather eye for Wolf Trap. As we ran abeam of it, I wondered how that innocuous sand bar managed to harbor a segment of the soul of Hatteras and make with some of the same high jinks. We crossed York Spit with the last of the ebb.

As a slight concession to the stubborn southerly and with the persuasion of a rising tide, we drifted up York River. *Princess* had a friend up there. Dr. Archie's water buggy was hitched to a stake up in Sarah Creek while the government paid him to play with their great big brand-new chemical set over near Richmond. We found his boat floating fine, and funny-looking as ever. The man said that Archie hadn't been around in a long time. Lord knows what was cooking up at Richmond. I nailed a note on it and went over to Yorktown to brush up on American history, and to sleep.

I slept first. Revived, I stormed the battlements of Yorktown Heights with a pocketknife, sat on the ramparts, and whittled. Triggered by a break in the clouds, the sun fired a volley of light down across the steep abutments, ricocheted off the river, and splattered the countryside with the fragments of fall. The monument to the men who gave their lives pointed an accusing finger at the sky. Its shadow, slowly sweeping the river, lay heavy on *Princess*. Suddenly the flag was lowered and folded; so were we in the anonymity of the night. Our island never seemed so far away.

It was back in the morning, nevertheless, like a chronic mirage, shapeless and transparent, forming like vertigo in the cold fog of the spilling river. Turned loose from her grip on the tall pilings of the ferry slip, *Princess* made good time with the tide down around Tue Point. We foamed along the flats. The wind had backed to the northeast during the night, and it lay on our beam all the way down York River. This favor of wind came wrapped in a light drizzle that tightened the bellies of the sails. We leaped toward Norfolk.

At Plumtree Point *Princess* faced slowly, regretfully away from the gray, gaping sea that waited beyond the wide portals of the capes. The deep acres of anchorage lay just around Old Point Comfort to the right. We tore across the veering rip, and the sharp bowsprit of *Princess* in a full thrust, a quick traverse, parried the bending blade of the tide. It fell before her as we stood into Norfolk.

The city was half hidden in a mist that lay about the ships in the harbor. It took almost two hours to cross the harbor. We ran along the busy docks, turned at Lambert Point, and nosed into the tiny channel that ran fast under a bridge. Exchanging courtesies, the bridge rose to clear our top, and we entered the municipal yacht basin.

I remember next to nothing of Norfolk itself. The water is my world. The ancient, high-pooped junks whose raucous sails cluttered the harbor of Karachi are clearer in memory than the play of lights on the balconies of the bazaar. Sails of dhows, purple and metallic, suspended on raveled stripes of turquoise and deep blue, are sharper in retrospect than the four dull corners of the pyramids. The spendor of the Taj Mahal would be lost on a sailor if it wasn't repeated in the mirror of clear water that lies confidently before it.

I remember Norfolk because I found something there that I loved. It was a little thing. I might have missed it in the clutter of boats that were tucked along the irregular border of the basin. Reminiscent of a kind of beauty I had pressed into the mold of my own desire, she lay demure and sweet in the light of the autumn afternoon.

It would be inaccurate to say that I couldn't believe my eyes. I am accustomed to believing my eyes. You have to when you're sailing alone. I looked again. It didn't seem possible, but there she was, an absolute replica, a sister ship of *Princess*.

My boat came about coyly and ran timorously alongside nosing the matronly tumble home of her identical twin. Held apart by the fabric of a fender, they clung to each other in sisterly embrace and gurgled in the happy Down East accents of the prodigal tide.

"She belongs to Captain Ackerman," said the watchman on the dock. "He'll be down around five or after. Always comes to see how she is before he goes home."

It was four o'clock. I furled sail and tidied up, stepping
ashore ever other minute to take another look at the pretty sisters
reunited in Norfolk. The sun came through and went down behind a worn knoll of earth. The stocky figure of a man in a brown
business suit took its place. He stood leaning forward, motionless.
His heavy arms were half bent and slightly raised away from his
sides. The brim of his fedora was bent up as if it faced a gale. In his
eyes was the startled expression of a skeptic come to grips with the
supernatural.

He hesitated for a moment eying the two boats, indistin-
guishable and abreast with my foolish little dinghy snuggled in a
tantrum of jealousy between them. He ran down, and the loose
pebbles rolled after him. "I don't believe it," he said. I watched
him staring fore and aft, down below and up at the twin trucks.
His head shook in disbelief. Then he said, "I'm Ackerman," and
held out his hard hand. I went home with him to dinner.

Captain Leon Ackerman lived with his wife in a modest house in the center of Norfolk. After many years at sea he settled ashore, built this little home on a tree-lined street, and went into the stevedoring business. It's a tough business. Captain Ackerman was tough, too, but with brains. He did all right. Well enough, I suspected, to afford any boat he might want.

Granted his was a superb sea boat, what did a well-to-do man want with an antiquated twenty-six-foot former lobster fisherman with its old-fashioned sail plan, its lack of headroom, and its clumsy overhanging bowsprit and boom? An artist might go for a deal like that. I did—it's romantic; it's a part of the poetry of the past; and it's a hell of a lot cheaper than any luxury yacht Nevins will whip up for you while you wait. So what was eating Ackerman? Could there be the soul of a poet behind that stevedoring jaw? What dreams lay behind his wide-open master's ticket with its innumerable endorsements?

Mrs. Ackerman was jolly as a little sea bird, and bubbling with surprise over the existence of another boat like theirs. "Leon was certain that his was the only one in the world. We've had her for fifteen years. We never saw anything like her." I had some more plum pudding and followed the captain to his chartroom.

His study was pine-paneled and lined with books about the sea. I began to understand. We talked about our sister ships, matching anecdotes frame for frame, timber for timber, plank for plank. Here in Norfolk, the old man had gone through every heartache, every wrinkle, and every exasperation of rebuilding a Friendship sloop that I had gone through around New York. Most of the work had been done at his direction in local yards over the past fifteen years.

"What did it cost, all told?" I asked him.

"I'm ashamed to say." He looked me in the eye, took a deep pull on his cigar, and blew out the round sum: "Twenty thousand dollars."

I believed him. Twenty thousand dollars. I went back to *Princess* talking to myself. I was staggered by the magnitude of my dedication. Twenty thousand dollars! I lay in the bunk and watched a star do a veil dance with a flimsy scrap of cloud. *Princess* nudged her sister ship with the slow, chafing sigh of familiarity. It was all right for Captain Ackerman, he could probably afford to indulge. But where did I come off, pouring that kind of money or man-hours on a girl who at best could never be more to me than a plaything? Twenty thousand, holy crow!

The years pass. The value of things we see and feel and love, spread over the swift or sluggish hours, makes up the total of our lives. I wondered what kind of job of rebuilding the captain had got for his twenty thousand dollars. Someday I would find out. I did. I came back to Norfolk intact after all the shooting. I came back with *Princess*. We saw her sister ship on the ways. The poor girl had a hundred short planks, some less than four feet long, and enough butt blocks joining them to build a castle. In a way Captain Ackerman was robbed. You can count the butt blocks in *Princess* on the fingers of one hand.

There was no way then to know that the years would double the cost and square the value of my vessel. All I knew was the kinetic surge of *Princess* and a ribbon of navigable water that cut through the land from Norfolk to join the Albemarle. Taking off again at the head of Alligator River, it bypassed the fury of Hatteras.

I hung around for a few days sweeping soot from the deck and sailing with the skipper and his wife on their Friendship sloop while my girl glared at us from the slip. The days of early October were mild and sunny despite all the air-borne putrefaction that lay like a pall above this busy town. One day the clean wind sweeping the Chesapeake coincided with the rising tide in the afternoon. I ran over to a gas dock and put a head on the half-filled tank of gas that must have been going flat sloshing around all these months. The engine, which was indispensable in an emergency, made no sense when there was any wind at all. It couldn't touch the wind for driving power even on a hard beat. We had come all the way to Norfolk using less than five gallons of gas.

With the tank filled and the galley crammed with provisions, I shoved off, knowing that I could hole up for the night almost anywhere along the Intracoastal Waterway. That part looked good after Wolf Trap. The bridge opened, and we were underway. The great steel structures of industry towered above us. There were hulking buoys on a dock, red as boiled lobsters, waiting to be opened and overhauled. *Princess* headed away from the noise of Norfolk into the quiet country. We turned to the left at Money Point and passed beneath the tight railroad bridge at the bottom of the S curve. It was tricky under sail, but we made it. The bridgetender was rooting for us. Two years later almost to the day, I made the same tricky turn, and I made money, too, starting at Money Point.

That second time I was a deck hand on a sixty-five-foot Army tugboat that was hauling a couple of landing barges around to Frisco. I had just come off a troopship that made the African invasion run, or tried to. I welcomed this inland trip as a breather. It was one of those little handouts you get during a war between the curtains of conflict.

The skipper of the tug was a deep-water man. This was the kind of thing he generally turned over to a pilot. The mate, who was gifted with the physique of a weight lifter, was less gifted in a more essential department. He had enough trouble trying to work a meridian altitude without straining his powers of comprehension trying to figure out an inland waterway chart. The second mate, referred to by the old man as the swamp admiral, was unlicensed. He couldn't read a chart. He couldn't read.

I was at the wheel as the little tug, dragging her barges like obedient ducklings, came to Money Point. There are three ways to go at Money Point. You can go up Julian Creek and join the rest of the wrecks that are foundered in the mud. Straight ahead will fetch you up in an abandoned ditch. The correct way is to the left. Except for a flashing red buoy at the intersection, there are no instructions on land, on the water, or in the air. You have to know how to read a chart. I looked around the pilothouse. The second mate was gone.

I made the turn, and the next one too. It was easy with all

that power. I didn't have to come about in the basin, as I did with my best girl. With the crisis averted, the doubtful second mate stormed back into the pilothouse and snatched the wheel away from me. Then he sent me for coffee. I was halfway down the ladder when he put her hard aground.

Desperate to redeem himself, the stubborn second mate clutched the wheel for days, hanging on like a drowning man. We couldn't pry him loose. He had been hired for his alleged knowledge of the waterway. All the way to Charleston we spent more time aground than underway. It was the mate, employing his vast physique, who finally tore him loose.

The next time I rounded Money Point, it was as master of an eighty-foot tug, hauling a monstrous wooden barge that measured one hundred and eighty feet by sixty. There wasn't room enough between the abutments of the railroad bridge to take the beamy barge alongside the tug. I had the barge made up close astern while we waited back at the dolphins for the bridge to open. Then we headed through. You could measure the clearance by inches. The tide that came along with us set the barge over to the left. The enormous momentum of that barge could tear down the overhead if we struck. There was no time to deliberate.

I rang full ahead. Six hundred and fifty horsepower packed in a diesel engine strained forward and increased the velocity of the barge; still she headed for the left wall of the bridge. I spun the wheel hard over to the left. The bow of the tug, which had already cleared the bridge, headed for the left bank, while the stern swung over to the right, just enough to nose the barge through. Jerked to the right by the tail of the tug, the barge cleared. Hard right and amidships steadied us, and the lights of Norfolk lay uneventfully ahead.

It was an old story. When you turn your bow, your stern turns too, the other way. It is a good thing to know, especially when you hear "Man overboard." *Princess* taught me that with her overhanging boom. She taught me how to play the tides, too, and when I played them out in the Atlantic from Norfolk to New York, that same barge and tug honored me by making the fastest known run of its kind.

But on that sunny afternoon in October 1940, neither the urgency of the dream nor the impending tide of war could hurry *Princess*. She listened only to the wind, and the wind began to whistle. We whipped down past Millville with the advantage of half a gale, the nervous tension of the tardy bridges, and none of the drawbacks of a pounding sea. There was a thirty-foot cruiser blown hard aground between New Mill and Samson creeks. I came about and tossed them my anchor cable, made fast to the rudderpost, and the northwest wind went to work.

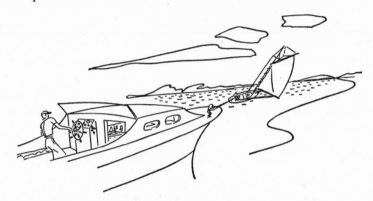

Heading east and heeled over, *Princess* exerted a force that was unrelenting and unbelievable. The cruiser came out of the sticky mud inch by inch till she was free. We entered the locks and rose up to the level of North Landing River together, and I waved the cruiser on its way when it became clear that, given deep water, sails were no match for her engine.

We ran the six straight miles of the Virginia Cut in exactly an hour and spent the night at North Landing. The morning of October 16, 1940, was gray. Congress had passed a law. Upon that day all males between the ages of eighteen and thirty-eight were required to register for the draft, or else. Men out on the high seas were excepted, providing they presented themselves immediately upon reaching port.

I looked around at the intracoastal ditch. I never saw anything that looked less like the high seas. North Landing River was high. We had to climb the lock to get to it, but it didn't meet the definition of a sea. There were no draft boards in the bush. Half-way through the next ditch in the middle of the North Carolina Cut lay the town of Coinjock. I had a date in Coinjock, and no joke. No wind, either. There were more than twenty-five miles to go. It was up to the engine.

It started on the first spin like a damn little warmonger, and we chugged down the marshy river, which opened to an expanse of shoal water. It began to blow from the northeast just before noon. Under sail, Coinjock was in the bag. *Princess* ran aground, and I was in the bag too.

I tried to blame it on *Princess*, but she just lay there and stared at the cat-o'-nine-tails in the swamp. This was no way to run a war or run away. I had to get off. Oddly enough, we were hard aground in two feet of water just above Troublesome Point. I was just about ready to sit that war out when the heavens opened up with a blast of wind that heeled us over, and we were off—to the wars.

It looked peaceful enough in Coinjock. There were no self-appointed Paul Reveres galloping off in all directions with lanterns to hang in belfries. There was just a quiet little schoolhouse with a rough, wooden floor and a slip of a girl in faded gingham sitting at an oak desk all alone with an American flag at her side.

21

I came out the same door I went in, waded through the oak leaves in the schoolyard, and looked down to where *Princess* lay in the canal. She looked like a great big gray seed that had devoured a man and sprouted a mast.

"Let's face it," I said, looking right at her, "you're only a boat." She didn't answer, and all of a sudden I wasn't sure. She pointed south with her bowsprit. There was no use getting into an argument. We shoved off.

I slipped my brand-new draft card into my wallet and tossed the billfold into the cold oven for safekeeping. There was a chance that it might slip out of my pocket while I jumped around the deck handling sail. The sky cleared, and we ghosted in a mild west wind down among the bends of North River. The channel is wide at the mouth of Deep Creek. If it hadn't been, that would have been the end of my worries about the draft and the end of any concern *Princess* might entertain about her own.

Without warning, the bow of a big inland freighter loomed around the point of the grassy marsh and headed right at us. I jibed over to pass to the right. The freighter had other ideas. Crossing the bow of my boat, the big ship cleared us by an inch, nipped the muddy corner of the marsh, and roared away without a sign or signal. We wallowed in her wake.

The west wind, which was diagnosed by a specialist in Coinjock as moribund, died at dinnertime. I dropped the hook in six feet of water just inside Camden Point at the mouth of North River. Spaghetti boiled in a bucket and a meat sauce simmered on the stove. Dinner was set on the cabin hatch cover with a view of the Albemarle as the sun went down.

I wondered how soon my number would be called. When would I know what fate would dish out of the fishbowl lottery? How hot was I? How hot? Good God! I dove for the stove and pulled my wallet out of the oven with a fork. The draft card was hot, and so was the money, but they were otherwise unscathed by this initial experience under fire.

It blew hard out of the south during the night. I shifted our position three times. It was easy with the hook down in a mere fathom of water. By morning I was an authority on the hydrography of Camden Point. I could have qualified as a pilot for the bar, through which a channel had been cut to the open Albemarle. I had no trouble getting out. I had plenty of trouble getting back in four years later with the same eighty-five-foot Army tug and that tremendous oil barge that spared the bridge up at Money Point. That time I had help. I had just a little too much help, in the way of an overzealous second mate who had been asked to wake me from my nap the moment we came abeam of the flashing white bell that lies in deep water one mile out from the bar. He didn't wake me. The tug did when she ran up on the bar. Before I could jump out of my bunk, he had backed the engine. The propeller cut the towline, setting the barge adrift. Winding up on the propeller shaft, the towline fouled the rudder, and the strain of it snapped the steering cable. The rudder was locked hard right, and we were still aground. I caught a glimpse of the barge starting to drift in the strong northwest wind. It was heading toward the mile-wide flats, from which we could never retrieve it with our nine-foot draft. It was four o'clock in the morning.

I rang full astern. The big diesel backed her off the bar. I rang full ahead. She went forward and turned. Confronted by the opposite edge of the dredged channel, I backed her briefly. Full ahead, and we were almost heading out. Once more full astern lightly and full ahead turning, and we roared right out to the barge. A couple of minutes after she was cut loose we got a line on the barge, dropped the hook, and had breakfast. The second mate had had no experience on the water prior to the war. Most of the water men, like the fishermen who tended trawls off Hatteras, were in the infantry. When the sun came up, the boys went over the side with galley knives and cut the towline clear of the propeller. I spliced the steel steering cable.

In the last year of calm, before the beaches were blackened with oil and the ocean diluted ever so slightly with blood, *Princess* waited to cross the Albemarle. We left with light airs in the morning.

For all the touted tales of brine, its fury is a kitten's slap compared to the tigerish claw of fresh water. It is slow to anger, but, once aroused, fresh water falls like liquid lead across the deck, gripping a leg or a man with a deadly drag that is alien to the buoyant and sprightly spirit of salt water. Salt water must be proud of boats. It holds them high. Fresh water hides a hull in its landlocked moods.

There are men who owe their lives to the caprice of salt water; men who were popped back on board by the sister wave of the one that washed them away. The nature of salt water breeds a hopeful race.

The freshwater sailor is something else again—brooding, tenacious as a man I met in Belhaven who lost a deckload of lumber and then himself in a bitter storm kicked up by the long shoal reaches of the Pamlico. He was sailing alone. After he went by the board he happened to grab a line trailing in the wake of the fast-moving skipjack and clawed his way through the shallow fury back aboard.

Where a saltwater man would have been glad to close for his life and to hell with the deck cargo, this bird spent the next eighteen hours getting "every damn stick back aboard." He grinned tight-lipped in the telling, like a man who killed a man in a fair fight. "It can get worse right here inside Hatteras," he said, "than it ever gets outside."

Disposed to be pleasant in the morning, the sound became annoyed by the stiff westerly and grew nasty mean by the time *Princess* got to the mouth of the Alligator River. Heeled over with the lee scuppers deep awash, we crossed the bar of Middle Ground and took our chances in four feet of water as the lesser of two evils. The waves were too close and sharp to come about and run over to the channel. One wicked wave crashed aboard as *Princess*, leaning, lifted her keel over the cusp of the bar.

We were joined by a bluff-bowed white sailing vessel that came out of Dismal Swamp. She had a deck cargo of cedar, and she looked for all the world like Captain Joshua Slocum's *Spray*. It couldn't be the *Spray*. The *Spray* had been lost with Slocum, whose last known words conveyed the unassailable sentiment that his way was better than an old man's home.

This reincarnation of the *Spray* that dabbled in freight belied the romantic convictions of Slocum. She had a motor, and she used it when it looked as if *Princess* would beat her to the Alligator River–Pungo River Canal.

Straight as a segment of a great circle, the man-dug road of water ran for seven miles, turned slightly for three and on again for another ten till its end was lost over the curvature of the earth. The wind became spotty, and we dawdled. The sight of the swing bridge was a welcome change from the sameness of the cypress swamp. It was late in the afternoon when we passed the second bridge and met the Pungo River.

Slatting around in the river, I got into a conversation with a fellow on a cruiser. He threw me a line and zipped into Belhaven. *Princess*, squatting in his wake like a fat heiress, loved it. We got there before dark, and I got a clump of oysters from a hill that was heaped against the wall of the cannery. There were half a dozen skipjacks tied up alongside, a black schooner named *Ptarmigan*, and that apotheosis of Slocum. My Friendship sloop was just what Belhaven needed to complete its inventory.

Speaking of inventories, the *Ptarmigan* was slightly overstocked. This handsome black schooner was being sailed to Florida for her owner by a newlywed couple and a hitchhiker by the name of Edward. Shunted somehow off the highways, Edward had taken to thumbing rides along the inland waterway.

Edward was the soul of propriety. He was quiet and well-mannered to a point of being nonexistent. Jerry, the new groom, was a navigator who had been around the world with Kaufman on the *Hurricane*, but to Jerry, just embarked on the loosely charted sea of matrimony, Edward was a symbol of a reef, unbreaking and ever-present. *Princess* and I were just what the doctor ordered.

All unsuspecting, I was entertained by the gay couple, had my jokes laughed at, my troubles given the most earnest consideration. Of course, I wound up with Edward. *Princess* stared balefully at the bay as he came aboard with his suitcase.

I might just as well have shipped the Sphinx. All down the Pungo River, not a word; across the Pamlico, windwhipped and silvered by the sun, not a word; becalmed for hours in the gloom of the ditch behind Goose Creek Island, not a word; morning, noon, and night, and not a word.

"Feel all right?" No answer. Maybe Edward was the listening type. I might as well talk. I started with the year one and talked till two. I took up at the crack of dawn and talked all the way down the Neuse River. I talked about art, about life. I told jokes, I delivered indictments, I rhapsodized, I poured passages, I waxed philosophic, I practiced polemics. I recounted impalpable adventures, pounded the profundities of Plato, swiped from Shakespeare, stole from Spinoza, doodled with Dante. In Adams Creek I ran dry. I waited, but not a damn word out of Edward. He *was* a good listener.

Edward was no dope. I had it straight from Jerry, who had carried him as far as Belhaven, that Edward was a graduate of two universities, a Rhodes scholar, a modern poet, an intellect of shining promise. But from Belhaven down across the saucer of the sound, through all the moody rivers, across the graceful bays to the last tedious canal that led us to the sea, to Beaufort and Morehead City, not a word. Nothing. Just that one atavistic gesture with the thumb.

It wasn't a bad run. Edward was steady at the tiller, and he certainly could cook. I came to wonder what the hell they taught at Cambridge, Heidelberg, and the Sorbonne. The last I saw of him, he was standing on the dock with his suitcase at his feet, making with the thumb. I wandered around the town and ran into Asa.

Asa was untutored. Asa was the foreman of the yard over behind Morehead City, where they build the big pogy boats. There was one on the ways in the process of construction. Massive oak frames coated with red lead stuck up into the sky like the innumerable raw fingers of a cupped hand. Here and there a man supported by a scaffold or clinging to a stringer swung a razor-sharp adz and the contour of the hull was faired. It was a good picture. I was trying to put it down on canvas. Asa watched over my shoulder.

"I'd sure like to have that painting," he said.

"It's yours." I gave it to him.

"Bring your little boat around, we'll do some work on her." That was nice of Asa. I brought *Princess* back under the bridge and came in the shallow channel of Calico Creek at high water. Asa hauled her and put a man to work painting and fitting her keel with an iron shoe to ward off the worms. While my girl was being groomed, I monkeyed around the yard watching them start to plank that two-hundred-fifty-foot fishing vessel.

"What is she going to look like finished, Asa? Can I see her plans?"

"We ain't got plans."

"No plans?"

"Well," said Asa, thinking, "come on, I'll show you her plans." He led the way into the shop.

By the light that sifted down through the grimy wall of windowpanes I saw a power planer, half buried in a heap of chips, a joiner, and a table saw. Asa came to the center of the shop and pointed down to a great semicircle that was scored deep into the old, worn planks of the floor.

"There's my plan," said Asa. My eyes traced the easy curve, which was accented by dirt caught in the crevice of the arc. "It's all the plan I've got. It's all the plan my pappy had, or my grandpappy, or my great-grandpappy before him."

"You build from this?" Asa nodded. I looked with awe and wonder at that mark on the floor, from which that immense vessel took its coefficient of fineness. This was the curve of the midship frame, the shape from which by eye and simple subtraction the ship was born. This mark was all the plan they had, this and a little boy's hand on a plane, helping his pappy cut to the line as the old eye grew dim and the young one sharp, generation after generation.

Princess came out of Asa's yard as if she came from a beauty parlor. Built Down East by the old man Morse in much the same way Asa built his ships, she sailed out of Calico Creek with something more than paint can give. We were closer than ever. The towering red frames of the pogy boat, like columns of a logarithm table traced by the stringers of sheer and chine, were silently solving their own problems of girth and motion as we turned away.

I came back to Calico Creek whenever I could. I came back during the following years aboard strange hulls built for war that were about as seaworthy as a drafting table. Across the broad expanse of a country plunged into a fever of war work, every shed and every yard that impinged on navigable water was loaded with work. Boats, rafts, landing barges poured out of every creek or bight that boasted a skilled hand. Calico Creek was idle. Asa was sitting on the steel table of the joiner, whittling a toothpick. His men were loafing in the yard or doing little odd jobs for the fishermen.

"Asa, how come you aren't building boats for the government?"

Asa looked up and smiled grimly. "We can't read their damn plans."

That was 1942. I could tell a mile away that the tide had turned in Calico Creek when I came by in '43. The place was alive. I saw massive mine layers fitted with every war-born gadget from radar to rocket launchers superimposed on gray hulls that were strangely reminiscent of the lines of a pogy boat. Jammed in the creek being fitted out or overflowing in clusters at anchor were patrol vessels, mine sweepers, war vessels fashioned of wood —not one couldn't pass for a converted menhaden fisherman.

There were uniformed guards and barbed wire around Asa's yard. I had to fish out my Coast Guard pass to get in. Asa was busy as the Assistant Director of War Mobilization. I caught up with him after a while. "What happened, Asa? I thought you couldn't read their plans."

"We still can't," said Asa. "We don't have to."

"You got men to read them for you?"

"No, sir," said Asa, looking a little put out.

"How do you do it?"

"We built a menhaden fishing boat for the fertilizer plant last year. The Coast Guard was kind of desperate for vessels of that size so they took it over. The vessels they had were designed to run best at fourteen knots. At fifteen knots they squatted. At less than fourteen knots they handled poorly, and they weren't too good acting at fourteen. They ran tests on our fishing boat, and they found out she was fine at fourteen knots, fine at fifteen, and fine at any speed you push her. Yes, sir, we're still building by that plan on the floor in the shop."

22

Morehead City was art-conscious. For a town of two thousand people, more of them were interested in the way paint is put on canvas than you are likely to find anywhere this side of the Left Bank. There was an old fisherman down there. Frankly, I can't recall his name. Call him Frankly—Jake Frankly.

Captain Jake Frankly had title to an old wharf. It was next to the dock where the big menhaden fishing boats tied up. Frankly was long, gnarled, weather-beaten and waterlogged like a branch of live oak that's been cast by the surf on the sands of Hatteras and recalled a million times. He was a big fisherman in his day. By the time *Princess* came to tie up at his wharf, Jake had slowed to a state of semiretirement. He owned a little party-fishing boat, and he made short trips for a fee, mostly inside the waterway.

I broke out my watercolors. Jake watched me paint. He watched the menhaden fishing boats take shape as if he were seeing ghosts. Art was something he read about. It looked like magic. At first there was nothing but a sheet of paper. Slowly a vessel he had known for thirty years came out at him. He looked from the little water color I was painting over to the real thing as if he was afraid the real thing would fade into nothing as fast as it came out of the fog of white paper.

I had barely put the finishing touches on my little painting when old Jake Frankly asked me for it. I wanted to give it to him. He was my host. *Princess* was tied up to his dock. I explained that I hoped to use it as a preliminary sketch for a larger painting.

"Let me have it for a little while," said Jake.

"Wait till I get the big painting underway."

"Just for a little while," said Jake. "I want to show it to somebody." I let him have it. The little while began to grow. I went looking for old Jake Frankly and my watercolor.

I went to Jake's house. Jake was not at home. His wife had no idea where he was. I inquired around and was told that I could find him in a bar halfway across town. When I got to the bar, Jake had just left.

The bartender said, "Jake had a little painting with him. Did you paint it?"

I said, "Yes."

He said, "Nice painting. Have a drink."

One of the boys in the saloon told me where to look for Jake. I went there. It was another bar. Jake had just left. Everybody liked the painting. A fisherman bought me a drink. By the time I got to the next bar Jake was still a bar or two ahead of me. Somebody gave me a bum steer, and I doubled back to his house —no Jake, no painting, no drink. Jake had doubled back to the first bar.

Six hours and several bars later I took a chance on his house again. It was late in the afternoon. His wife said, "He's in bed."

It was still broad daylight. "May I see him?"

"No," she said. "He's drunk." That's what she said. I was definitely sympathetic. I was unquestionably plastered.

"Did he have a painting with him?"

"He had something with him."

"It belongs to me," I said. "I would like to have it."

"Just a minute," said Mrs. Frankly, "I'll go look." She disappeared into the house. After a while she came out with the picture in her hand. "Is this it?"

That was it—crumpled, beer-soaked, and tattered. "Thanks," I said, and lit out for Frankly's wharf, where *Princess* lay. Just before sunset Jake came down to his wharf. I could see him coming. His mouth was set grim. He stomped along the worn planks of the dock, halted alongside *Princess*, and looked me hard in the eye.

"I know what you are," said Captain Jake Frankly, "you're a spy." Jake was country. For a city fellow, I'm kind of country too. We got along fine. Old Jake and I got to be friends. We did a lot of fishing together. Whenever I see a blowfish, I think of Jake. He caught the first one I ever saw close up. We fished right there in Beaufort Channel with the tide rising.

A blowfish is a hard fish to deal with. It's got a hide as tough as shoe leather. It's got spiny points that stick out all over. If you hook or cross a blowfish, it pumps itself up till it's three times its size and as round and hard as a soccer ball. It bristles.

I had a lot of sympathy for little fish that were getting swallowed all the time by big fish till I met up with the blowfish. Now I don't know. I pity any fish that swallows the blowfish. I pity the blowfish too. They both die.

When we weren't fishing, I was painting. I fixed up that watercolor painting of the menhaden fishing boats for Captain Jake, and I painted a picture of every other fishing boat in town. The *Ptarmigan* showed up with Jerry and his bride, and I painted pictures of it. I was a painting fool in Morehead City, and they paid me to paint. I never saw such a rush on art.

The fishermen in Morehead City couldn't get enough.

They had me working night and day. When they saw how their boats looked in paint, they wanted to see their wives, their wharves, their kids, and the whole caboodle in two dimensions. I painted everything in sight. I made a small killing. Paris was never like that.

Neither was Charleston, for all its art galleries. It took some doing before *Princess* got to Charleston. Jake didn't want us to leave. "There ain't nothing south of here," he said. He could have been right.

In the Southwest they speak of a "blind side" when they talk about livestock or life. The sea came near climbing on my blind side in the long run through the wilderness between Morehead City and Charleston. The thing that blinded me was the all-over feeling of peace. The long run down Bogue Sound lay behind us. The night was spent in the little town of Swansboro. *Princess* left with light airs, fresh eggs, and a pound of chopped meat soon after the grocer opened his shop on the hill.

The current of tide pouring through the inlets flushed the channel and cut through the coastal morass. Sweeping in and out as we passed, it contrived to help more than hinder in the absence of a sensible wind. The high reeds whispered. There were little drifting clouds, the kind you see in children's books, made out of puffs of cotton. The sun was lifting little by little like a picture to be hung on the wall of blue sky. Just below Bear Inlet *Princess* pushed her nose into the mud.

We were in no particular hurry to get off the bank. *Princess* was all there was in the way of traffic. I hadn't seen another vessel for two days. The inland waterway seemed like a relic of a race that evolved by accident in some primeval time and left the same way. The red triangles and black squares pinned on posts might have been symbols of some old forgotten faith.

The tide lifted a fallen leaf from among the reeds and sent it turning slowly along the dredged bank. The big mainsail of *Princess* hung straight as a curtain in the quiet air. Flies buzzed, landed on the hot deck, and buzzed off. The silky cotton genny clung to the heavy staysail. Brushing past it, I picked up the boat hook and swung out on the bowsprit to try poling *Princess* back into deep water.

Sometimes it works. Standing on the sprit reduces the draft back where the keel is deep. It didn't work this time. I went back aft and took the boathook along. Down below I gave the engine a spin, choked and another. It roared. I reached under the bridge deck from the cockpit and pulled the lever, shifting into reverse. Then I swung the tiller hard over, port and starboard, right and left, to rock her loose. She didn't budge. I felt under the bridge deck with my foot and kicked the shift lever full ahead. That's when it happened.

I wish I could forget what happened. I never will. I have come up out of sleep covered with cold sweat time after time, tortured by thinking of it. It's the thought of that half-inch rope gripped around my middle like a noose of steel, drawing up fast, to cut me in two.

The rope was caught on the propeller shaft. I ducked. The loop of line shifted its grip to my neck and shoulders. I dove for the deck. It drew down on my hands, scraping skin off my forearms, and it snapped the hickory boathook like a parlor match. The engine roared away, winding rope on the shaft till it wrenched itself off its bed. The engine coughed dead. It was all over in a split second. I was alive.

The sun stared deadpan in the sky. The nursery-book clouds, like dopey sheep grazing in blue clover, were where I left them. Small birds still sang in the tall oak on the bank. Nothing much was changed by this isolated incident that came so close to closing the careless pattern of my life.

The propeller shaft was bent, the staff of the boathook was broken and the mainsail hoist, wound fiddletight on the shaft, held the engine up against the overhead. A sail is one thing; a motor is something else. When they're both in the same boat, power and sail can help each other, but they can also hack away at each other with all the jealous fury of civil war, and God help anyone who gets caught in the middle.

I had no one to blame but myself. I sat in that unearthly calm, benumbed, wondering just how far the fates will go to teach a fellow a lesson. I should never have left that coil of line in the cockpit, where it could dangle down the hatch and get caught on the shaft. The halyards should have been made up as neat as if we faced a force-ten blow on Beaufort's scale.

The sympathetic tide took us off the mudbank, and the wind broke down and helped us along the inland waterway. We would have been better off outside. It would have been better to risk the terror of Frying Pan Shoals than to endure the fire of my own forgetfulness.

There isn't much that comes back about the rest of the run to Charleston. The shadow of that episode lay like a pall over *Princess* for days. She had done a lot of things to me in the three years that we had been together, but nothing like that.

The thing that hurt the most was the place she chose to do

it. We were as far from people as we had ever been. If that was the way *Princess* felt about me, what was the sense of searching for an island where we could be alone? I had seen another facet of her nature—dark, unpredictable, cyclonic. What was even worse was the realization that I loved her all the more.

She was in bad shape down below. I dropped her hook in mid-channel and cleared her propeller shaft. The engine settled back on its bed. I hammered the shaft till it was straight enough to turn. There was more vibration when the engine ran, and more leak than ever.

I didn't dare run outside. We tied up at the wharves of Wrightsville for lunch and ran the ranges of Cape Fear River under sail in a moonless night to see if it could be done. We ran aground halfway down. I kedged her into deep water and waited for morning.

Cape Fear River runs. It doesn't meander or mosey. The dredged channel leading from the canal entrance to Southport heads every which way. In daylight hours a vessel can find its way from buoy to buoy; at night it must follow one range until the next one comes into alignment and so on down to Southport. Without the key of a chart it is a bewildering puzzle of lights. There are lighted buoys in the river and lights on the bank that back them up as ranges.

Equipped with a compass, a flashlight, a chart, and the faith of a martyr, you can make it. I did it with a tug and a barge years later. It's kind of fun. Never do it without a witness. No one will believe you did.

There was a sizable inland freighter tied up at Southport, broken down and waiting for an engine part. I talked to the pilot about the waterway. I asked him if he knew by heart every jutting reef between the ports of Jacksonville and Norfolk.

He said, "I've been on every one." That's the way I learned about a lot of them. The rest I have come to respect by searching out and minding every speck or dot the boys of the U. S. Coast and Geodetic Survey have seen fit to record on the paper channel of the chart.

It rained into the dredged channel all the way to the head

of the Waccamaw River. *Princess*, reaching with the peak of her mainsail for a cut of the northeast wind, startled a little pig that snorted up the bank and disappeared in a high field of collards. Winyah Bay bounced with the cold light of November as we turned into Georgetown. A great iron, square-rigged vessel with all the appointments of a yacht lay in mothballs at the dock. Tied up beneath her bowsprit, *Princess* nestled out of the wind while I walked among the stately white houses and sensed the certainty of war.

In the morning we raced along the waterway to cover the sixty miles to Charleston. It was nip and tuck. It looked as if the bottom might drop out of the boating business any minute.

23

Princess came in the back door to Charleston like the help, picked up a gale of wind in the Charles River, curtsied to Fort Sumter, and made a grand entrance in the Municipal Yacht Basin under full sail. You'd have thought she was sixteen days out of Cape Town or fresh from the Azores, the way she came in.

It was nice to talk to somebody besides *Princess* or myself after that long, lonely stretch through the canals of the back country. I walked into town. Charleston was beautiful—beautiful beyond comparison. The people who lived in Charleston didn't seem to have the slightest suspicion regarding its almost sinful perfection. The Charlestonian made me think of a man who marries a great beauty in order to forget her.

There is no place in America where the story of how men

once lived is so well told. The proud façades of the old buildings speak. The lavish grace of column and portico leaves much to be wondered at and nothing unsaid. It's all there in the visage of its architecture. Nothing is lacking in the way of evidence except that which might explain the wherewithal.

The money for all that high living came in part from rice, Carolina rice, grown in the low plantation country through which *Princess* sailed on the way to the city. They might still be living high in Charleston if it weren't for all the rice in China.

Whatever the reasons, the ships that carried the rice are gone. There are no square-rigged barks moored side by side until the wooden catwalks that cut across them stretch for a mile out into the bay. The bounce of empty barrows over the returning road of wood is silent. So is the creak of heavy-laden wheels and the chafing groans of the impatient clippers. The ships are gone like husks of rice, and the forest of spars is all gone. *Princess* was a lifetime too late.

All we had was the hollow chaff of Charleston and each other. I sat on her deck and painted pictures of the city, a proud city, a city possessed by the vanity of recollection. I roamed through town, dipping into my paintbox for the sake of art and into a bottle of muscatel for the sake of my circulation. It got around. The Carolina Art Association offered to hold a one-man show of my paintings.

The exhibition opened on December 17 at the Gibbes Memorial Gallery. It was a great success. Nobody showed up—nobody except a critic from the *News and Courier*, which was published in a little building across the street. All I know about my one-man show is what I read in the paper. It said, "Mr. Richards paints those important things that are visible to the spirit rather than the eye."

I still don't know whether that meant modern art, the muscatel, or ghosts. The important thing was that the turnout was visible to neither the spirit nor the eye. People stayed away in droves. I got awfully homesick for old Jake Frankly and that art-loving gang of hard-drinking fishermen up at Morehead City. Jake was right when he said, "There ain't nothing south of Morehead City." There was nothing to talk about, nothing but an island pinned like a brooch to the bosom of the Caribbean—nothing but a dream, peppered with stars, way out of reach and too far to find.

I wasn't the only one searching for that dream. The three guys on *Pauline* were looking for it too. *Pauline* was a white forty-foot ketch that lay alongside *Princess* in the Municpal Yacht Basin. *Pauline* was no debutante. Her age was written in the rust that bled at every fastening of her hull. She was lucky to be safe in port. Some fishermen found her bouncing around on Frying Pan Shoals, fetched her off, and dragged her in to Charleston. She came near to breaking her back out there.

Pauline was all that was left to show for a lifetime of effort. Her owner was a prodigal young man who had inherited a piece of property known as a taxpayer from a frugal uncle out in Akron. This young man from Akron, whose interest centered on the sea, converted the taxpayer into cash and squandered half of the proceeds along a primrose path that led from Akron to Norfolk. The rest went for *Pauline*. With two fellows who were nice enough to help him get rid of his cash for crew, he set sail out of Norfolk, bound for an island—any island.

They actually rounded Hatteras in that trap. There must have been a moderate sea running. Cape Hatteras has work to do. It steers the great stream of the Gulf, turning its warmth toward the north of Europe. Cape Hatteras has time for little favors too. Let a skilled navigator or a staunch vessel breast the tempest that's bottled up along the rips and reaches of her shoals, and Hatteras will let him have it. Let a seedy ketch come by, manned by three birds who have never seen salt water in their lives, and Hatteras will put on her party manners. That's what she did for these guys from Akron. Hatteras stretched before them demure and gentle. I have known men to round Hatteras in a tiny, top-heavy harbor tug—men who must never have heard of Hatteras or didn't believe, men who were like to die in after years thinking of the chance they took.

Frying Pan Shoals is not so fussy. It will hand anybody hell at almost any time. It called the tune. *Pauline* danced, and the boys didn't know the steps. They got sick and went below. The fishermen were kind of surprised when they found out, halfway into Charleston, that she was not abandoned and they couldn't claim her as a prize. She became a fixture in the Municipal Yacht Basin.

Pauline was no prize, anyway. Her mainmast, which had snapped during her ordeal on the shoals, had been sawed off neatly at the height of the mizzen till she looked like a bald-headed schooner. Her inventory of sail was as bare as the shelves of a department store after the January white sale. Her big mainsail blew out and carried away. All that was left was a jib that was now much too long along the luff, a scrap of staysail, and a shredded mizzen; otherwise, *Pauline* was fairly well found.

Pauline had an engine, and tools to fix it, but no gas to run it. She had a galley complete with pots and pans, dishes and silver, and a refrigerator with nothing in it. She had charts and instruments for piloting, a pressure lantern, and extra blankets. She had a magnificent collection of spare bronze blocks. She was loaded. She even had a canvas-covered cedar dinghy that was named *Pauline II*. She had everything but money. *Pauline* was in peril of being sold to satisfy the supermarket.

The owner took off. The boys said that he got a job on a houseboat heading south. He left them with power of attorney to sell *Pauline* and pay off the pyramid of debt. They tried to sell her, but *Pauline* had no takers. One look at that rust-stained hull, and no one would pay the couple hundred dollars it would take to send the boys back to Akron without the sheriff on their tail.

Black paint is cheap. So is a little ad in the *News and Courier*. I contributed both in exchange for the pawn ticket to retrieve the barometer and my pick of the boat's gear that would not be too sorely missed. The important thing was to dress up *Pauline*. As soon as the hull was painted black and the rust stains were no longer visible to the eye, I entered into the spirit of our agreement.

First I swapped that monstrosity that I had dragged all the way down from Cambridge, Maryland, for the neat little namesake of *Pauline*. I appropriated the pressure lantern and a wonderful set of bronze blocks. I had the least misgivings about a gallon of white semigloss that *Pauline* would never need by virtue of her new *décor*.

Emboldened by the power of attorney in their pocket and the smell of Akron in their nostrils, the boys gratefully loaded *Princess* till there was no room for me. I took a good part of *Pauline* back to her before the customers showed up. *Pauline* went for four hundred dollars, which satisfied the lien and bought Pullman tickets back home to Akron. There was enough left over for a big time in Charleston for all hands before the train pulled out.

Now I had the Caribbean island all to myself and enough gear off the decrepit ketch to furnish it. The trick was to get there before the war got to me. It was time to shove off. I left in a light and variable easterly, taking along some bird from the medical college who had a couple of days of free time before his mid-term finals. We slatted around in the idle air, taking a whole day to get to Edisto Island. *Princess* was pretty proud to have a doctor aboard, even if he had six months to go before he was ready to intern. *Princess* was fairly fit, all but the dribble in her sternpost. Except for being gun-shy, I was sound of wind and limb. There was nothing for the doctor to work on but the weather. Except for the funny stories he told, he did very little to help. The wind was failing fast. Finally it passed out cold, or hot as the case may be. It was so calm that even our respiration seemed artificial.

Tied to the tip of Yonges Island in the Wadmalaw River, we were having lunch in the sweltering stillness of the swamp. There was a spur of track drawn from the Atlantic coast line out onto the island, and a freight train was loading up. The doctor ate with one eye on the train. In the middle of pie and coffee the doctor shrugged, grabbed his little bag, and hopped the freight, leaving me with the corpse.

No sooner had the accelerating clack and clatter of the train wheels died away than the patient revived. It blew like crazy. It blew a gale straight out of the north. It blew the birds right out of the swamp and a bone into the teeth of *Princess*.

Through the tempting slues that led to the sea, I glimpsed

in passing the mountainous waves kicked up by the muscle in the sky. *Princess* roared along with a rash of little ones. She got in on the ground floor with the tide, and up she went with it, up the rivers, through the connecting cuts, and down. Her wash threw a wake that pounded the banks like a powerboat, and grounding made no difference.

When we hit the mud, we hit standing up and reaching. We got off close-hauled and heeling. When she ran aground I had coffee. Sometimes I ran aground to have coffee. It was easier than fooling around with the anchor.

The rain came down at the top of the tide and the Coosaw River. We hopped down to Beaufort with it. I got a wet impression of a stately southern town and shoved off again. It cleared a bit, and the wind gave every indication that it was willing to work.

The wind was also working for a couple in a fancy thirty-five-foot ketch-rigged double-ender and an old fisherman in a ten-foot punt with a scrap of burlap for a sail. I chased the double-ender all day. The fisherman chased me. I ran off into a creek, lost a mile, and made it up. It looked as if *Princess* would win. She caught the double-ender off Port Royal, but the couple took the wind out of our sails by dousing theirs and dropping the hook about the time that we were fixing to overtake them. I dropped my hook too, and the fisherman went on to win or to wherever.

As I lowered the gaff I dropped the folding boom crutch over the side, and the outgoing current took it away. I jumped into the dinghy and went after it. It was the new dinghy off *Pauline*, and it rowed nicely. I rowed nicely too, but when I recovered the boom crutch, I couldn't make any time back up against the tide. It started to rain. It grew dark. I rowed and rowed and rowed up the river, like in the song. I rowed for miles, but I just couldn't make the hundred yards that separated me from *Princess*.

There didn't seem to be anything to do but drift over to Saint Helena Island and lie there in exile till slack water. It was a nasty prospect after the hard day's sail, singlehanded and wet. I thought of hot chow and warm blankets, and I pulled like a horse.

There was plenty of horsepower in the double-ender at anchor near *Princess*, and I was hoping that they would pull up their hook and come for me. I hollered, but they didn't understand. After a while they got the idea and got their engine going. Meanwhile, I rowed up the river, row, row, row. Little by little the hook on the double-ender came up, and at last, in their own sweet time, they came and got me. While little *Pauline* was being hauled back to *Princess* by the kind couple who hated to lose, I slumped over a thwart like a man who has just lost the single-sculling championship of the world.

Hot soup can snap a man back fast—hot soup, a nap, and the sound of taps in slow, clear cadence bugled across the wind and the river from the Marine Corps barracks on Parris Island. The north wind wiped away the rain and gave the stars a snappy shine. This was no wind to waste. I hauled up the hook and took the last hour of the tide to clear Beaufort River. I crossed Port Royal Sound at slack water and ducked in between Pinckney Island and Hilton Head. I found still water at the southernmost tip of a little island that was about the size of the one I was seeking somewhere over the hill.

24

Anchored in the lee of the unnamed island, *Princess* stretched her cable and waited within earshot of the surf that slammed against Hilton Head. Her shrouds hummed like the strings of a strummed guitar as the wind went by. A lot of wind got away while I slept.

Fair wind is fuel. To sleep while a fair wind blows is the same thing as running the engine of a boat with the lines fast to the dock or the anchor locked in the mud. It woke me, and I got up in the gray equivalent of dawn. The reeds on Pinckney Island were bent over before the lash of the wind like stick people stuck in the mud. The big mainsail went up before breakfast and it helped with the hook. We fell off into the raging northerly wind and stormed down Calibogue Sound.

Between Calibogue Sound, Cooper River, and Bull Creek there are so many opportunities for the tide, it's a wonder it can figure out which way to run. The tide, for some unaccountable reason, becomes a thing of enormous consequence around the Savannah River. There is as much as ten feet between low and high water. The low adjacent lands provide a vast tidal reservoir that is filled and emptied by the Savannah River in the course of a single day. The ten feet of high water that is alternately invited in and tossed out gives the river a bad name.

When we came into the Savannah River, it was letting the ocean have it. The river was all for letting the ocean have us, too, and there was damn little that the wind could do to prevent it.

There are many islands in the Savannah River. The last one is a strange, dragged-out affair that divides the mouth of the river like a ten-mile tongue. It is called Elba Island at first and as the miles go by it becomes forgetful and calls itself Bird Island and after that Long Island and finally Cockspur Island. Separated and made independent by the rising tide, the sovereignty of these islands is abridged at low water.

There have been changes made. There is a channel now that cuts across the island. When *Princess* came by, there was nothing but a lighthouse and a dock with a longboat in davits about a mile above Fields Cut. It was a long mile. Heeled over by half a gale and driving up against the torrent, we logged at least six knots and stood still. I got the engine going. Hauled by the feuding team of canvas and combustion, which pulled under protest in tandem, we finally got within heaving distance of the dock. An old man threw me a line and snubbed it quick. The place was known as the Waving Girl Station.

There wasn't any girl at the station. There was an old lady, and she was just as sweet as they come. She was the sister of the old man who maintained the station. I had to stay for lunch. She took one look at me and said, "Come with me, young man." I followed her like a good boy.

The lighthouse keeper's sister marched me into their kitchen. She filled a tablespoon with some stuff that looked like white gunpowder and tasted like yeast and made me swallow it. It was wonderful. I felt like a new man.

"The government gives us a supply of this powder in case we can't get the right kind of diet." The old lady looked at me searchingly. "What kind of diet have you been getting?"

We had roast beef for lunch and yams and collards and all I could eat, and believe me, I could eat. "You've got an awful nice government," I said.

"It's your government too," she said: I stared at her and felt for my draft card.

The United States Government has maintained the Waving Girl Station since the days of the clipper ships. It got its name from the wife of the first lighthouse keeper. She was a Georgia girl, and much too pretty to be isolated on Elba Island. Even Napoleon managed to get back into the swim. The waving girl didn't have to. A world of ships came to know her as they rode the tide into Savannah. She became known all over the globe, and she was loved. She spoke to the ships, and they edged closer to hear her voice. To men home after a long voyage, the magic of what they heard was not so much in the news it conveyed but in the voice itself—a woman's voice.

The original waving girl grew old. Her husband retired and took her to live in Savannah. The men who manned the new steam vessels called for her as they went by. They cut their engines to hear her voice, but there was no reply. The old-timers searched the knoll with a long glass from the quarter-decks of the windjammers for the sight of her familiar figure. They came near colliding out there. The wife of the new lighthouse keeper was finally forced to perform the role of the waving girl. She got to like it.

While we were having lunch the eight-cornered house shook with the blast of a ship's whistle. My hostess ran to the window and hung halfway out, calling and waving. She was the third in line of succession. Her age was about to wave her out too.

She talked about a little home that they were building in the back country in a place called Snake River. She looked out through the southeast window at the tall swamp grass that tumbled to the wind. She spoke of retiring to their new home, and she wondered aloud about what the people in Washington were going to do for a new waving girl.

The lighthouse keeper walked out three times during lunch to look after the lines holding my boat. There was a noticeable flirtation going on between *Princess* and the old man. He couldn't take his eyes off her. When the tide turned, we had a time dragging each other away—me from the waving girl and the lighthouse keeper from my baby.

I did a little watercolor of the place while I was waiting for slack water. I gave it to the waving girl. "Now I know where I've seen you," she said.

She climbed upstairs and came down with a clipping from the Charleston *News and Courier*. It was all about my recent one-man show of paintings, and it had a photo of me. I was amazed. "How did you happen to save that?" I asked. Her brother laughed at my question. The waving girl looked flustered.

"My sister saves every word she reads about art. She clips them out and puts them away. She has boxfuls of clippings on art, trunkfuls of clippings on art, and bureau drawers overflowing with the stuff. It beats me," he said. His sister looked at me kind of helpless.

"Well," the old man said after a while, scratching his head with his hat. "I guess it's better than collecting pancakes, especially in this climate."

The last time I saw them, they were standing on the knoll alongside the station. She waved to me. Her brother was no waving man, but he lifted his hand as *Princess* drew away. Then the sun came out. The river glistened as the north wind curried little waves like loose scales of a fish and sent them flying. It took one port tack to cross the river. A starboard tack took us to the bend of the Right Channel. Over the top of Elba Island we caught the brunt of the breeze.

We passed down the undecided tide of Wilmington River through miles of ruffled marshland and stopped at the docks of Thunderbolt. It began to rain. It was enough for one day, a day that I kept going on three hours of sleep and a teaspoonful of powder. Down below I found a jar of the vitamin stuff that my friends had stowed as a parting gift in the galley of *Princess*. I guess they thought I'd wind up with beriberi from the way I was living.

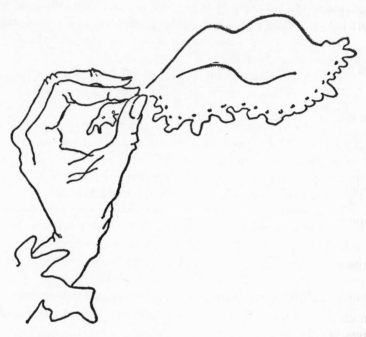

I liked the way I was living, even if the waving girl didn't quite approve. She thought that an artist should have the better things of life, like a hot meal now and then. Most artists I know would go along with her on that, but what are you going to do with a guy who lives for the throb of the wind on the luff of the jib or the surge of the keel as it cuts on a bias to the selvage of the sea? The tide ebbed with the end of the day. I put out long spring lines on the fishermen's wharf so *Princess* wouldn't get hung up, and I went to sleep.

It was dark when I got up, darker than I had ever known it to be along the mirrored edges of the water. There is always some light that gets bounced around where the sea is faced with land. This was black. I lay there in the starboard bunk looking out of the hatch at the total blindness of the sky, and all at once I was seized with fear. I was sure that my baby was caught under the dock.

I sprang out of the bunk, positive that the top of the mast had lifted a plank or poked a hole up through the wharf. I was sure that my boat would be pinned by the dock beneath the next engulfing tide. It was half dream and half the darkness that did it. A truck, turning on the highway to Savannah, put its headlights on the *Princess*. I saw enough in that moment to know that we were in the clear. It was silly, anyway.

We never were in danger. The top of the dock is only fifteen feet above mean low water. The mast of the *Princess* is nearly double that. Nevertheless, there was no way that I could explain the total absence of light except by a frantic recollection of being trapped in a closet as a kid or caught under the high wharves of Thunderbolt. I must have been dreaming of the towering tides of Bristol or the first wave of the incoming tide, called a bore, which can outrun a horse when the tide sets in along the flats of the Bay of Fundy. Maybe it was just the name of the place—Thunderbolt!

All the draggers left in the morning. There were seven of them. The fishermen shifted the lines of *Princess* without waking me. The wind, more boisterous than ever, was still fair out of the north and threw its weight a little to the east when I cast off the lines. We rounded the islands and took off. Jibing around the hairpin turns, I saw the red bottoms of boats turned down like empty glasses in the cold rain.

The tide seemed synchronized to our motion. We moved fast through the Georgia marsh country, which is feathered with soft grass and probed by the brackish fingers of the sea. We ducked along behind the islands like a bird on an endless belt in a shooting gallery, and the ocean took pot shots at us as we crossed the intervening sounds.

The day was fading when we came down Old Teakettle Creek and poured across Doboy Sound. I had spent twelve long hours with the tiller in my hand, hauled hard over on a reach. I had eaten what I could, when I could, out of a can. I had used up four charts, and we were a hundred crooked miles closer to a dream that presumably lay before us. That's when it happened. That's when we got all fouled up just above Rockdedundy Island, right in Rockdedundy River. I have no idea how it happened. I don't even know what Rockdedundy means. I was groggy to begin with, and groping when I ran aground. Between Thunderbolt and Rockdedundy the names were getting me down.

The light flashed red twice in a group every four seconds, and its number was 182. I spent the better part of two hours trying to get around it. I can get just as stubborn as any channel marker stuck like a mule in the mud. On the way south in this part of the Intracoastal Waterway, every red light, nun buoy, or triangular marker is supposed to be kept on the right. This was a triangular marker, it was painted red, and, just to make sure, it had a red light. I took it on the right-hand side, on our starboard, if you please. I ran aground. I broke out the mud hook, kedged *Princess* off, took a good look at 182, and ran aground again. I went through this routine several times, with identical results. Then I took the sounding lead and the dinghy and went looking for the channel. It wasn't.,

At least, the channel was not where it was supposed to be. I went off in the dinghy looking for it in the dark while *Princess* waited in the mud. The wind seemed to have shifted one hundred eighty degrees. That's what provided the first clue to the solution of the great mystery of Rockdedundy River. With this slender lead to go on, and with rain pouring down my neck and hunger and fatigue numbing me, I solved the mystery of the missing channel. The light was on the left of it.

Princess had gone clear around a little island while I wasn't looking. My baby was heading back toward New York. For a moment that seemed like one hell of a good idea.

25

Princess acted as if she knew what was best for both of us. The sea didn't have the foggiest notion. The wind was raving like mad. She kept ducking around, trying to get me to go back. The wind put her up to it. It was no fun unless I could get my girl to let tomorrow take care of tomorrow. She wasn't too hard to handle. She responded as quickly to the touch of my hand on her tiller as she did to the force of the gale.

The wind came out of the north. It was still blowing after five days like a storm on the coast of Maine, and it carried the perfume of pine, Georgia pine, which was strong enough to turn her head or mine. My baby listened mostly to me. I kept her heading south; I still had an island in mind.

Unburdened by an excess of cargo or conscience, my boat

was broad enough to be steady in a blow and tender too. We ran down Little Mud River in the dark. The rain pelting the deck sounded like the amplified patter of reef points on canvas. Almost every garment I owned was wet. The only pants that weren't belonged to a tuxedo, and I wore them tucked into the tops of the last dry pair of wool socks.

I had constructed an armless shirt with the last dry Turkish towel. I hadn't shaved in a week or combed my hair. I wore the tuxedo vest over the towel, a sou'wester with a hole in it on my head, and a square yard of canvas over my shoulders. That's the way I looked when I ran into that covey of top people behind St. Simons Island.

Princess churned up and down the rivers in time with the tide. It was uncanny the way we caught the flow at the bottom of every twisting river and the ebb at the very top. There was no tide table on board *Princess*. It was luck, and it added two knots or more to her speed. We moved.

We climbed Fredricka River hand in hand with the obliging current and were doing dandy when I dropped the last box of matches into the bilge. I didn't mind being wet; being hungry didn't matter too much; fatigue was my constant bedfellow— everything was tolerable till the matches went in for a dip.

After that there was no smoking. The fire in the stove was out. I had no way to make coffee or to heat a can of soup. I was beside myself. The rain ran across my eyes like water flowing over a couple of fancy pebbles. Through streaks of it I caught the gleam of white pilings. It was a dock. *Princess* huddled against it, and I made her fast. I saw a light in a house up along a path that led off the glossy white wharf into the bush. It looked like a hunting lodge constructed of logs. I caught a glimpse of a tremendous fireplace and a fire to fill it. I knocked.

A man rose from a long sofa that faced the fire, leaned a shotgun he was cleaning against the fieldstone of the hearth, and came to the door. "I'm the Fuller Brush man," I said. The torrent of rain ran in a steady stream off the stubble of my chin.

The man peered at me for a moment and then he said,

"Come in." There were several men in hunting clothes in the room. "You'll find a razor and a fresh blade in the bathroom."

After I shaved away the brush he introduced me around. I met a Supreme Court judge. I met the head of the fish and wildlife branch of the Department of the Interior. I met an internationally famous financier. I met the Surgeon General, and I met a very important man in a short white coat who sure knew how to roast a pheasant.

I stood around dripping little pools of water till somebody suggested that I take off my disguise, wring it out, and hang it up to dry in front of the blazing fire. While I was at it I went out to *Princess* and got a bundle. My socks were hung on the mantle and the spare furniture was decorated with wet dungarees. I borrowed a shirt and a pair of pants from the Supreme Court judge till mine got dry.

The men had been hunting pheasant and wild turkey all day. The way they hunted was nice work if you can get it. It was like shooting fish in a barrel. Sea Island is a game preserve. For all practical purposes the pheasants and turkeys present themselves to be shot. Roasted, they tasted as good as the birds the Pilgrim Fathers hunted while the Indians were hunting the Pilgrim Fathers.

We all sat at a long scrubbed-oak board and we ate fabulously expensive food served in bunkhouse style. The conversation drifted around to war. That was what I was waiting for. I figured to find out from the top what I could expect at the bottom. I had heard all the gobbledygook. Now I was going to hear the top boys talk turkey.

They didn't mince words. The war was on and we were in it. There was no question about it. Declaration was a matter of a provocative occasion. It was a formality. These boys were discussing the technological advancements that were going to accrue to mankind as a result of the war. The more I listened, the more I ate. I ate like a doomed man. The man in the white coat slipped me a spare pheasant. He felt sorry for me. Potentially I was a foot soldier, even if I did have my feet in the Surgeon General's socks.

"Look," I said, "I don't want to be a wet blanket all dressed in your dry clothes, but I'm draft material. I'd just as soon forego the technological improvements and try to get along without the war."

Everybody was quiet. The coffee was served. The rain beat down on the roof and doused the deep woods. I looked up out of my coffee cup for a sign of resistance. There was none. My victory was complete—too complete. "Maybe it isn't that simple," I said, backing a bit.

They grabbed the scrap of amnesty I offered and goofed off talking about a wounded turkey that got away during the afternoon and about the Gullah people on these isolated islands of the Georgia coast who still talk the African mother tongue. I gathered up my clothes and said, "Good night and thank you."

The man who picked up my tab said, "See that you do as much for someone else sometime." Then he looked as if he were sorry he'd said it, and so did I.

Princess came down the Mackay River first thing in the morning. She crossed the sound as the wind backed to the west a bit and blew up. The sun came out in midmorning just as we came out from behind Jekyll Island. Sunlight splashed in the transparent shallows of St. Andrew Sound. The wind must have been blowing forty miles an hour in bursts. We came about at the bend in the Cumberland River and ran aground. *Princess* was heeled over closehauled at the time. When I spilled the gale of wind out of her sails and she righted herself, her stern went way up, like a cow getting up after a nap.

Up forward the bowsprit pointed sternly down at the reef. Going aft was like climbing a mountain, but the boathook helped. *Princess* drew almost five feet of water, and there was only a foot of the stuff under her. We had gone on the bar at the urgent behest of a gale. It would take a gale or better to get us off. I tightened the mainsheet and raised the genny, drew the genny close, and waited. A couple of minor puffs got us nowhere. The wind seemed to be slowing, and the tide was running out fast.

But we got off—all it took was one burst. I haven't the

faintest idea where that burst came from. After six days of blowing, it was hard to believe that there could be any more wind left up north. It rolled us off the reef and out of Georgia. Wrapped in its exultant breath, we were carried down to the last island of the coastal chain that links Charleston and Fernandina.

When we tied up at noon, the assorted islands lay behind us like precious stones set in the prongs of the hurried rivers. Fernandina was as nice as its name. Favored by the deep channel of St. Marys Entrance and a long line of deep-sea fishing families, it prospered. At the post office I picked up a couple of letters that had followed me from port to port till there was hardly room enough on them for another forwarding address. One, postmarked Virginia, was from Dr. Archie.

Archie wasn't happy. He was a chemical engineer, and the government insisted that he work at it. Archie was spoiling for salt water. Most of all, he didn't relish being locked up in a hush-hush project. About hush-hush he said, "To hell with that noise." The whole business smacked of the beneficial side dishes of war that I had heard so much about up at Sea Island. It wasn't Dr. Archie's cup of tea.

My cup of tea was the warm saucer of the Caribbean. Nothing stood between *Princess* and the Caribbean but the bridges. The War Department was in charge of the bridges, and I was very touchy about the War Department. Our paths crossed at embarrassing intervals all down the length of Florida.

There is a break in the Bahama Banks called Northwest Providence Channel; it leads into the Caribbean. Cross the Straits of Florida, which are policed by the Gulf Stream, and there you are. The place to take off is Fort Lauderdale.

The run down the coast in the sun was dream stuff. It would have been paradise enough if it wasn't for the bridges. We had been spoiled by the reticent islands of the Georgia coast and the unobstructed overhead of its rivers. Down we came with straining canvas in open collusion with the wind tide and the moon tide. We came about before every bridge and waited in irons and agony while a passage opened. The bridges opened when they were good and ready, and another length of water lay before us.

We almost met our Waterloo just above a little place called Wilbur-By-The-Sea. It was also my birthday. It was a hell of a note. Heedless of the moon and possessed by the wind, the tide ran fast out of Ponce de Leon Inlet. I saw the bridge start to open. I saw unbroken water beyond it. We were coming down wing and wing, blustering and puffed up, when the engine that turned the bridge conked out.

Princess had time enough to turn. She beat up into the wind and I dropped her hook. The anchor dragged. I lowered sail and paid out anchor cable. It still dragged. Nothing would hold in that sand bottom. We dragged right down onto the bridgehead just above Wilbur-By-The-Sea.

Kicked down the long body of Halifax River by the ten-day gale, the water lifted and pounded *Princess* against the viaduct unmercifully. We couldn't get out of there. There were pilings, broken and sharp, just beneath the surface under her counter. The frames of a derelict lay like jagged fangs before her. The mainsail, lowered in a hurry, got caught between the topside and bridgehead and was badly chewed.

I did what I could. While the vessel heaved and crashed against the viaduct, I ran off and found an automobile tire on the beach for a fender. There was a four-by-four timber along the footwalk of the bridge. I stood on the road and eased the shock by holding her off with the end of it. There was no way to draw her back out of the clutch of that pocket—the wind and the current were too strong. I was sure that *Princess* would break up. She didn't. I had rebuilt better than I knew. It was the two oak strakes along her sheer that saved her, but I could have cried to see the punishment.

The bridgetender was very sorry. I asked him what happened. "I don't rightly know," he said. "It's my first day on this job."

"You had to pick my birthday," I said. He went off to call the Coast Guard.

We got out of there. After a while the Coast Guard came and pulled us out. They pulled my baby sideways with a line bridled out to her bow and stern. Since they already had a line on the bow, they let the stern line go and kept on hauling all the way down to New Smyrna. Then they turned us loose.

The north wind died in Mosquito Lagoon at the age of ten days. Out of respect, it was quiet from Cape Canaveral to Fort Lauderdale. We ghosted down Indian River, tacking into a diffident southerly that grazed the Everglades. I remember Eau Gallie and a tiny harbor that nested in Spanish moss. I remember Fort Pierce: old people playing shuffleboard in the sun and a pretty girl flying around *Princess* in a moth sailboat while I lay below consumed by the flame of influenza.

I remember a physician in Fort Pierce, owner of an able Bluenose schooner, who had chummed away his practice and taken up shark fishing for the sake of getting its liver. There were other things, too, like the heavy industry of Nature and the feel of the tiller in the fragrant dark. I remember New River, Fort Lauderdale, and *Princess* swinging like a balance wheel in the ponderous escapement of the tide.

26

I remember an apple tree that grew in our back yard when I was a kid. I used to lie awake at night and listen to the wind in that apple tree. It sounded like the ocean. They cut the tree down, and I went to sea. It was a coincidence.

It blew like hell one night in the Pacific. Breaking combers clipped the ports of the pilothouse like the white knuckles of a fist. The tug shipped a green sea. The freeing ports couldn't handle it. I grabbed the wheel and spun it up into the wind. We started over, over, over. I rang full ahead and held the wheel hard up. I closed my eyes and waited. I could hear the hiss of a curling comber. It sounded like the wind in the apple tree.

It was 1944. I had come to the halfway mark in the war, midway in my quest for a tropical island. The Pacific, overrun and bristling with determined tourists, was poor pickings. Fortunately, I had a choice.

My job was to pick up little harbor tugs in New Orleans and deliver them to islands in the Pacific. Sometimes, when I had to take one around to New York, we would pass a mile offshore, where *Princess* languished in wet storage. Those war-built tugs would break down at least once every forty-eight hours, but never near Fort Lauderdale, where I might have had a reason to run in. It was almost as if they knew. A tug can be bitchy too.

Suddenly one evening I found the island in the Caribbean. I was taking a lively little cargo vessel from New Orleans to Panama when I found it. The island is called Southwest Key, and it lies forty miles off the Honduran coast.

It was crescent-shaped, and a full moon came with it. It had a lagoon that abounded in crawfish. There was a profitable stand of coconut trees, and a spring on the property. It had a little wooden shack. It was perfect, absolutely perfect—except for the rats.

The rats had emigrated from the mainland. They swam ashore and nested in the coconut palms after a fisherman scuttled his vessel in the lagoon to get rid of them. Their numbers were held in check by periodic hurricanes that combed most of them into the sea.

The island belong to an Englishman by the name of Hunter who lived in Belize. He wanted seven hundred bucks for it. The price was firm, but when I got back and took it up with *Princess*, it wasn't the same. She hadn't been with me when I found it. You know how women are.

It might have been different if we could have talked it over alone, but there were two guys off the tugboat with me when I found her waiting in Fort Lauderdale. The tug was up in the inlet at Palm Beach. It took a hurricane to make this brief reunion possible—a hurricane, engine trouble, and the sour-ball schooner, God bless her.

The captain of the sour-ball schooner didn't owe me a thing. If it hadn't been for the drag of his ship on the hawser we were pulling, our top-heavy tug with its stingy forefoot might have pitchpoled us into oblivion.

The sour-ball schooner plied between Cuba and our mainland. Despite all the talk of war shortages, an embargo had been placed on foreign sugar. It was O.K. if you came in with candy. The Cuban schooner was loaded to the hilt with sour balls, but what happened to that candy on arrival would break the heart of any kid: It was broken up and melted back into simple syrup.

We were both in the axis of the Gulf Stream heading north along the Straits of Florida when the hurricane struck. She was just a speck on the horizon when I first saw her. I took her for the Settlement Point Lighthouse on Grand Bahama Island till she leaned with the force of the wind. Battered by the gale, the sea jabbed and clinched in explosions of spray. The eye of the storm gouged huge pits and hollows in the sea. It was no place for either of us. The bottom had dropped out of the barometer.

The sour-ball schooner doused her canvas as we overtook her. She took the end of a six-inch cable bent to her heaving line. The mate made it fast to the king posts that embraced her bowsprit, and the old man with the full-rigged beard eased her helm. We headed for the inlet at Palm Beach.

By the time we made the sea buoy with the two-hundred-foot schooner in tow, the wind was beyond gale force. As the surf drew back, the rocks of the jetty were bared like teeth to gums of mud. The rocks were lost in a topple of foam as the sea lunged across the breakwater. It was one for the books. We made it straining full ahead to keep from broaching. Bridled in the lee of the steel and concrete warehouse, we braced ourselves for the brunt of the blow.

The captain of the sour-ball schooner walked across the dock, his white beard stuck straight out in the gale. I shook his hand. He thanked me and I thanked him. He insisted that his was the burdened vessel. I insisted that we owed the tug and our lives to the existence of his schooner. He didn't speak enough English, and I didn't understand enough Spanish to carry on a sensible argument, but we stood there in the howling gale, each roaring our indebtedness to the good offices of the other. He gave me a paper bagful of sour balls.

When the hurricane struck, I sat in the pilothouse of the tugboat and ate sour balls. I ate quite a lot of them, and it was a good thing I did or I never would have found the bottle of rum at the bottom of the bag. They tell me that it blew over a hundred miles an hour that night. In the morning I gave the leftover sour balls to the kids in the trailer camp.

We had saved a lot of simple syrup from the sea. It gave me an idea—one with saccharine overtones. It was a crazy notion to haul my sugar back to New York. The Army had registered no objection to my hauling the sour-ball schooner in a pinch. I resolved to declare a personal state of pinch and haul my boat back home.

The storm tapered and the sharp sea was ground to a dull swell by the long, abrasive beach. That's when I went down to Fort Lauderdale by bus to get my boat. I took along a couple of deck hands off the tug to help me bring her up through the inland waterway to Palm Beach. I could hardly wait for the Army tug to get a line on her. She was a hell of a sight better-looking than that tub which hung from davits behind the fiddley, and she was a better sea boat, too. If we ever tangled with a submarine or caught a shell, *Princess* could pick up all hands and round the longest barrier reef like a lady.

Princess was always a willing boat. Here was her chance to make a direct contribution to the war effort. She was no less willing when I faced her that summer, the first time in four years since I had set eyes on her. We had no time for sentiment—this was war.

In a war of this kind, a war small enough to fit within a war, the thing to do was to try and get around the Coast Guard, which patrolled every inch of shoreline. A pleasure craft like *Princess* would be suspect the minute she showed her nose outside. No matter how well supplied I was with documents, gold braid, and the give-a-damn attitude of petty authority, some yeoman bucking for a stripe would be sure to turn me in.

The Gulf Stream waited off Fort Lauderdale like a blue-carpeted escalator to carry *Princess* up to Palm Beach. My girl was forced to pass it up. We had to go up the back stairs of the inland ditch and slat around in the mangrove swamps while enemy submarines, drifting to save fuel, disported themselves in the limpid depths of the Stream and waited for sizable prey.

It wouldn't have been so bad if we could have got her engine going. I should have brought the chief engineer along, or at least an oiler. Gummed up with inactivity, the old rock crusher refused to offer its valves a seat. The wind died, and it was hot. We slatted around all afternoon. Somebody going a mile or so gave us a tow.

As soon as the sun went down behind the impenetrable wall of the mangrove thicket, out came the mosquitoes. It was murder. We should have worn long underwear, long coats, long anything, or dressed like beekeepers. We should have stayed on the tugboat, which was equipped with screen doors. The warhead of a torpedo seemed tame compared to the proboscises that dove at us from every quarter.

There is a superstition to the effect that if you scratch the mast and whistle, you can work up a wind. We whistled, we scratched, and suddenly it blew. We were too busy whistling and scratching to man the tiller. *Princess* jibed over and ran aground in the narrow channel near Pompano.

I put the boy with the big muscles to work rocking the tiller and I took the other fellow out on the bowsprit for the sake of his weight. *Princess* drew five feet aft. The end of her keel grounded first. Out on the bowsprit, we pushed against the tangle of mangrove roots with a boat hook and our feet, and we swung by the forestay to rock her loose. I heard a sharp crack.

I looked back. There was the muscle-bound deck hand with the tiller in limbo. He had broken it off. A piece of the rudderpost about two feet long came up out of the rudder well with it. The rudderpost, after being submerged for five years, was waterlogged and heavy, while the top of it was dry and brittle from the years of sun. It had broken off at the water line, and we were still aground.

I hated losing the main part of the rudder, but what with the mosquitoes and the advancing darkness, I had to let it go. There was no time for a diving operation. I would have liked to have its exact dimensions. After all the authentic rebuilding that I had done on *Princess*, it was a shame to have to guess at the lovely curve of that perfectly designed part, but such are the casualties of even a small war. There was no time to mourn. We needed assistance, we needed DDT, we were desperate for coffee.

The day was gone, and it was dark. Leaving *Princess* lashed to a mangrove, we piled into the dinghy and headed for the light that twinkled like a glowworm caught in the underbrush. Garnered from a half-forgotten schooner, the dinghy still bore the inscription that related to her original owner. Little *Pauline* gushed so effusively when the three of us stepped aboard that it was only by dint of feverish bailing with a bucket that we managed to cross the channel to the highway side before she sank. We waded ashore, dragging the dink, and trudged toward the light. We approached in a spirit of truce—before us lay a Coast Guard station.

They had coffee, screen doors, and a picket boat that was just the thing to pull *Princess* through the swamp and tie her up safely to the lovely white wharf at Delray Beach. I deployed the boys back to the tug, which waited in Palm Beach, and for the first time in four long years I slept aboard *Princess*. She was very sweet.

She had a present for me the next morning. I found it when I went over the side for a dip. It was the main part of her rudder, hanging on by a sliver of wood after that wild, ten-mile tow by the Coast Guard picket boat.

They told me about a good place to haul *Princess* in Lantana, which lay just below Palm Beach, and a fellow with a motorboat offered to tow me there for the cost of the gas. The big war was waiting. There was no percentage in fooling around. *Princess* followed the motorboat to Lantana. I unstepped her mast in the basin of the yard and lost a pet wrench over the side in the process. The corroded silver dollar from the slot in the mast step went to the old Englishman who hauled her. He cherished it for years —that and a little hydraulic jack with which he could waltz the mightiest vessel around the yard. I had a moment with *Princess* alone. Then I caught the bus that took me back to my place aboard the Army tug.

The sour-ball schooner was still disgorging her sweet cargo, and the chief engineer of the tug, who installed three new oil-injector springs in the diesel, was wiping his hands with cotton waste, sorting his tools, and matching them to the penciled outlines on the board above the bench.

We shoved off that night. Before I left I walked across the dock to say good-by to the captain of the sour-ball schooner. I had described *Princess* to him, and he knew about my plan to haul her back to New York. He seemed relieved for my sake that the plan had failed, and in the poorest Spanish imaginable I managed to communicate the reason.

The old man was sympathetic. He loved all sailing vessels as he loved the one he commanded. He offered to bring me from Cuba a piece of *madera* ten feet long that was *mucho duro*, something just right to fashion a new rudderpost. I thanked him for the rum and the candy. He wished me Godspeed in his own tongue, and I left.

The sea was quiet, ominously so, when we passed into it from between the granite-spiked jetties. Grateful for the protective shield of the moonless night, we turned north and east in the favor of the Gulf Stream as the phosphorescent miles to the southwest came quickly between me and *Princess*.

27

I didn't see her again until the war was over. It was spring, and the year was 1947. I picked up an old car and drove from New York to Florida to join her.

She was still hauled up under the shed in Lantana. When I got to the boatyard, I left the car on the pavement and walked across the sand. I was afraid she might resent the car. She had a legitimate gripe. Except for one hurried visit, I had been gone for seven years. I had known other little boats during those years. I didn't expect her to trust me even with a business coupé.

I didn't trust her, either. As a matter of fact, I could see right through her. Her seams were wide open. She had spent the last three years of the war laid up with a couple of fast lapstrake party boats. If it hadn't been for the memories we shared, we might have called it quits right then and there.

In the shade of the shed she lay in the penitent position of all Friendship sloops that are hauled without regard for their shoal draft forward. She was down by the head. She offered me a leg up with her bobstay. I climbed aboard her dusty deck and went below. They say that the body of a man is renewed every seven years. This isn't true of a boat. Whatever life is given to a boat is due to the bounty of man. The years had taken their toll. There was work to do.

Work didn't come easy. For one thing, I couldn't keep up with my tools. Drop a chisel and it was gone. A hammer sank out of sight in the sand. Even the saw, half buried when it fell, was turned under by the wind that curled off the lagoon. For every stroke of work there were six lost looking. I combed the sand with my fingers. It was all right to use my fingers. There was no company.

One by one I found the tools I lost. I also found a spool of nine-thread fishing line. I tied the tools ten feet apart along the fishing line. If I lost a caulking iron or a plane I grabbed anything that showed above the surface of the sand and jerked the line. Out jumped the tools like the guts of torpedoed ships. Some guy saw me, laughed, and went away. He must have told somebody else. I became famous in a small way. People came from miles around to see me work. Sand is a serious problem in Florida. The whole state is built on it.

Coming back after all those years, I looked at *Princess* with love and retraced her lines unabashed, corroborating by eye her every check and flaw. Her mast lay alongside. Leaning there, I drank in the moment like a wine taster, stacking it against the endless rehearsals of anticipation. It was good.

As good as she looked to me, *Princess* was in no shape to go to sea. I ruled as most immediate the replacement of her broken rudderpost. I bought a length of oak from the local lumber mill. Fixing to shape it, I suddenly remembered something about a piece of *madera, mucho duro*, that the white-bearded captain of the sour-ball schooner had promised to bring from Cuba. I never doubted that he would. You just don't go around doubting the word of an old man with a long white beard.

When I got right down to doing the job, the memory of the old man's promise haunted me. Was it possible? Three years had gone by. It would be too much to believe. Even if he had brought the timber, would it still be there? It was worth the try.

I dropped the oak timber purchased for the job and lit out for Palm Beach and the little harbor at the inlet. The jalopy burned up the highway. I don't know what the big hurry was, after the interlude of years, but I made the distance from Lantana to Palm Beach in Daytona time. The jalopy came to a screeching halt alongside the dock. I jumped out and raced over to the first man I saw, who happened to be the only man there, and for a good reason—he was the watchman.

"Did the old man on the schooner bring me a piece of wood?" The watchman stared at me. "You know," I said, "the captain of the schooner. Did he bring me a piece of wood from Cuba?"

"*Santa María!*" said the watchman, gripping my arms with both hands as if I were a long lost son. "For the love of God, you have come at last. This piece of wood I have guard with my own life. It is long years that have pass. You come at last, God be praised!" He led me to the timber. "The captain say, 'Pedro, take care of it, someday he will come. It is a promise.' "

The timber lay alongside of the corrugated iron wall of the warehouse. It was covered with dust—dust and sugar. I tried to lift one end. It wouldn't budge. With all due credit to Pedro, nobody could have stolen that big red dog in a hurry. The timber was ten feet long, six inches wide, and fourteen inches thick. We had a hell of a time dragging it over to the car. We lashed it to the rear bumper, and I headed back to Lantana with the front wheels of the jalopy occasionally in touch with the road.

I was real proud of that piece of wood. I showed it to everybody. Everybody consisted of the manager of the boatyard, his wife and kids, the man who ran the sawmill, the mechanic, the two boat carpenters, and the old Englishman who moved the boats. They all liked the piece of wood. It had a story, and I never tired of telling it. I suspect that they tired of hearing it.

After several tellings the millman said, "Yeah, but it's no good for a rudderpost."

"What do you mean?" I said.

"It ain't got the strength."

"Why not?"

"It's mahogany," he said. "What you need is oak."

"It can't be mahogany," I said. "Feel the weight of it."

"That's a lot of board feet."

My bubble burst. According to this expert, my piece of tropical wood was too brittle for structural purposes. I agreed to swap it for a piece of oak of similar dimensions. I should have had my head examined.

The process of learning to distinguish good wood or good guys from bad was complicated by the kind of thing the old man on the sour-ball schooner did for me. After that I figured that I could trust anybody. I even trusted the millman, the one with the covetous eye for my tropical timber.

Paul saved me—Paul, who owned the boatyard in Fort Lauderdale where *Princess* spent the early years of the war in wet storage. I was down there the next day, looking for some of the gear that had gotten away during my absence. I had told the story of my piece of wood so many times that it had become a habit. I couldn't help telling it once more. Paul listened, drooling.

"Has it got a rich red color?"

"Yeah."

"Is it hard?"

"Yeah!"

"Does it hold a fastening like grim death?"

"I guess so."

"That's horseflesh, run back and get it," said Paul. "The millman has swindled you." I ran. The piece of wood was still intact. The millman gave it back to me without an argument. I returned his piece of oak. It dropped on his toe, quite by accident. I apologized. The millman said, "That don't help my toe none."

You ought to have seen that piece of wood when it came out of the planer. It was beautiful—I have never seen color and grain like that. It would have made a table fit for a king. It made a new sternpost fit for *Princess*. Compared to the pains I took surveying to get the hole for the propeller shaft in that part of the keel accurate, Lewis and Clark had a picnic. I was in terror of ruining the gift of wood given me by the captain of the sour-ball schooner. I had nightmares about it. I could see the old man coming at me in a rage, his long white beard doubled back and clenched in his choppers.

I checked and rechecked. At last the moment arrived. I tightened the clamps that held the timber and threw the switch to start the motor. Down came the drill. Up came luscious, cherry-red curls of horseflesh spilling out on the floor as the drill sank from sight.

At last it came through. I could hardly wait to see where. I backed the drill out. The clamps were made loose and wrenched off, the timber turned over, and there was the hole, true as a whole day of careful figuring and a boatload of luck could make it. I was in seventh heaven. Slowly *Princess* took shape. A new rudderpost was fashioned of oak. A couple of new planks were faired, and over in the machine shop the old rock crusher was getting another lease on life.

The mechanic had his troubles, too. The engine needed three-eighths-inch piston rings. I took the car and went looking for three-eighths-inch piston rings. There was a fellow who knew a junk dealer who had piston rings of all sizes. He led me to a barn.

Have you ever seen a barn just past haying time? That's what this barn looked like, but instead of hay it was heaped to the rafters with piston rings, which incidently ain't hay. I said, "Are any of these three-eighths-inch?"

The junk dealer said, "Go look." I took off my coat and started digging with a micrometer. I dug all day. The mountain of surplus piston rings held every diameter and every size except three-eighths of an inch. There were literally millions of piston rings, and most of them were three-sixteenths. I took it up with the junk dealer.

"Is it all right to use two three-sixteenths-inch piston rings alongside each other?"

"No," he said, just like that. I kept looking.

By sundown, covered with grime and still unsuccessful in my quest for three-eighths-inch piston rings, I went back to the mechanic. "What are we going to do?" I asked. "All they have are three-sixteenths-inch piston rings."

"Why didn't you bring me a handful?"

"How come?"

"We can use two of them side by side."

"No!"

"Sure. That's what they do in all the finest foreign racing cars. Gives you more compression."

I went back to the barn with plenty of compression. This time I took along a pitchfork. Anything good enough for the finest foreign racing cars had damn well better be good enough for *Princess*.

224

28

The longer I looked, the more I realized that no other boat could ever take the place of my baby. There was no doubt about it, we were still in love. *Princess* was pushing sixty. I am no spring chicken myself, but in girls and boats such age must be considered a romantic liability.

Girls are touchy about it, but boats are not above having their admirers whittle away at their age. Thus it was that each new part that I fashioned, using the old part as a template, made her that much younger. When I wasn't involved in this process of rejuvenation, I lay on the sugar-white sand and stared up at her heavenly form.

Sometimes I dozed, dreaming of other little boats, boats I had known during the seven years of separation from *Princess*. I sprawled in the sun and smiled, thinking of the souped-up babes that had given me the time of my life, time and again through the war-filled years. I wondered what had become of the tugs, the ones we took to the far Pacific, the one we left in Honolulu, the ones that were earmarked for invasion. Where were the aircraft-rescue boats, and that honey of a little cargo vessel whose job it was to supply the islands adjacent to Panama, the innocent isles that bristled with antiaircraft?

I lay in the lee of a sand dune, sun-drenched and safe, dreaming troubled dreams of troubled seas, of giant combers, and of darkness that can obscure the imminence of a fatal capsize. I wallowed in the extravagance of fears that I could never afford at sea. In the agony of these delayed reactions I became half afraid to put to sea even in *Princess*.

Fortunately, dream storms also pass, and I remembered coral lagoons and the sun-clipped façade of volcanic rock that yielded a gracious harbor like an unexpected cup. I remembered the intemperance of Nature, teeming and steaming, and the bugs. I remembered the bugs best of all.

I had been looking for the tropics, and thanks to the war I found it. In its embrace I learned things I never knew about pasture land quilted with snow and printed with the random design of rabbit tracks. I came to hunger for the cold cake of rock walls and the feathery icing of new snow. I learned in tropical Fahrenheit about the amnesty of temperate winters and the God-given armistice of bugs. It was good to be back. *Princess* was heading north, and there was nothing to worry about but living. As worries go, that was a distinct improvement.

From where I lay, things were literally looking up—that is, until I got fixed to step the mast. It was a dark moment when I discovered that the stick was riddled with rot and that two thirds of its girth at the truck would powder away to the touch. There is probably nothing in the state of Florida so difficult to come by as a spruce stick. I even looked with a covetous eye at the coconut palm in the boatyard. Staring hopefully up along the curve of the tree, I wondered whether its shape might not also offer the key to some dynamic principle that would revolutionize sailing. I fell to wondering if the war had provided mankind with all the technological improvements that were expected of it. All I had to show for the war was a rotten mast, a consciousness of Hiroshima, and some vague expectation that the world would be saved by the plastics industry. That's when I got the idea.

It wasn't really my idea. I got it from an old man, an inveterate patcher of old boats who had taken the time to follow the far-flung technological front. He reminded me of phenol resin glue. It stuck like billy-be-damned!

Jack Collison did most of the gluing. Jack was a wartime shipmate, a yachtsman, boatbuilder, and knight in shining armor. He took as a personal affront the ravages of time and inroads of rot from which *Princess* suffered. He wandered into the yard and, seeing the condition of her mast, demanded the right to rectify the situation then and there. He rolled up his sleeves and went to work. He worked like a demon. I never saw anything like it. He worked sans pay, sans rest, sans sense.

Grabbing an adz and standing astride the stick, Jack chopped out the rotten part. Then we went looking for wood to make what boatbuilders call a fish, which is nothing more than a length of wood tapered at each end to look like one. That kind of fish is spliced into a spar or mast as reinforcement. Scrounging behind the shed, we kicked up a wicked-looking snake called a coachwhip, which slithered away into the undergrowth, and we came up with a ten-foot length of spruce spar. It was part of the gaff of a schooner that had foundered off Cape Canaveral years back. The sinking ship had unhinged the jaw of the gaff from its mast and sent it thundering down the back eddy of the Gulf Stream covered with survivors.

Most of the spar had been used to brace the shed. The short end lay in the sun, half covered with sand, and a deep check extended all the length of it. We decided to split it at the check. Jack drove the first wedge. I drove the second. Jack drove another one alongside these two. Then we scoured the yard for wedge-shaped metal. We buried every loose scrap of iron in that check, but there was no splitting the log. The words of the old canvas man came back to me: "We could thrust our arms clear to the shoulder into the checks of the old spruce sailing-ship spars and never fear for them in a hurricane." We wound up substituting oak wedges for the iron ones and sawing that indestructible log lengthwise with a two-man saw.

When at last the plane rested on its side and the setting glue oozed in the clinch of clamps, Jack Collison shoved off. He wouldn't even let me buy him a drink. It was a revelation to me. I had completely forgotten about that way of pleasing people, of letting them break their backs working on your boat. It was positively indecent. *Princess* at least should have known better, but in that respect all boats, whether they be sail or power, are cut from the same cloth.

As for cloth, seven semitropical years spent baking in a hot loft had cut into the sails of *Princess*. Her mainsail was ready to go at the slightest provocation. The genoa jib and spinnaker, which were sewn of Egyptian sailcloth, were in good shape. I began to get an inkling of how the Egyptian mummies managed to stand up over the long, hot years. The stiff storm trysail was still intact. Hand-sewn and stout, it could contain a hurricane. It never got soft with age and easy to work but stayed stubborn till it shredded, like some sort of sea-horse shay.

I wish I were that durable. The years had taken something. I could feel it where a boxer feels it first—in the knees. I wondered if I could hop around the deck in a blow the way I used to. I knew darn well that I couldn't, and I was scared. Sailing alone is a tricky business. Besides, I had the car to think about.

That took some thinking. Cars were not easy to come by in 1947. I had endless offers which made me all the more determined to hang onto the old jalopy. Come what may, I resolved to bring the car and the boat back to New York. It was a matter of principle. New York was where I was when the whole thing started, and I could hardly consider the matter closed until I had got back.

Princess could hardly wait to get going. She was shaping up fast. Her stick was now firm, and her status as a sailing vessel was unassailable. The mast was stepped. She was caulked, painted, and petted. She was ready to go. It was the end of April. It was high time. When the yard bill was paid, the ancient Englishman with his little hydraulic jack was ordered to start her rolling down the long incline. She splashed and floated off into the tree-lined basin. My baby was in her element.

It had been a long time. In all her years, that had been the longest spell spent on the beach. *Princess* had a hell of a lot of swelling to do. I could almost feel her drinking salt water. I was like the man who heard spoil bubbles crackling under his hull and went screaming into the night that the torredoes were gobbling his love. After *Princess* had made up a bit and I could give the pump a breather, I began to make plans.

Progress had to be a leapfrog affair, with the car running a poor second. The nice part was to have the use of the car in every port. The tough part would be hitch-hiking back to the port of departure to get it. One way or another, I would have a boat or a car in every port, and part of the time both. The way it worked out, I lived like a harrassed millionaire. The boat leaked. The car developed a rash of flat tires from running roughshod into boat yards to get to her before she sank. I had all the disadvantages of convenience.

The last thing I recall of Lantana was the little coal stove off my boat, discarded in favor of the clean convenience of alcohol, smoking away under the palm trees while the yard owner's kids stoked it with palm leaves, playing house. The damp years had done it in. Rust had eaten through the walls and toppled the grate. All there was left of that seagoing central heating system were the endearing words "MARINE HOUSEHOLD" on the oven door.

Princess had not gone very far when she fell in with a couple and their little daughter sailing north. Theirs was a tiny decked-over snipe. By contrast *Princess* seemed like an ocean liner, but they managed somehow, urged by an excessive love of salt water and one another. I can't remember a happier little group. For reasons that escape me, the little girl called herself "Goosen."

She was about six, and sometimes she sailed along with me in *Princess*. I told her stories, and she said that she'd marry me someday when she grew up.

Sailing north along the inland waterway after all the years at sea was like finding a reel of half-forgotten film and watching it projected backward. One by one, the little coastal towns fell behind. There were moments of great beauty and peacefulness.

In one town I asked the man behind the counter of a bean wagon whether he knew Pat Hennessey. Pat was a native of Florida, and a friend of mine. He was a Marine. He was a natural athlete, and he could write. They put him in public relations. He used to talk about a redhead that he wanted to meet someday. Red hair was a must, and she was bound to be beautiful. I found out that night in the bean wagon that Hennessey never met her. Big, handsome Pat put in for paratroops. He was picked off in the air over Iwo Jima by a Japanese sniper crouched in a palm tree.

There were palm trees along the Indian River. There were people. There were vast stretches of beach and sky and splashes of sunlight. I was in no hurry. It was kind of wonderful, and at the same time sad. On the third day after leaving Lantana, after a rough run from Titusville, I met a tugboat captain on crutches.

There's a channel marker with an arrow on it just as you leave the yacht basin. Cutting corners, I snagged my mainsail on the arrow and tore a three-foot strip from head to foot along the leech. I had to cut the boltrope to get loose. *Princess* headed across the last shoal gasp of the Indian River with that strip of sail flying like a tremendous pennant from the peak.

The wind was dead ahead out of the northeast. I had no decent chart of the area. I tacked back and forth across the shoals with a gale of wind holding my baby so far over that she drew scarcely two feet of water. I got stuck coming about. A plane zoomed low at the silly sight of our predicament and the twenty-odd feet of white streamer that underscored it. A burst of wind coincidental with the backwash of that plane rolled *Princess* into the channel. I lowered sails, fetching in the loose ends, and proceeded under power for Haulover Canal. The bridgetender's wife put a long seam in my mainsail with her sewing machine, and we were off again. At sundown I asked a man standing on crutches on the deck of a steel barge if I could tie up alongside.

He asked me aboard. I had coffee with him in the warm galley of the tug, and I had a piece of pie. The old man had broken his leg two days before. He had the nerve of a brass monkey. There he was, with his leg in a cast clear to the hip, wrangling the longest layout of steel barges and deep draft tugs ever to negotiate the inside waters from Miami to Jacksonville. I don't remember the dimensions of each barge or how many there were, but the whole outfit stretched over a thousand feet. He was taking these oil barges clear to Norfolk, but he anticipated no difficulty from Jacksonville on north, where the controlling depth was eight feet —but it was only six in Florida, and the tug drew more than seven.

For all their bulk, the barges drew only eighteen inches of water. To complicate things, the tug was shorthanded. I offered to help. The captain said that he'd be glad to tow *Princess* for the sake of an extra hand tying up. It was a deal. I slept like a baby that night. My only regret was that I didn't have the jalopy along. It would have been hardly noticed on the deck of one of those huge barges.

Next day was sunny and brisk. The wind was strong from the east. I helped the old man make up the tow and swung down along the anchor cable of *Princess*, made fast to the after end of the last barge. The tug got underway with a cataract of foam. She had plenty of power, enough to dredge her way through any bar. I was content. I made the bitter end of my anchor cable fast to the mast, and settled down to the long freeload to Norfolk.

I stretched out on deck for the first hour and watched the scenery. This was it—no work, no fuss, no feathers. Our speed was about six knots. I steered for a while, and then I let the tiller go. It seemed like a waste of time. There was a book to read. I reveled in my luck.

What had we done, *Princess* and I, to deserve such good fortune? I made coffee and decided during the process that this was the long-awaited opportunity to brush up on her interior. To begin with, the engine needed a coat of paint. Idling the motor, I scraped the flywheel with a bastard file held like a lathe tool. I had opened a can of vermilion enamel and started dabbing when we struck. I bolted out of the hatch, covered with red paint like a stuck pig. What I saw I couldn't believe. Bushes were going by. They made strange, scratching sounds along the bottom. *Princess* was traveling across dry land.

After the first shock, I grabbed a hatchet and jumped forward. The tug was still moving, but slower now. Should I cut the line? No! The barges, veered by the wind, had short-cut the channel and climbed right across a bar, with Princess faithfully behind them. If I cut the line, how would I get off dry land? I waited. The straining tow line drew *Princess* into a few inches of water. I could see the furrow that we had cut across thirty feet of mud. The tug pulled with all her might. The barges inched forward. *Princess* found two feet of water under her, and down came the ax.

We had had it. The strong easterly heeled us over, and with the shortened draft and all sails drawing we made for the channel going north.

29

Neck and neck, *Princess* and the jalopy inched northward. Jockeying back and forth between them, I began to sense a terrific rivalry between the Friendship sloop and the business coupé. *Princess* was registered as a pleasure craft. The coupé was all business except for one pleasurable feature: It had nothing to pump except tires, which sank at the mention of boatyard nails.

The boat had one leak that had me running in circles. It didn't figure. It would start for no reason at all and stop for the same reason. One day *Princess* was bone-dry, and the next day she was doing her level best to founder. It seemed like some sort of spite. I got the uncomfortable feeling that the boat was just plain jealous of the coupé, but I had to abandon that notion when the ja-

233

lopy got three flats in a row while rushing dockside to keep the boat from sinking.

Anyway, peace was wonderful. It was fun to fret over silly things that didn't involve dying—or did they? After all, the boat might sink in bad water. The jalopy could blow out a tire on a curve. These possibilities were the best I could do now that the war was over and I was fresh out of enemies. To play safe, I ran up the Intracoastal Waterway, which was safe, sane, and teeming with hostile natives who did their level best to kill me with kindness.

Kindness can take strange forms. If I asked for directions, I was rewarded with the most specific instructions, which I followed, and sure enough ran aground. If I got a tow from some goodhearted tugboat skipper, he ended by short-cutting the channel and dragging *Princess* right up over a mudbar. I couldn't win. Peacetime was evidently just another form of war.

Generally, when folks travel they have the means of transportation waiting on them hand and foot. My travels were undertaken in behalf of the means. Both the boat and the car were as demanding as spoiled children. After all the rebuilding and the effort of getting underway, I was a candidate for a rest cure. If I hadn't been braced by the quiet hours back in Eau Gallie, I would have thrown in the sponge, the towel, and the titleholder too.

Eau Gallie was good for me. Certain places can do things for you. Sometimes it's the expanse of a vista. Another time it's the sense of sanctuary. *Princess* came into Eau Gallie with half a gale behind her and all sails set. There is a winding channel just before you get to the bridge. I ran it at sundown on the way into the tiny basin, set in Spanish moss like a silvered mirror half hidden in long hair. I can't put my finger on it. It may be the live oaks, the curve of the low hills, or the name itself, but Eau Gallie has it.

It did it for the boat, too. In the two days that I was gone to get the car, she didn't leak a single drop. Well, one drop maybe, but it had evaporated by the time I got back. I had to throw a bucket of salt water into the bilge of *Princess* to keep her sweet. It was a mistake. I guess she figured that I was never satisfied; she started to leak in dead earnest. By the time I got to St. Augustine, I had to beach her.

There's a creek that turns in behind the town, a smooth stretch of sandy bank, a sharp incline suited to the need of her design, and enough tide to clear her at low water. I ran her aground at high water early in the morning just below a dock where a farmer-fisherman had a trawler tied up. That's where the hunt for the big leak began.

The tide was halfway out and still no signs of the leak when I spotted a trawler roaring up the channel, throwing a tremendous wash. I yanked off my shirt like a man marooned and waved frantically. Fortunately, real water people understand. When the fisherman saw *Princess* on her side, they slowed for fear of pounding her hull with their wash. By noon the tide was out and so was the leak, right in plain sight. It was a butt in the garboard on the starboard side that was guilty. A piece of caulking cotton that hung out or flopped back into place acted as a moody floodgate. I fashioned a new butt block with a tapered edge that reached down to the rabbet in the keel. It provided something to caulk against. *Princess* also got a quick coat of bottom paint.

I was busy daubing away when the farmer-fisherman came striding along the beach in a kind of limping gait occasioned by the steep incline of the hard-packed sand. He stood staring at *Princess* while he fished in his overall pockets. "That's a Down East vessel," he said, "built over Friendship way. Had a boat just like her. Quite a time back it was." The old man squatted in the sand, squinted up at the hull, and scratched a parlor match on the seat of his pants. "Swapped her for a cord of wood," he said, drawing on his pipe.

"I beg your pardon?"

"Yep," he said, "that's what I did. Swapped her for a cord of wood. Good little boat. Let a fellow have her for a cord of wood." The old man stared at the boat for a while, and then he said, "Come on, now." He pointed to a house up on the road. "Got a place set for you at the table. Been watching you all morning. You didn't take time to eat. Tide's out. Won't be the wash of no vessel to bother your little ship. Hurry now, Maw's waiting. Dinner's on."

I put away the rest of the bottom paint, cleaned my lunch hooks with gas, and hurried after the farmer-fisherman to the little house on the bluff. It was an elegant meal served by a very proper old gal in a frilly apron. She could sure dish it out.

The old man sat at the head of the table, framed by a china closet. He dished it out too—badgered me all through the mid-day meal about the Friendship sloop that he swapped for a cord of wood. "Tell you what," he said. "Why don't you leave your boat on the mud flats around the bend? Won't no harm come to her. You can come and get her any time." Then, looking at me sharp, he said, "Between that boat and a car, you got more than mortal man can stand. 'T ain't good for your health."

I hadn't noticed it till then, but I was kind of on the skinny side—more than a little overworked, too, leapfrogging a car and a boat all the way up the coast. The man from the state of Maine and his old lady did what they could for me. They did as much for other people, too. I wish I could recall his name and hers, but no matter, their neighbors will know.

For myself, I knew that the long, tedious watches on the Inland Waterway were getting me down. I knew that I ought to make one long run or give up—St. Augustine to Charleston, for instance, would help. I was ready to chance it outside if my baby was willing. The tide came up in the afternoon and proved she was. She didn't leak a drop.

The folks on the veranda of the little white house on the bluff waved, and we moved out with the tide to the town pier, where *Princess* made immediate friends by docking herself nicely in a tricky wind. Four of her friends were small sailing vessels being made ready for the same run that we contemplated. There was a thirty-foot sloop with a young couple in command and a Bluenose schooner that sported bulkhead-to-bulkhead carpeting in the main cabin, with a pile deep enough to wallow in. There was another sloop owned by a fellow who was in a business that I could never understand. He bought and sold the boats he sailed. There was a yawl, the strangest-looking vessel I ever saw.

The yawl was built by a former submarine commander who must have found some sailing qualities in pigboats that nobody else knew about. The frames of the hull curved up, forming an overhead that was planked just like the sides. The deck, streamlined by this method of construction, offered nothing but a catwalk running fore and aft to get about and handle sail. The anchors were rigged so they could be raised and lowered from the cockpit without going forward. The inspiration for this innovation was the incidental fact that one man had already been lost trying to handle ground tackle from the slippery, snub-nosed bow.

Provisioned, we all left St. Augustine at noon in what might loosely be called consort. It sure as hell was no convoy. Everybody had a different idea. Most of them ran up close along the coast, tacking in and out with the puffy easterly. *Princess*, being the only single-hander, lit out for the Gulf Stream and deep water, where, if need be, I could get a bit of shut-eye without running the risk of being drawn in on the treacherous, outlying reefs by the pull of the tidal rivers that abound along this marshy section of the coast.

It is safe enough with even two on board running watch and watch. Alone along a coast breaking and alive with swirling currents, fatigue is fatal. To go it alone, a man must have sea room. The wind was northeast. Close-hauled, *Princess* made her easting by dusk with the boisterous Stream kicking her along faster the nearer she got to the core of it. The wind freshened. Harnessed to the drive of her vast mainsail and the fierce pull of her genoa jib, my boat tore through the troubled sea.

I lit the gasoline lantern and the running lights. The cabin looked cozy from the cockpit. I lashed the tiller, and *Princess* held her course. I curled up in the cockpit with a can of soup and prepared to make a night of it. It certainly was a relief to get out where the old girl could steer herself, within reasonable limits. No such thing is possible in the narrow confines of the ditch. The wind came kindly around to the east, which took the top off the sea and gave us another knot or two. At this rate, Charleston by morning was a lead-pipe cinch.

With the Gulf Stream as a partner *Princess* was really in business. Leery of a night on the open sea, three of the sailboats had turned on power and disappeared in the spume and fog that lay along the churning coast. The yawl was still under sail, and as her peak faded in the night it gave way to the intermittent green glint of her running light. At last that too was visible only through a glass.

About ten o'clock that night I saw a blinking light where the green running light had been. The light, flashing against a surface of sail, could be nothing but the yawl. I blinked in reply, inquiring by code if she needed assistance. Either the crew didn't read code, or they were too troubled to try. I thought about her streamlined deck and the man who was lost trying to handle an anchor from such a perch. Obviously, there was nothing to do but come about and go in among the reefs to assist her.

All the way in I flashed to let them know that I was on my way. Running back the wind was dead astern. In one hour the distance gained in a long, ten-hour beat against a cross sea was gone, and I spoke the yawl. "What's the matter?" I yelled.

"Nothing," came the reply. "We just wanted to know if you were all right."

It took all night to get back into the stream. We had to buck a strong east wind and a southerly set. The wind veered to the north the next day and blew half a gale. Nature got in on the act and kept us constantly on edge. By nightfall I had put in close to thirty-six hours at the tiller without sleep.

There was no sextant on board and no chronometer. A little portable radio that had the characteristics of a direction finder gave me a rough fix. It showed our position to be about sixty miles offshore and southeast of Savannah. I just had to get some sleep. I was willing to close for one hour.

Some of the time for some mysterious reason, the wind moderates at the moment of sunset. I counted on that moment to shorten sail. Instead, the wind went wild. Exhausted, I let the halyards go and clawed my way about the heaving deck, tying the reef points. I'll never know how I got the mainsail up again or how I managed to gather in the billowing genny. With the tiller lashed, a bright light hanging in the hatchway, and the bowsprit pointing northeast, I went below for a catnap as night fell.

I woke with a start. The sun was in the middle of the sky. Thirteen hours had passed. The wind had moderated. I jumped up on deck and looked at the compass. *Princess*, God bless her, was still heading northeast.

30

It's a small world. On the surface, most of it appears to be sea. Here things stand out as a mole might on the face of the Mona Lisa. Standing out on the face of the broad Atlantic, for instance, was a commercial fishing vessel that I knew, out of Thunderbolt, Georgia. Men at her windlass were breaking the surface with a net that flashed with catch in the morning light.

Princess, still reefed, had nothing to say about the night. It was kind of embarrassing. The old lady had held her course for almost fourteen hours while I slept. The least I could do to show my gratitude was shake the reef out of the mainsail and give her back the genoa jib. She responded in the light morning air by overtaking the preoccupied trawler, which supplied us with matches, more fish than I knew what to do with, and a clue to our approximate position.

According to the fishermen, we lay east-southeast of Savannah, Georgia, and some twenty miles offshore. If the wind had shifted during the night while I slept, it might have been touch and go. Still, had it blown hard enough from the proper quarter to drive us all the sixty miles in to the surf, such a wind would have opposed the direction of the Gulf Stream. As dead as I was for sleep, a sea kicked up by the clash of these elements would have brought me to. At any rate, it was a dandy morning to split hairs.

I sat at the tiller in my skin and stared down at the uninflated rubber life raft that lay in the cockpit. Having no dinghy, I had purchased it in St. Augustine as a sop to safety. A little cylinder of carbon dioxide came with it. I took comfort in the realization that it stood ready to jump to my rescue at the turn of a valve.

Princess idled in the light winds. There was no hurry. The mouth of the Savannah River lay a scant twenty miles to the west and north, with a whole day to go. I spent what was left of the morning cleaning and cooking fish. I fried some in oil, baked some with a garnish of onions and tomato sauce, and chopped up the rest for a Down East chowder with plenty of pepper and condensed milk. I could have fed a regiment. I fed myself and fell to napping. My boat was getting nowhere. The wind was the puffy kind you get sitting next to a swinging door in a corner saloon. We slatted in the long, slick swells. I had a chart of Charleston Harbor, which was my original destination, but nothing for the mouth of the Savannah River except one of those seagoing road maps.

It was evening by the time *Princess* knifed her way in among the range lights that delineate the main channel. We were under power with the old rock crusher wide open, bucking the tide that had just turned. The chart was never intended for the use I put it to. I missed the main channel and ran up a dead-end channel behind Tybee Spit. Turning to correct the error, I headed over to the right. Tybee Spit reached out like a rough hand and grabbed *Princess* by the bottom. We were aground.

The tide went out too fast for us to get off. When it was

out, it left my baby high and dry, higher than I knew, and dryer. Granted the grace between ebb and flow, I got out in the dark with a flashlight and climbed down for a look. It was quite a climb. *Princess* was up a tree.

Standing on the spit, I gawked up at her like a scenery stiff. She was actually up in a tree. A big tree of oysters growing in progressive clumps supported my boat as an apple tree supports a robin's nest. I looked close. The crunching sound when she ran aground was nothing but the noise of cracking oyster shells giving way as my boat was bedded down. They made a perfect cradle. *Princess* was safe, and more comfortable than she might have been supported in boatyard chocks.

I climbed back and folded the rubber raft with the cylinder of carbon dioxide. Someday the tide would come back. I thought about all those oysters and wished to hell I had a little horseradish sauce.

The tide went out so far and so fast it looked as if it was going out for good, but it came back the same day, as it always does. While I waited I got some sleep in the angular trough between bunk and bulkhead. When I heard the tide creeping around,

I got up and looked out on a day concocted of sunshine and fog. *Princess* dribbled between her top strakes as the tide began to lift her. I pumped a bit and eased her up with a wooden beam thrust down between the port chain plates. Everything lifted at last: my boat, the fog, and my spirits. Down we went around the black breakwater of granite rocks, from which *Princess* had been saved by the intercession of Tybee Spit. We made the run to the Coast Guard station on the Savannah River with the rapid current, and tied up.

It was good to get in. I petted the old girl, saving a friendly pat for the rubber raft and that ever-ready cylinder of carbon dioxide. There was a lot of comfort compressed in that bottle. Through high seas and high winds, past reaching reefs and tidal slues, that rubber raft and a quick turn were all I needed. Now that we were in, I gave the valve a playful twist. It went *p-f-f-t*. Call it faith—it buoys you up even when it's based on an empty bottle of carbon dioxide.

Back down the coast by thumb, I picked up the patient car at St. Augustine and drove in a couple of hours the span that had taken four days to cover by water. All together again, I got squared away for another go at it. This time it was the forty-mile run to Charleston. As I warped the boat about at the dock, *Princess* got her nosy bowsprit caught between the pilings. Her sprit was an original member in which years plus the natural bent of the wood caused a visible curve. I watched fascinated as the tremendous force of the Savannah River broke that big oak spar like a matchstick. I could easily have saved it, but I wanted a made-to-order reason to replace it with a straight one.

They had a straight one in Savannah, and the jalopy took me downtown to get it. It was a cruddy-looking piece of live oak that had lain for years as the base of a big pile of pine in the process of being cured. Somebody bought the pine that day, which brought the length of live oak to light. When it came out of the planer, it looked like marble, and it was just about as hard.

That piece of live oak could hardly be drilled by hand. What was more amazing (when you consider how live oak grows), it was as straight as a die for ten feet, with the core of the grain dead center at each end. The boys at the Coast Guard station put it in the big drill press at the shop. When it was set in place of the broken one and secured, I knew that I had a bowsprit to conjure with, or joust. No sailing vessel that ever jousted with a quartering gale had a better spar.

I left Savannah River with the tide and the best wishes of the Coast Guard station gang, who had borrowed my jalopy and were driving it to Charleston for the ride. The run to Charleston was without incident. We cleared the breakers off Folly Island. My baby clawed her way along in a strong onshore wind, as she had Down East so many times before. It was dark by the time *Princess* reached the mouth of the Cooper River. The tide was running out, and a chop was built up by the stiff breeze.

There are places where a tidal flow coming out of a system of rivers will run strong enough to act as a breakwater. Such is the case off Charleston. The Cooper River, joined by the flow of the Ashley and Wando rivers, forces a jet of water out into the open ocean that cuts down the surf set up by the prevailing southerly. Behind this wall of running water, *Princess* found a calm spot. I dropped her hook and slept.

When the tide changed, I got up, ran in past the old walls of Fort Sumter in a gray dawn, and tied up at the Municipal Yacht Basin. I found the jalopy in the morning waiting for me in Dr. Joe Waring's back yard. It was good to find old friends, and a very agreeable new one in the person of a ship captain and a big pal for *Princess* called *'Orrible 'Orace*.

'Orrible 'Orace was the nickname he gave her. She was a Liberty ship whose rightful name was Horace something-or-other. At the close of hostilities she lay at anchor in the Cooper River. Her master was a young Virginian who sported a full-rigged beard. He had his orders. *'Orrible 'Orace* was bound for the boneyard that lay up the James River from Norfolk.

'Orrible 'Orace had been home to her skipper for most of the war years. Compared to the quiet hills of Virginia, it had been home in a tough neighborhood. Ships had been sunk all about her.

Submarines that had decimated her convoys had disdained her bottom. Planes had picked off adjacent ships, leaving her unmolested. *'Orrible 'Orace* had come through unscathed. She was the ugly duckling type. *Princess* is beautiful. It was natural that these ·two should gravitate to each other—*'Orrible 'Orace* for the pleasure and prestige that lies in the aura of great beauty, and *Princess* for reasons native to her sex. They were introduced by the bearded skipper in a ritual that smacked of insanity.

Possessed in much the same way I was by the horrors of peace, this captain had found an anodyne for safety. He developed a taste for riding up and down from the deck of the Liberty ship to sea level perched on the deck of his star sailboat, no hands. This was no small tribute to the skill of the bos'n who handled the controls of the windlass during these gymnastics.

The chief engineer of *'Orrible 'Orace* was not to be outdone. He owned a class boat, too. His was a comet which he picked up in Bari, Italy, for peanuts. They told him in Italian that he couldn't beat a star with a comet, but he was all for trying. He kept her shining like a cylinder wall, and whenever sheltered water was found to sail the star, the chief broke out the sling for his comet and followed suit.

Taken from their cradles and launched in a likely harbor, these little vessels vied for the honor of their respective departments. Lined up along the bulwarks of the mother ship were the deck monkeys and the black gang, cheering them on. These contests were attended with the *sang-froid* one finds on yacht-club verandas during regatta week. There were no vulgar displays of enthusiasm, and practically no broken heads.

Into this slightly superior atmosphere came *Princess*. She tossed imperiously, lifting her head like a blooded charger as preparations were made to lift her out of the Cooper River and set her on the deck of *'Orrible 'Orace*. I bent a sling from some new, three-inch cable borrowed from a barge and passed it under her counter. Passed again under her clipper bow, the ends were joined in a bow line. She was ready for the hook that dangled alongside the steel wall of ship in the roaring tide.

With her little engine pounding wide open to keep her abreast of the current, I swung *Princess* over to the accommodation ladder of the Liberty ship to take the old man aboard.

"Want to ride up with me?" said the captain of *'Orrible 'Orace*.

I declined. Grabbing the accommodation ladder of the ship with one hand and bow line from my boat with the other, I left the destiny of *Princess* in the capable hands of this young patriarch. He fastened the sling to the hook, and, standing on the stern of my sloop with one hand in his pocket and the finger of the other rotating in a signal to lift, the bos'n took up the slack and my boat began to lose contact with her natural element. I began to lose contact too. This was strictly dream stuff. Up she went, sixty feet into the air, all five tons of her lifted like a feather by the ship, which was riding light. At the top of the arc I gasped as *Princess* shifted suddenly in her sling.

Down below lay the treacherous swirl of the Cooper River

horsing out to sea. Looking up from the platform of the accommodation ladder, I could just make out my friend, poised without benefit of hand line or stanchion, crouched like an acrobat. The sling held. I raced up the ladder and met *Princess* as they eased her down alongside the hatch. She came down pretty as you please, with her spacious chine leaning on the hatch like a chin on a table, while the very young old man unassumingly stepped off. Lashed fast, my boat would be all set to round the rigors of Cape Hatteras while I moseyed along to meet her in the jalopy.

I was busy expressing my gratitude to the audacious master of *'Orrible 'Orace* when *Princess* gave a lurch, skidded out, and landed with her bottom on the iron deck. There was no great harm in her pratfall, so we left her that way lashed down to the deck, ready for the worst that could happen off Hatteras.

I watched them, *'Orrible 'Orace* slipping out past Fort Sumter with a guilty look and my baby snuggling alongside the number five hatch, her shapely bilge pressed against the steel plates of the mighty ship. You could tell by the way they left that they were bound for no good and Norfolk. They left me with nothing but my old jalopy.

31

Sometimes for brief periods it's kind of fun to make believe that you don't own a boat. We got a chance to get acquainted again, just me and the car. It acted perfectly. I responded by double-clutching and otherwise showering it with oil and attentions in a silly, overprotective way.

There is virtue in a car. They are loyal, steady, and obedient. They may not be as pretty as boats, but they don't go off unchaperoned on the decks of Liberty ships. Lord only knows what was going on off Hatteras with that loose star, that dizzy comet, and *'Orrible 'Orace*, to say nothing of the wild-eyed chief and the bearded old man. There was actually nothing wrong with the car. It had its points. It also ran. But what can a car mean to a guy who's crazy in love with a boat?

Once out of town, the jalopy burned up the road. I was anxious to get to Norfolk to see how my baby made out rounding Cape Hatteras. It was the early part of June. It rained. Crossing through Dismal Swamp country, I waited in a downpour for the same bridges to close that I used to pray would open. I got to know how the other half lives, the motoring half.

One night was spent in an old hotel, the hub of a little southern town. All night the rain pelted the tin roof of the portico outside the tall, arched window of my room. The big elms hung limp in the soft streetlights. Down alongside the curb in a river of rain, my old car shone like new. Somewhere out beyond the Pamlico, far outside the Albemarle, my little boat was doing with another that which we never dared to do alone. Hugging the deck of a giant ship, she was clearing the far-reaching reefs, the dreaded Cape Hatteras.

The sun came through in the morning. The window was all leaves and sunlight, like a stained-glass window leaded with black branches. I had coffee on the portico, and so insistent is habit that it was all I could do to keep from sauntering down to the canal as if to go aboard my boat.

I drove to Norfolk through the freshly laundered atmosphere and the gentle offshore breeze of the morning. I spotted 'Orrible 'Orace from the dock. She was the Liberty ship in the anchorage, the one with the Friendship sloop canting on her afterdeck.

Hampton Roads was alive, crisscrossed by the bow waves of little boats that ran from ship to ship and from ship to shore. I left the car on the dock and boarded a bumboat that took me out to the accommodation ladder of 'Orrible 'Orace. It was lowered far down to a point just above the playful flick of the harbor waves.

On deck I was greeted by the bearded captain. We went aft together, and I saw my baby. She was untouched by her experience. "Hatteras was as calm as a lake," said the old man.

My boat looked kind of sheepish nestled against the hatch with her bowsprit down like a silly pup with its nose between its

249

paws. In the calm of Norfolk harbor we rigged a boom and lowered a hook to the rope sling that was still draped around her like a shawl. We lifted *Princess* to her feet and left her there, barely dangling. I went forward with the old man to his quarters. While the captain's black Scottish terrier, named Whiskey, nipped and frolicked at our feet, we also had a nip. "My second officer is paying off," said the skipper. " *'Orrible 'Orace* should be here a month before she goes into mothballs up the James River. You have papers. Do you want the job? There will be some overtime."

I took the job. It meant doubling up as captain of *Princess* and navigating officer of *'Orrible 'Orace*. Even with the one at anchor and the other hauled out, it was a tricky position for a man to be in. I had rivals. Every man on board wanted to play with my boat. Every time I turned around there was someone sanding her spars or laying another coat of government semigloss on her topsides. *Princess* never had it so good. The cook paid off the day after I joined the ship. Galley-wise, it was every man for himself. Nonetheless, I doubt whether I ever had it so good either.

In my spare time, and on such a ship it is mostly spare time, I too worked on *Princess*. The deck of a Liberty ship is a boatyard to end all boatyards. It was clean. There was no dust, plenty of power, a well-equipped machine shop, a carpenter's shop, and forty guys climbing all over one another to help. *Princess* began to look like something fresh out of Nevins. Working on her bottom was the best part. There was no need to stoop. If there was work to do on her keel, I hit the controls of the electric windlass and up she came. I never bothered to walk, either, but, like a barber with flat feet, I spun her around at will.

Except for one stormy night when I had occasion to pilot *'Orrible 'Orace* singlehanded back to the spot from which she had dragged her hook, the weather was all fair. *Princess* was shaping up fast, and so was my pocketbook. With my boat on board and nothing in Norfolk too attractive, I put in all kinds of overtime.

The month aboard *'Orrible 'Orace* passed like a week. I picked up a new mainsail for *Princess*. It was one of those rare bargains. The sail had been fashioned for a larger vessel before the war. The old sailmaker cut it down to fit my boat. He said, "It was half paid for but never called for. I can't very well charge for what's been paid on it." I got it for the balance, and it was worth fourfold.

Painted and polished, her new white canvas bent on, *Princess* was a thing of beauty. Forty pairs of admiring, even envious, eyes watched as she was lifted off the deck of *'Orrible 'Orace*. Set in a sling like a jewel, she was lifted by the windlass, sailed through the air, and set down alongside the Liberty ship. There was no one to ride her. The skipper of the ship had already left in my jalopy for his home near Washington. As much as I loved her, and still do, when she's airborne or off Hatteras, *Princess* is not for me.

Cast loose from not so *'Orrible 'Orace*, who had been something of a sugar daddy, I waved gratefully as *Princess*, without a backward glance, lit out for the harbor entrance and the Chesapeake. We had company. It was the schooner *Scaramouche*.

The *Scaramouche* was built by Ramon Novarro and named after the vehicle that spread his fame, but the steady beat of her staysail luff meant no more to this matinee idol than the flutter of a million feminine hearts. The *Scaramouche* soon passed into the possession of other men, all manner of men in whose care she picked up an assortment of ailments, none of them fatal but all aggravating in varying degrees. The optimistic couple who took her for the yard fee in Florida and sailed her north canceled out her jinx with a black cat and a police dog. These took to a spot between the runners of the cabin hatch cover, which was referred to thereafter as their office.

The cat was always the first to go ashore in port, leaping from the scuppers of the *Scaramouche* to a piling and clawing her way up like a lineman on a telegraph pole. She was never about at sailing time, and the dog was invariably dispatched to round her up. It was a great thing to see him bark her aboard as the boat undocked.

Princess, running in consort with the *Scaramouche*, was steadied by an even westerly. The couple signaled for me to come over within earshot. "Our stove is busted." I acknowledged the message, came alongside, and lashed the tiller of my boat, and stepped aboard the *Scaramouche* with my stove. *Princess* proceeded on her course unattended.

Hour after hour my little boat sailed herself up the dead center of the bay while I lunched aboard the *Scaramouche*, stretching out in her commodious cockpit and expanding on the obvious virtues of my own vessel. Slowly *Princess* drew away. The schooner *Scaramouche*, whose bottom was heavily bearded with marine life, fell behind. She was no match for my boat under sail. When it became time to return to *Princess*, I started to take a more than academic interest in the proceedings. The engine on the *Scaramouche* refused to start.

At last, in the gathering darkness, with my boat almost out of sight, the engine coughed and came to life. We overtook my independent little ship, and back aboard I went, stove in hand. Down below, I prepared my evening meal with *Princess* still unmindful of my existence, still steering herself.

I lit her running lights and, standing in the warm companionway, watched her cut a constant furrow through the fragrant summer sea. It was uncanny. I wondered what had come over her.

She was never that good. Something must have happened off Hatteras. She wouldn't say, and I'd be damned if I'd ask.

The rain let up. The days were fine. Passing Wolf Trap under power in a dead calm, I veered over at the memory of its violence in a blow. Damned if it didn't bounce as bad in a calm as it did in a storm. It was fun to come back and poke around, but somehow I began to look longingly for the end of the voyage. It had been a long time and a long way. Now the excitement of coming home seemed to blur the final hours. I found the sleepy indentation of Solomons Island changed by the war into a vast air-sea base. Beating in at night, *Princess* was met by the blinding lights of a gigantic seaplane that took off and barely cleared her truck, heeling her over in a backwash of wind.

The kids encountered in Annapolis had gone off to war or wherever. The drudgers, untouched by the upheaval at sea, were still tonging oysters in the deep sanctuary of the bay. There was a new highway astride the canal, and the Delaware still ran back out like hell.

I drifted into Smyrna. My friends were all gone, and the strange sailboat built by the brothers up country and lugged lovingly to sea was a broken derelict on the edge of the tidal marsh. Inquiry about the folks who tended the bridge brought shrugs and vague references to bad things. "Didn't you read about it?" they said. "It was in all the papers."

How could I have read all the papers? It didn't matter. I didn't want to know. I gripped the dream and kept moving. There were Ship John Light and Cape May. There were the open sea, the open sky, and the Italian fishermen off the Jersey surf who sing hauling seines as they sing off Sorrento. There was a bad night off Manasquan Inlet when I ached to run in at sunset but didn't dare. All these things have been robbed of detail by the will and the desire for home port. Nothing is clear except the last dark night, when sheer fatigue lent the turbulent Atlantic the illusion of protected waters wherein I seemed to sail as if in a deep, wide channel between kindly banks.

At last it was morning, and the sun lay fair on the hills of

Atlantic Highlands, and the surf cut a kinky white line between the gold of Sandy Hook and the color of the morning sea. The wind died and the late spring sun beat down. I sprawled in the heat of the plywood deck and dozed while *Princess* made a coy and skittish entrance to home port, turning every which way in the tricky embrace of the tide.

I must have dropped off for longer than it seemed. When I looked up, the span of a bridge threw a bent shadow across the path of my boat. Could it be that The Narrows had been bridged in so brief a time? It hadn't. That was Rockaway Bridge. *Princess* had drifted way off course.

Now half the tide was spent, and another hour would be lost before we could regain the main channel. Thus it was that the little engine had its final say. It drew us back against the tide to mid-channel. Whatever wind there was was aft. The unprotected cockpit was a hotbed of sunlight. With the big sail reaching and the engine at half-throttle to steady her, I rigged a line to the tiller and went forward out of the heat. While I stretched out in the shade of the genoa jib, *Princess* ripped along through the busiest harbor in the world with apparently no one at her helm.

The island of Manhattan lay dead ahead. The Statue of Liberty, on her own little island, was still carrying the torch for all men who dream of islands on the million-windowed island just across the bay.

BOOK TWO
Key Biscayne

I

An old dream is a tough thing to kill. It can hang on. An old dream about an island is all but indestructible.

Old or new, any dream worth dreaming will skip little issues like "Where is the supermarket?" and "What do we do about a doctor?"

All you can count on is sunshine, coconuts, and fish. Every conceivable kind of fish. Snappers, blues, mackerel, lobster, and turtles, too. No schools (except schools of fish). No theaters. No libraries. No bowling alleys. No pizza parlors. None of the jazz that makes our world a dream world to a tropical islander.

If you've got the dream, chances are you've got a boat. It's a sign of the malady. It's the way to get to an island. I had *Princess*.

We went all the way, almost. I rebuilt her. I sailed her to the tropics. I went off to a war sailing other boats, and I found the island. But not with *Princess*.

Finding the island alone was bad enough. Finding it with another boat gave *Princess* an edge. It also gave the dream a lease on life. *Princess* bided her time. For a guy like me, *Princess* could afford to wait. Even if the guy now had a wife and two kids.

My boat was hauled on the banks of Pugsley Creek. The headwater of Pugsley Creek is a municipal dump. A tiny spur of Eastchester Creek, Pugsley turns through a dozen acres of swamp-grass that flowers at twelve feet. This elastic little river, which doubles its length when pushed by the tide, lies seven miles north-east by north of Radio City as the crow flies.

There are no crows in Pugsley Creek. The little wilderness of tall green reeds abounds in pheasant, snipe, mallards, kingrail, and a kind of gooney bird with long red legs, a white neck that describes a parabola, and a green bill that describes everything. I never bothered to look it up. Someday I will, on account of the green bill.

While I'm at it, I'll look up Pugsley and find out what kind of a bird *he* was. Named in his honor, this wildlife "sanctuary" in the dog-eared corner of the Bronx lies fair within the bounding lines of the City of New York.

The glob that is fetched out of the recess of the river by the probing tide is of a very fancy composition. I read about it one time in an engineering journal. They were quite excited about it in a highly technical way. It can chew up a canvas cork fender in three days and digest it in a week. The suction of the muck plucks caulking cotton right out of the tight-lipped seams of a vessel and swallows it predigested. It can swallow the vessel, too, with a neap tide as a chaser.

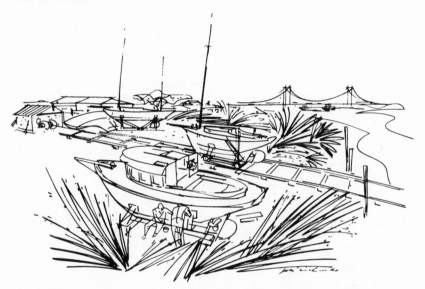

Moored in the river, a boat of any consequence must lay on the bottom while the best part of the creek is out rounding up a fresh tide. Lured by all kinds of false promises, the clean salt water advances sedately into Pugsley Creek, buoys up the boats, spills onto the soggy marsh to the south, and climbs over the debris to the northeast, wondering all the while what it got into.

The yard my boat got into was at one time the home of one of the first boatbuilding families. The main building and show-room faces the shore road. Its big cracked plate-glass window is angled to mirror the dusty process of depositing fill in the cavities of the swamp. A standard-gauge railway bisects the yard. It travels down for a hundred yards out along a wooden catwalk and partakes of Pugsley Creek. Its rusty car looks like it took one too many.

An independent line that runs between two worlds, it originates in the gookum of the creek, climbs through a jungle of reeds, and terminates at a solid brick winch house. Figured in freight miles, this is one of the most expensive carriers in the world.

There were six boats in the yard that were seriously interested in salt water. *Princess* was one of the six.

Spring was years away. There was a nap of snow on the decks of the boats and dusted over the bald spaces of the yard. It blew hard out of the northeast during the long winter nights, but deep in the crosshatched ruts of Manhattan you never knew it. It takes a full gale to wiggle a window shade in Manhattan. An old sixty-foot launch with curved plate-glass windows and hand carved mahogany interior was blown off her crutches, down into the reeds. The high tide of grass would cover her by mid-summer, and a sudden grass fire would devour her in the fall.

There hadn't been a grass fire on our bank of Pugsley Creek in many years. There had been one the autumn before along the south bank of the creek, leaping like a wall of prairie flame while we waited with worn brooms and buckets for the windborne spark that never came. The tide, deliberate and unhurried, rose up and put it out.

There were ashes and snow in the upper reaches of Pugsley Creek. In the spring the snow would melt and run off. The ashes would stay. It all belongs to the City, and the City wants avenues and houses. One day the trucks of the Department of Sanitation would come down and pile their fill right to the mouth of Pugsley Creek. Someday kids would play stickball on Pugsley Street.

2

It was spring, and it was hot. Too damn hot to work. The garboard plank was out on the starboard side of *Princess*. A cool breeze came off Pugsley Creek, and I fell asleep dreaming of an island. Any island. Like Little Corn Island, which has no taxation, no representation, nothing but the life of Riley.

Little Corn Island is a territory of the United States. Eddie Reinecke is a citizen of the United States. So am I. Riley is the guy in the saying.

Eddie Reinecke and I had an idea that we were fighting for the United States when we stumbled onto Little Corn Island. Technically we were not fighting when we ran across it; we were working. The United States was engaged in World War II.

Working and fighting were pretty much the same thing.

The way it worked, if we got killed, we were fighting. If we didn't get killed, nobody knew what the hell we were doing, least of all Eddie and I.

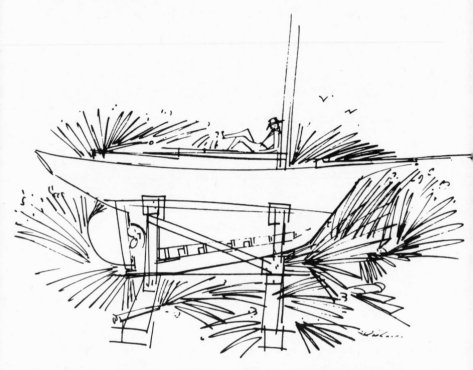

We had tried to enlist when the war started. We were told to go back to the ships we came from. That was where we were needed. That was where we could do the most good. So long as we were in the Merchant Marine, we could not enlist on account of the War Manpower Act. In order to be drafted, a sailor had to stay off ships for at least a month, during which no one else could hire him, on account of the War Manpower Act. There was no way for Eddie or me to get into the armed forces without going on the bum.

Draft or no draft, a seafaring man had to be rich or frugal to get into the armed forces. Seafaring men are hardly ever rich, and never frugal. After a big time in port, they go back to the ships where they came from.

That's what Eddie did. So did I. We went back with pleasure. You could hardly blame us—the ship was a beauty. She was a tops'l schooner designed by Herreshoff and built by Nevins. She had sailed around the world, and she had won the Bermuda race. She carried a yard on her foremast for a square sail, was a hundred feet on deck, and drew ten feet of water. The fellow that owned her must have had a lot of jack. When the war broke, he gave her to the Army. The Army gave her to us.

I was her skipper. I had orders to take her to the Canal Zone. The Army hired a bunch of guys to help me. One of them was Eddie Reinecke, Executive Officer. I gave the orders. The first order was to paint the vessel gray. Eddie turned the crew to. The crew smeared war gray all over the mahogany brightwork, the white topsides, the teak decks. I watched the process as long as I could, then went ashore and got drunk.

I have a certain affection for sailboats. I love the glassy reflection of the sea on a varnished counter. I love the gleam of the tall sticks and the light golden lines of running rigging that cross and recross the clean pattern of sail and hull. The day they smeared gray paint all over that schooner was my first taste of total war.

In a total war you employ anything handy. A schooner does the same thing. She employs the wind. The wind is handy. It's a good thing to have around a submarine, because it's quiet. There was a small auxiliary kicker, but no big engine in our schooner to tip off the ears of a submarine. She was quiet and she was lovely. She was the loveliest bottom the Army owned.

The Army owned a lot of bottoms. It had twice as many as the Navy. A great deal of the Army's tonnage consisted of small vessels like that schooner. The Army hired Merchant Marine sailors to man their bottoms, and the Navy made up the sailing orders.

There seems to have been a notion in Navy circles that small boats should stay close to shore. If small boats must go to sea, the least they can do is keep out in deep water, where they are not likely to get caught in the turbulence that bounds the land. Any canvas man will tell you that. The way the Navy orders read, it was a cinch to see what was going on. It was just a question of time before the Navy would have more tonnage than the Army and there wouldn't be any more Merchant Marine sailors.

Somehow this never bothered me. It might have been because I never bothered with sailing orders. I put them away in the drawer of the chart table and sailed to the place where I was supposed to sail, just as if it was peacetime. In that sense I was a patriot. I helped win the war. Before I had my own command I sailed with Captain Erbe, and Captain Erbe showed me how.

Louis Erbe was an old-time square-rigged skipper with a mile of pilot endorsements appended to his license. His license was the ninth issue of a master's ticket for sail and steam. They don't issue that kind of ticket anymore. The examining inspectors wouldn't know a stuns'l from a crossjack.

Erbe was a patriot, too. You can get very sentimental about your country out on the high seas. He got very sentimental. He ignored Navy orders. For every Navy order he ignored, he got two letters of commendation. The other ones were from the Army. That's where I got the idea. That's how we both survived.

The obedient were lost. They succumbed to the injunctions of the Navy and broached on reefs. Sometimes a sub will give you time to launch a boat. You can expect no such favors from a reef —and if you're in the Caribbean without a lifeboat, the fish will come and eat you. Punctured by a coral pinnacle, a vessel may release a lifeboat hours later, like an afterthought. This boat will land on a beach somewhere, like the one that landed on Little Corn Island. The natives found it. The natives drew a bonus of charred bodies in the boat they found. They wondered what the hell was going on.

The people on Little Corn Island weren't there to get away from it all; their forebearers had been dumped there by slave traders. Their only contact with the outside world had been a taciturn bird from the United States Weather Bureau who landed a couple times a year. He came and released little yellow balloons from the station on the hill to see which way they would go. They always went northwest by north—which any of the natives could have told him. The natives would have been happy to barter that information for a little talk about the outside world, but the man from the weather bureau was all business and balloons.

When the war got underway, the man with the balloons didn't come around any more. The wind still blew into the northwest by west out of southeast by east, just like it had for Henry Morgan and Christopher Columbus. Outside of that, no news was good news on Little Corn Island. It was the same way in the Merchant Marine. And it was the same on the schooner I was taking to Panama for the Army.

We left Tampa in the middle of the night and ran way out in a strong northwesterly under reefed main and jib to skirt the mine fields and Dry Tortuga. The following day the wind backed around to the west and steadied. The schooner seemed to know more about sailing than anybody on board. With any kind of a wind forward of the beam, she sailed herself. Jam the chair from the doghouse under the wheel and she would hold her course like an Iron Mike.

The weather was postcard stuff. The crew lolled about the deck like passengers on an all-expenses-paid cruise. One night, off Yucatan, they were reminded of the war when a plane made a bombing run, dropped a flare, and went away wondering. From the air, in the dark, the schooner must have looked like a sub on the surface.

I rigged a line with a lure fashioned out of a piece of towel and trailed it aft. We caught bonitas. We caught many bonitas. We caught too many bonitas. The line was rigged with a weight that took the shock when the fish struck. The weight, which was borrowed from the lead ballast used to trim ship, came near pounding a hole in the deck. Near sundown something struck the hook that drew it out straight as if it was cold rolled. Eddie tied two hooks together. The lead weight pounded the deck, and both hooks came in straight. Something was hitting those hooks hard. Three hooks held. It was a dolphin.

Nothing swims faster than a dolphin. It is impossible to estimate its speed. It can hit a hook at well over seventy miles an hour. The belly of the dolphin is a lively lemon, luminous and dappled with green dots that turn to gold as they merge into a fiery emerald. The vivid green yields to the royal blue that tops the dorsal ridge. The colors die with the dolphin, fogging like slow film. It was good eating. In the morning Little Corn Island lay off the port bow.

There was no call to stop at Little Corn Island. There was no shortage of food, water, or fuel on the schooner. Whatever need prompted me to come about and drop anchor in the silent lagoon was a personal matter between an island and a man.

The dinghy floated toward the tide line like a cloud. The sea was so clear that the little boat seemed to float suspended in midair toward the slope of the beach.

Eddie and I were hauling the dinghy up on the soft dry sand when a native came running toward us, floundering like a man in a snowdrift. He was black, and the sand was white. He was excited. He said, "Wha' hoppen, mon?"

It was the morning of January 10, 1944. The latitude was 12 8' north and longitude 80 45' west. I looked at Eddie. Eddie looked at me. Then we looked at this black guy waiting wide-eyed on the beach. We had just heard the great question of World War II.

3

My wife could tell the minute the dream set in. She'd say, "Let's take the kids and go up to the boatyard." I loved her for that.

We went over the bridge by way of a lumberyard in Brooklyn that had the most beautiful boat lumber you ever laid eyes on. We picked up a length of Sitka spruce thirty feet long without a knot or a blemish.

I asked the foreman where the branches grew. "They start at a hundred feet," he said. That stopped me. I never bothered to ask him how the tree got started. Anyway, it was nice bendy stuff. We wrapped it around the car and headed for Pugsley Creek.

My wife, Betty, held the plank while I planed, and Seth and Suzy went hunting wild animals among the mysterious tall reeds that made that beat-up old yard a wonderland for all wildlife, especially kids. They climbed through the ancient hulks that had been spared a sinking at sea.

There was another sloop abandoned in the yard. She was a thirty-footer, and, if such a thing is possible, she was in an even more disreputable condition than *Princess* had been. Her keel was rotted out. Her stem trembled to the touch. Her rudderpost was almost a memory. Her frames alone were reason enough to let her go.

Still, she was an authentic Wilbur A. Morse Friendship sloop with the original fashion piece at the bow and something of the grace that makes a beautiful thing seem endlessly in motion. Mastless and immobile, she careened through the reeds with the froth of flower like a bone in her teeth.

Whenever Betty wanted to find me, she knew where to look. I'd be back in among the reeds, staring at that relic and wondering why in hell there wasn't someone willing to have a go at her. Dreams have sister ships.

When the dream was too insistent, I'd goof off by myself and go out to Pugsley Creek. I could always find some congenial monkey out there. Someone with the dream, the syndrome, or both.

Minelli had the dream, but no boat. He worked on Jack's boat and hung around like a fifth wheel when Jack went sailing. He had to be part of something that was part of the sea.

After watching him break his back working on Jack's boat for years, somebody called Minelli a zombie. Minelli blanched. I found him later staring at that bedraggled Friendship sloop. He had to have a boat that he could call his own. Being called a zombie had sparked that need.

"You can't do it, Minelli."

"Why not?"

"You've got to strike a balance. So much work and so much fun. Working on Jack's boat was too much work for the amount of fun. It would be the same thing if you worked on my boat. But this would be all work and no fun for years."

"There would be satisfaction." Minelli had the bug.

"Look, Minelli, I was a damn fool to buy my boat. There are all kinds of new materials coming out of the laboratories. One day soon you'll buy a boat that will never need caulking, never need fixing, and damn little painting. Think of it, a boat that will never give you anything but fun."

Minelli looked at me. "Fun?" he said.

There was a long silence while he ran his hand across the scroll that said "WILBUR A. MORSE, BUILDER, FRIENDSHIP, ME." "I had fun working on Jack's boat."

"Yeah," I said, vaguely.

"What do I do now? Wait around for a chemical engineer to stamp me a plastic boat like they have in the dime store, only bigger. Is that fun?"

I looked at Minelli. Here was the descendant of Balboa, Columbus, Vespucci, dreaming of the days of his forebears while he licked the wounds of a technological revolution. "Let them make motor boats," he said.

What can you do with a guy like that? Or with a guy like John? John phoned that night. I hadn't seen him for fifteen years. Not since an evening on board *Princess* when she lay alongside Paul's Boatyard in Fort Lauderdale. We watched the little alligator that basked on the far bank of New River, and I expounded on the faults and virtues of *Princess*, the wonder of Walt Whitman, and the guts of Gertie Stein. John never forgot.

John was the boy wonder of the small-boat competitions in Florida. You would never think that a guy that big could get about on a moth sailboat. He built his own boats and sailed them, and won every race he entered. For a big bruiser, it was a thing to see. He was quick as a cat to come about, and he knew where the wind was before it blew. When the war came he went into the Air Corps. When it ended, he became a pilot on an airline running to New York.

"Is this the Joe Richards that owns *Princess?*" I allowed that it was. John came to dinner.

The world is a thing of people, of places, and of little things. The arrangement of these fragments, like the arrangement of these letters, spells the story. Looking at John while he told us of his new vessel, I had an uncanny feeling that this guy held the key to our dream island.

It was the way he went on about that boat. He had built it with a cousin who was a mathematician of top rank—an atomic scientist of unquestionable genius. They planned and plotted. They figured and connived. They built an elaborate model— and for all their know-how and skills they came up with a dory, a fiberglass miracle of technology and technique, but for all that still a dory. A great big dory that you could walk fore and aft in down below with a top hat on. Like all dorys, she would not stand up for all the cement and iron punchings in her bilge. They hauled her and attached an enormous concrete bulb on her bottom. That did it.

Now she was so heavy that it took a little lifetime to get her underway, and all the know-how they could muster to slow her down. They were planning again, this time for an air foil like the wing of a plane that would make the old sail seem as old-fashioned as sailing itself. Contemplating *Princess* while he talked, I felt as archaic as Leif Ericson.

"Tell you what," he said, looking around at our rookery. "Why don't you folks come on down to Key Biscayne for the Christmas holidays. You can have our house down there. We will come up here and use your place during the same period. My kids would love New York."

You read about this kind of thing. Here it was come true. "You've got a deal, John," I said.

Now all we had to do was wait. We had five months to think about it. John came back with pictures of Key Biscayne, insular paradise in its own right, pictures of his vessel, pictures of his kids rollicking in the Bahamian sunlight. They had all been to the islands by boat. We sat watching while the slide machine turned the wall of our New York apartment into a magic door to freedom, sunlight, surcease from snow.

I launched *Princess* that fall. The yard at Pugsley Creek had yielded at last to heavy industry and the city dump. All the boats were gone. Minelli's problem was solved by the grass fire, which swallowed the other old Friendship sloop. We hauled *Princess* briefly in Joe White's yard to recaulk a bad seam and took off for our old home at Rosenberger's City Island yard.

The nice thing about being an artist is that you have no steady job (and, incidentally, no steady money). This creates a state of permanent imbalance that any canvas man can understand. John's invitation to Florida created a vacuum in the southern sector, toward which we toppled weeks before our invitation was in effect. We arrived in Key Biscayne around the first part of December. We were taken in like long-lost cousins. The dream island suddenly seemed just beyond the hill. But *Princess* was still back in City Island, New York—a mere detail to an artist with no dough.

Our times teem with so many miracles that the spirit staggers. Nonetheless, the fact that we made it to the dream island in the Bahamas, all of us, aboard *Princess* still seems like one of the cockeyed wonders of the world.

4

I was in millinery. The way it happened was so painless, I didn't know I was in it till I was in it up to my ears.

My wife cut her hair short. Why? Because somebody else cut *her* hair short. Then she grew it out. That took longer. It took longer on all the girls. That's how I got into millinery.

The scraggly ends looked like hell—like Irish tassels on a Bristol fashion furl. What she needed was a neat little sail cover to hide the loose ends. She built one with all the know-how of a sailor's wife. She called it a chignon hat and wore it on her pony tail. Women followed her in the street. Women with post-Italian-hairdo messes. Betty came home all aglow.

"Don't stand there blinking on and off," I said. "Go sell it to Lord and Taylor." She did.

And to Saks and Bergdorf and Gimbels and on and on.

If you've got an off-beat engineering problem, take it to a sailor. I rigged a jig. An inverted bowl with a light on it. Punctured with holes, it provided a form for similarity and a key to speed. Our place turned into a sweatshop. I made another jig. The kid who delivered liquor took one into the basement of the grog store and started a subcontract business between deliveries. It was wild. Betty made them out of leopard skin, leather, chintz, gunny sack, and gossamer, and I stood around smoking a big black cigar.

Then suddenly John Charlton showed up and the bit about the dream island swamped us. We went off to Florida.

Princess was left to her own devices at Rosenberger's City Island boatyard. We lay on the white sand of Key Biscayne and stared across the Stream toward the magic island that beckons all men with boats.

Our host, who must have invented Southern hospitality, took us sailing between stints as an airline pilot. His boat, called *Aquafoil*, was a revelation. Any off-beat boat that does as well as a conventional boat is a revelation. John could better have used his talents in a moon hop or millinery. The boating business is overflowing with inventive minds, tycoons, cosmic poets, and kooks.

I made an angle out of my arm, propped my head on it, and watched Suzy and Seth make a living Serrolla out of the sun, sand, and surf. How in hell was I to take those kids back to the bitter winter of First Avenue and Fiftieth Street? I knew I couldn't—I wouldn't—and it bugged me. I sneaked off and got a job.

It was a good job. I held it for one day. Betty said, "Where have you been?"

"Working," I said with the pride of a forty-year-old kid with his first pair of long pants.

"Go to work and quit," she said. "We're going back to New York."

I quit. The boss said, "Don't you like us?"

I said, "I don't even know you. My wife wants me to lie on the beach."

He looked at me and massaged his nose. Not everybody

can have a rich wife with no money. But, after all, *Princess* was still in New York. The millinery business was still in New York; so was the art business. But what about the kids and the sun and the surf?

I lay on the beach. Christmas came, and John and his family went off to inhabit our apartment in New York. I had known the tropics and I was back. In style. The long clean sweep of beach with a lighthouse at the point was island enough for anyone. There were doctors, too, and a supermarket. There was the magic of isolation interwoven with convenience. It was an intermediate heaven.

But it wasn't the dream.

A dream island is a very personal thing. You can share it, sure, but then it isn't *it* anymore. There were nine hundred families on Key Biscayne. There were a million families on the mainland.

A long causeway led ten miles out to sea over Virginia Key —and past Bear Cut through the dense parkland to that tiny hamlet that invested the last sweet corner of the Key. It must have been somebody's dream island way back a long, long time ago.

It was seventh heaven for the kids, this old coconut plantation with palm trees soaring eighty feet into the sky and exploding in a dazzling burst of fronds. I lay puffed up with contentment and chow, floating on my back in Hurricane Harbor, staring at the sky, and wondering what in hell they were doing in New York and why. We lay in a bed of pine needles, soft and fragrant, and marveled at the architecture of the trees. We swam. We sailed. We lived.

Christmas in Key Biscayne was gone. Our friends came back from their visit to our home in New York, and the hour of departure was at hand.

"Too bad I didn't keep the job," I said to Betty.

"Yes," she said.

I got another one. A better one. We rented a little house, put the kids into school, and wondered what in hell to do about our apartment in New York, our boat in City Island, and a life in New York that suddenly was no more.

On a frenetic trip up to New York over a long weekend, I got rid of the apartment, took all our gear, millinery, art, and everything else out to a shed in Rosenberger's boatyard. I went back to Florida—and then came the boat show.

It opened at Dinner Key, just across the bay from our new home in Key Biscayne. I caught every booth.

There was one display that kept pulling me back. It was called "Kenosha Auto Transport." They moved boats. Here for sure was another fragment in the over-all plan to capture the dream island.

"How much do you want to trail a Friendship sloop from New York to Key Biscayne?" I knew it was expensive. "Roughly," I said.

The man in the booth looked at a chart, scratched his head, and said, "About two hundred and fifty dollars."

"You've got a deal," I said.

"Call me tomorrow and I'll verify it."

I called him. "Sorry," he said, "I had my figures wrong. It's more like three hundred and fifty. Call me tomorrow and I'll have it for sure."

I called tomorrow and tomorrow and tomorrow, and every tomorrow added a hundred dollars to the cost. It leveled out at six hundred and fifty dollars, which may have been a bargain for somebody, but it was to hell and gone out of reach for me.

"What's the name of the boss man in Kenosha?" I said.

"Nicholai," he said, "John Nicholai."

I wrote him a letter. It described the plight I was in. It pleaded the cause of *Princess*. It enclosed a short version of my story, and it ended by offering some money to help.

I got a wonderful letter back from Kenosha. Jack Nicholai knew all about *Princess*. He believed that *Princess* and I should be together.

It's a funny story, the story of *Princess* and her overland run from City Island to Key Biscayne, sometimes at the rate of eighty miles an hour. A sharp little rebel named Carter drove the trailer truck. They briefed him before he left with some nonsense about *Princess* being a famous boat. Carter assumed that *Princess* had been around the world. That, at the very least. Then his imagination took off.

Wherever he stopped he regaled the denizens of the local diner with wild tales about me. How I fought cannibals in the South Sea Islands. How I found sunken treasure off Zanzibar. My romance with a golden princess in Timbuktu. About the night I was assailed by hostile natives—I sprinkled tacks on the deck and watched them come and go through the peephole in the o.

The o was the o in 10 D 705, her registration number. On the starboard side a knothole in the plank coincided with the o. I had found a piece of plexiglass, ground it to the size of the knot, and plugged the hole. It made a dead port in the forepeak, a nice little source of light in that dark corner. From the outside it glinted like an ominous eye. Carter made that the basis for his wildest yarns.

One night he had a little adventure of his own. He had been rolling all day. At dusk he parked the rig and took a nap in the cab. At midnight he could have sworn that he had company. He did.

He looked out. There were pigs, hundreds of pigs, swarming below *Princess*, attracted by the stench of the sea life that clung to her bottom. They came in waves, a sea of pigs like surf, snorting, grunting, and climbing all over each other. They were all bucking for a seafood dinner, which is plenty hard to come by in the Carolina mountains.

"I gave them a blast," said Carter. "You ought to see them scramble."

Carter called me from Lauderdale. I drove up and waited for him at the Cloverleaf north of Miami.

They came down the highway sparkling in the sun. *Princess*, her bowsprit jutting out over the cab in a motherly gesture, was squatting on a jerry-built cradle on the flatcar. She was as beautiful as ever.

We came over the long sweep of causeway that separates Key Biscayne from the mainland, and she saw the bay, the long blue bay of Biscayne that would be her home port for many years. Carter parked the rig in front of our house out on the key and promptly went to sleep on the glider in the Florida room.

I walked around the trailer and stared up at my baby. I couldn't have been more dumbfounded if she had come from the moon.

She had sailed thousands of miles. She had swung sixty feet in the air at the end of a steel cable before she rounded Hatteras on a freighter. She had been dragged across a half mile of dry reef by a mighty tug, and now she had just completed thirteen hundred miles of highway travel through nine states and at a breakneck rate of speed. She was a lady with a wild past. And a wonderful future.

And she was handy. They may not know it out in Kenosha, Wisconsin, but when I opened her hatch I found the cabin jammed with every stick of furniture, every household appliance, every book, painting, and possession we owned. Even the hats. Good old Eddie Rosenberger!

5

For the record, a dream island has never been the sole objective of my life.

My aim was to get my kids through school, keep my married life on an even keel, paint some pictures, and keep out of hock.

If I could do all that and squeeze in the moment of magic that lies like a luminous halo on the silent reaches and secret recesses of a tropical island, I felt I would have had my portion. I had a damn good start.

Princess was back in Florida, ready for another go at it. So was I. So was the whole family. Not only that, but I had a job that would keep us until the moment of departure. It looked like we would really make it this time.

And if we didn't, Key Biscayne, where we lived, was so close to being paradise that we were inclined to shrug off the ultimate island as one of those improbable baubles, like an Hispano Suiza or a castle in Spain.

After all, we did have *Princess*, big as life out in front of the house on a huge trailer, with the man from Kenosha blanked out on our glider snoring his head off.

While he slept, *Princess* disgorged her cargo. Drawing table, lamps, mattresses, pots and pans, ironing board, books, toys, pillows, boxes of winter clothes, ladies' hats, children's gear, bicycle, and bilge pump. *Princess* had everything but her engine. Her poor old Kermath, after fifteen years in my service and Lord knows how many years in others', had finally died. I had drained her, but the cake of rust that clogged her innards was porous. It became a rusty chunk of ice. She had cracked her block that last winter in New York. *Princess* was once again the simple sailing vessel that Wilbur A. Morse intended. Which was no way to get to an island.

She had to have an engine. She had to have a new mast. The old one was beyond repair. She still had to have a new keel, and garboards. Lord know what all she had to have before we could take off in good conscience.

The Gulf Stream, buffered by a barrier reef, lay demure and gentle off to the east. The million maelstroms it contained were swept along in a torrential flow. It was no place for a boat with a leaky keel.

Carter, the man from Kenosha, awoke at last, rested from the travail of ferrying *Princess* overland from New York. I had scraped the seafood dinner from the bottom of my vessel, and she soon had a coat of paint.

We all had lunch, Carter jumped into his cab, and the big diesel banged off with a mighty snort to Santana's across the Bay.

Princess was launched by sling, just like hundreds of boats are launched every day at Dinner Key.

The cradle, empty of its burden, came apart like a house of cards. Without *Princess*, the eight hundred pounds of iron in her bilge, and the chain to hold it together, the whole deal would have taken off. *Princess* was living lucky.

With the boat back in the water, we breathed a sigh. There she was, right in Biscayne Bay, with scarcely a dribble of the clear blue-green in her bilge.

We said "so long" to Carter. Now we had to get the old girl back across the Bay to Hurricane Harbor.

With a borrowed outboard and a dinghy to clamp it to, we started out across the Bay the next morning against the whisper of an easterly. The whisper began to talk out loud, and by midmorning it was hollering.

I had known the wind to come up suddenly in the flat lengths of the tropics, but it didn't have to do it the very first day, when Princess had no sails to handle it and no power to oppose it.

A man, like a tree, or the configuration of a coast, is conditioned by the acts of nature. The tyrannical pirates of this area were rendered mad by the ferocity of the wind and the dogged insistence of the seas.

Imagine the frustrations of a privateer aiming to make port in a leeward island. Sailing three months in the Atlantic circle, out around with the Stream, back down with the Trades, and on up with the Gulf Stream again, only to miss the island by a mile and have to go the three-month ordeal all over again.

No wonder they dropped one hook, kedged another hook between long boats, and inched back that mile against the flow of the current. No matter if it took three weeks to beat back that last long mile.

I knew that morning from the violence of Biscayne Bay that if we made it to the islands, it would be by guile and not by brute strength.

Getting across five miles of Bay was suddenly rendered impossible by the mercurial nature of two lovely elements—the crystal-clear water and the dust-free air.

A guy came by in a speedboat, threw us his ski line, and snapped us into Hurricane Harbor. Too bad he wasn't around to do it for Blackbeard and Henry Morgan.

Tethered to the mangrove roots with a stern hook in the holding muck of the harbor, *Princess* was a lovely centerpiece in the pines and fronds and the fading light of a February afternoon. Monday morning I went back to work.

It was a time of stocktaking, of contemplation, of planning for the push. *Princess* would have to be dry-docked. I would need a month or more to get her ready for the crossing.

Who knows, it might take a year. And who really cared? My wife had an expensive tan in lieu of a mink stole, and the kids were living like millionaires, and almost as sassy.

The big break came at last. I got fired. I was fired by an imaginative guy named Jack Green, who said, "Here's a great big art job—go home and do it."

I did.

In three weeks the art job was done. I had the bundle. Off we went to Dunn's Boatyard with *Princess* at the end of a nylon cable and John Charlton's wonder boat popping away up through the maze of vessels that lined Miami River. *Princess* came regretfully up out of the river and found a corner of the yard all for herself. I could hardly wait to get at that leaky old keel. I had most of the screws out of her garboard before the bottom was even dry.

The next day the garboards were off. I reinforced the chocks and got ready to drop that old oak keel right out of the bottom. I sold the iron ballast for ten bucks to a local junk dealer. He came looking for more. It was Swedish iron in its purest form —the equivalent of the finest tool steel. To a guy without a blast furnace, it was still just junk. So was the keel.

When I finally got it out, I saw the terrible reason for my years of pumping. The keel was so porous that it acted like a sponge, squeezing water into the boat with every rock and roll. It was fit only for termites; no self-respecting torredo would touch it. *Princess* shivered, swaying on chocks above the ugly spectacle. I went looking for a timber for a new keel.

I didn't have far to go. There it was, right on Harbor Drive in Key Biscayne, a block from our house—a great big mangrove log thirty feet long and just as straight as a die. There was another one, but smaller, for a keelson. They had been unearthed in the process of laying a new water main on the Key. Bulldozed underground ten years before, there was no sign of rot or blemish on them after those years in the muck. I was going to have a keel to end all keels. A keel for a thousand years. A keel born and raised in salt water that would fight off the attacks of torredoes as well in deadwood as it did in live. Now, if I could only get it milled.

It was as hard as that Swedish iron.

I don't know how old Blackbeard or Henry Morgan were with an adz, but I was no match for the sinews of that wood with a hand tool.

Meanwhile, up at the boatyard, *Princess*, sans keel, lay suspended in space. I went about my business.

One night early in spring Betty woke me. "Joe," she said, "you've got to get those mangrove logs out of the yard. They stink."

They did. Like a sewer. An evil, sulfurous miasma hovered over them like the breath of hell. I hauled on my pants.

Somehow I managed to sling an old shroud from *Princess* around the logs and drag them with the old jalopy to an empty lot near the harbor. Then I went back to bed.

At four o'clock I jumped out of bed in a panic. "My God," I said. "Somebody will steal those logs!"

By five o'clock they were back in the yard, nice and safe and smelly as ever. You have to be tough. Like Blackbeard. Like Henry Morgan.

By ten o'clock they were back in the empty lot by the harbor.

When I wasn't too busy, I went looking for a place to have those mangrove members milled. A saw big enough was hard to find. So was a sawyer who would tackle mangrove in his mill. There was a little easy-going guy who made noises like he might, down the river at the Miami shipbuilding place. I dragged the smaller log over before he could change his mind. "Dragged" is just the word for it. It was too heavy to lift. Mangrove has the reputation of being the third hardest wood in the world.

I dragged it at the end of a cable all the way down Crandon Boulevard, which had a gravel surface set in tar like an endless belt of sandpaper. Held in position by two stumps of sawn branches, the log ran down the highway until it had a dead flat side, which was perfect for the table of the saw. Where the highway police were that day I never will know. The road was no more to me than a shimmering highway leading to the isle of dreams.

Over in town the traffic got too thick. I had to jack up that big red dog and go the rest of the way with the log on top.

It went through the giant band saw just as nice as you please, I thought. The little sawyer didn't. He told me why when I came around with the big log for the keel.

"Hell, no," said Charlie, "I wouldn't touch it. The last one took the temper out of the band-saw blade."

"But Charlie," I said, "I've got the other one in the boat for a keelson and I've got to have this one to finish the job."

"I've got problems, too," he said.

I left the big mangrove log alongside the shed and went looking for bigger and better sawmills. I found one, too. After more than a month of looking.

"Take it down to Miami Wood Treating," the man said, "They've got a steam saw down there that's big enough to cut anything."

I went, with the mangrove log tied to the bumpers fore and aft and with me sitting way over to keep the car from capsizing. Seventeen miles.

Talk about being affable—the man in the office of Miami Wood Treating must have been the head "treater." He met me at the gate, all smiles.

"Just put it here," he said, waltzing around.

"Stand clear," I said, letting it go. It went.

The man jumped the wrong way. The log landed on his

toe. I was beside myself with empathy, sympathy, sorrow, and chagrin.

He hopped around like a chicken with its head off. "It's all right," he said.

"Let me see it," I said. "Let me see it." He simmered down, unlaced his shoe, and drew off his sock. There was a little blood. "It's nothing," he said.

"But look at your toenail," I said. The big toenail was standing straight up, attached to the toe by a shred.

"That's nothing," he said.

"Nothing!"

"Yeah, nothing." He ripped off his other shoe. Then the sock. The other toenail was standing up the same way.

"Come around Tuesday," he said, "—we'll mill your log."

6

The Miami Wood Treating Company is not an educational institution. It is a big lash-up dedicated to the task of preparing trees to become fine upstanding telephone poles, but you can learn something down there.

There is a tremendous steam boiler under an open shed with the chimney poking through the roof. The boiler is fed with wood scraps. It powers a reciprocating engine that turns a great wheel of blade alongside a geared carriage. It also supplies pressure for a long tank which drives the asphalt tar deep into the grain of the wood. If it wasn't for the bugs that infest the land as well as the sea, the whole outfit wouldn't be worth the powder to blow it to hell.

So far as my mangrove log was concerned, there was no

need for tar or pressure. Nature had contrived to build into that wood a combination of sulfur, salt, and tannic acid, a stinky bone-hard log destined to discourage the most ravenous appetite any old wood borer could muster. It had to make one hell of a keel.

As far as the stink was concerned, I couldn't care less. It would always be under water.

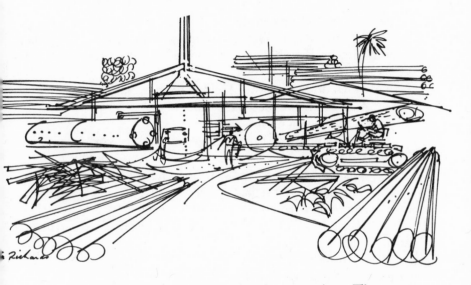

I was down at the plant Tuesday morning. The steam boiler was all stoked up. The head sawyer turned a valve, and the saw blade began to spin. The great carriage geared to the track came up with an imaginary log.

The man with the wild toenails was keeping the books. A man by the name of Moses was sitting on the high seat of a tractor with steel claws for picking up logs.

The head sawyer gave the high sign. Moses rumbled over with the tractor and picked up my precious mangrove log. It came down on the geared carriage. The body of tree was cleated down, a lever was pulled by the sawyer, and the great saw dug into the wood with the carriage feeding it to the teeth with inexorable determination.

A segment fell away. The log came back. The sawyer reached over and felt the heat of the saw blade with the back of his hand. Moses rolled the log over, flat side down. The sawyer adjusted the gauge to an eight-inch cut and off it went again. Hard, hard wood against carbon steel.

Four times it happened, and four times the sawyer felt that whirling blade with the back of his hand. Moses watched him leaning on the handle of his cant-hook.

It came out a thing of beauty—dark, red, square, and clean. Moses let the cleats go and helped me drag the timber off the carriage.

"What do I owe you?" I said to the head sawyer.

"You don't owe me a damn thing."

"What do you mean?"

"You can't use that piece of wood," said the sawyer.

"Why not?"

"That's not mangrove." I froze. The sawyer turned away.

I had already installed a keelson of the same stuff. If it wasn't mangrove, what could it be?

"What is it?" I said, tailing the sawyer as he went under the shed.

He turned. "That's Australian pine," he said. "It will rot out under you before you can turn around."

The voice had spoken. A feeble protest found its way to my lips.

"But . . ." I said and gave up. This was the head sawyer of a mill that had been cutting local wood for years. It would be damn foolishness to argue.

I turned away and helped Moses throw my log on the scrap heap. My jalopy, crunching softly down the sawdust road, took me out to the highway and home.

It was one of the darkest days I have ever known. Months of work. Months. Months of searching had gone into the business of milling those logs. The smaller log, presumed to be mangrove, had already been milled and installed as a keelson. The agony of milling both members, the sheer stupidity of it. Australian pine. Holy crow.

The light of early afternoon playing on the tender top of the blue bay, the laughter of my kids, the commiseration of my wife, nothing could mitigate the pain. It seemed the hand of fate was set against me, that the road to the ultimate island was cut off forever.

I wandered around in a kind of fat fog, half blind to the highly advertised beauty of the Key, the copywriter's caress of fronds, the PR caper about sunlight against pastel walls, and all the gobbledegook relative to purple paths that lead to silver sands and the limpid lousy sea. I ended up at the home of my friend John Charlton. John, who knew all about mangrove.

Jewel, his pretty wife, was ironing clothes. The kids were hooked to a TV tube. John was on a trip.

"Jewel," I said, "I guess John was wrong."

"John wrong?" said Jewel, "I doubt that."

"I mean about the log."

"You mean the mangrove log?"

"Yeah," I said, "I had them milled. The small one is installed in the boat. I threw the big one away."

"Why?"

"The head sawyer at the mill said that it's Australian pine."

"John will love to hear about that," said Jewel.

Jewel was wrong. John damn near flipped when he heard it.

"Joe," he said, staring like he meant it, "I spent all my boyhood ranging with a hatchet and a transit through these woods. I've hacked at everything that grows. My father was a civil engineer. He had a hand in building this area. I know what I'm talking about. That log of yours is mangrove. Go back and get it. You couldn't have a better keel."

I didn't sleep half the night, fretting. Had the hot maw of the boiler down at the wood-treating plant devoured my mangrove? Would it be there in the morning?

Dawn came; pretty as a postcard: goofy palm trees against tropical clouds piled up like a four-dollar sundae. I took off down through Crandon Park, for which the causeway to the Key was built. The cool sea paled to dead white in the tiny coves around Bear Cut. I was too concerned to be hungry, but my eyes drank in the bay for a blue breakfast. I scuttled across the causeway past Virginia Key in that tired old car and joined Dixie Highway going south.

I was almost the first one at the wood-treating plant. Moses opened the gate for me. "Moses," I said, edging over to the scrap pile, "I came to get my timber." There it was, right on top of the heap.

Moses eyed me and shook his head. He said, "I told the boss. I told him that that wood was no Australian pine."

"Well, what wood is it, Moses?"

"Man," he said, "that wood is cherry wood."

"*Cherry* wood?"

"That's right, cherry wood."

"Well, Moses, according to a friend of mine who ought to know, that piece of wood is called mangrove."

"Don't care what they calls that wood down here, but up in Alabama, cherries grow on that wood." He looked at me with the fierce conviction of the statue of Moses by Michaelangelo. Then he helped me tote the timber to the car.

I did owe the head sawyer something for cutting that piece of wood. Like money.

Something made me feel that money just wouldn't be right. It had to be something that would suggest that he might be wrong. Like a photostat of a degree in forestry from an agricultural college, or maybe a book. I was fresh out of photostats.

I left a copy of my book about *Princess*. Moses was impressed. He promised to give it to the head sawyer. I took off with the new keel.

All the way to Dunn's boatyard, where *Princess* was hauled, my magic island loomed like a double exposure in the sudden heat of late summer.

Back at the boatyard I showed my prize to Wes Hempstead, his old man, and his uncle, all seasoned boatbuilders. Then I stowed the precious member in the shade of *Princess*, covered it with a coat of Cuprinol to keep it from checking, and went back home.

It wasn't till the cool of late fall that I was able to get back to the boat. It was wonderful to go out to the boatyard in the dead of winter and work in the shade of *Princess* just as if it was a June day along the coastal hills of Long Island.

I was among friends. The Hempsteads, who were running the yard, were a Connecticut boatbuilding family that had gone into the salvage, boat repair, and storage business on Miami River. There wasn't a power tool I couldn't borrow.

As I jacked the great mangrove keel up to the keelson and set an enormous mangrove knee at the sternpost, old man Hempstead came by, got down on one knee, and peered along the line scribed for the rabbet.

"You've got a dandy piece of wood there," he said.

Hempstead knew about all the agony connected with getting that mangrove member milled. "Just about every old-timer in these parts has looked at that piece of wood," he went on. "Wasn't a one that didn't agree that it was mangrove."

"I had a time with the mill man," I said. "He claimed that it was Australian pine, which is hard enough but rots like hell."

"I don't know about that," said Hempstead. "They say Australian pine makes a fine keel if you keep it under salt water."

I quit for a minute and looked at all the old boats rotting in the yards. "If it's mangrove, it should last for a thousand years."

"That it should," said Hempstead.

"I know where there's an even bigger one. It's out on the Key. Do you want me to bring it to you?"

"What for?"

"Make a wonderful keel. Last a thousand years."

"Now why in hell would I want that," said the professional boatbuilder, "when the rest of the boat will be gone in thirty years?"

7

For *Princess*, an island was the pot of gold at the end of the great circle of sailing. Now at last she seemed sound enough to have a go at it.

She had a new keel. She had a new keelson. She had more natural mangrove knees and floors bolted to them than she needed or deserved. Not even Wilbur A. Morse had done that much for her. She had everything but a means of propulsion.

Princess had no mast. She was innocent of engine. She was a barge, a float, a dock. I had to give her a sense of direction, a will to live like a boat. I bought her an engine.

It made her happy. It made me happy. It made the bird who sold me the engine delirious.

It was a wild-looking red dog with an enormous upright dimension. It had valves in the head, an incredible bore, and a gigantic stroke. The valves were hung on the side and there were pipes, springs, and gizmos all over. It was a plumber's dream, a study in dimensional impressionism, or both.

I was formally introduced to this monster by the yard foreman. He was as suave as Duveen. He must have recognized in me an affinity for antiques, curios, objets d'art. It was a slow courtship. I had other pressing things on my mind. Like that damned bronze bolt that I had pressed down through the mangrove keelson and keel—almost. It got stuck.

It wouldn't come through. It wouldn't back out. Morse would have left it there for a drift.

With a passion for perfection (and a solid day's work) I managed to extract it. It took a twenty-ton jack and a fierce groan from the sinews of that wood. I should have left it there.

I should have left the engine there, too. The owner had removed it from his converted Navy launch. Hopefully, he asked a hundred and fifty dollars for it.

Suddenly I forked over the dough.

He jumped. Then he hung his head and mumbled something about a new pump. "She heats up," he said.

"I know all about water pumps," I said, letting him off the hook. "I own an old boat."

The engine was an old Doman. They were great little engines, known the world over. Some of them are probably still running on the Yangtze, the Nile, and the Mississippi. They never wear out. They hardly ever quit. After the outfit that made them was sold, the engine came to be known as the Falcon.

Whatever the name, it had plenty of compression and no play in the bearings. Best of all, the valves were out in the open, where you could kick them if they got stuck. All you had to do was jump on the rocker arms and away she'd go.

Off she went. Right in the shed at the boatyard. I ran it for a minute with a soup can of gas. Then I gave the man the money. He never looked me in the eye again.

After the usual all-night vigil in the river while the boat

was adjusting to her new members, I started up the old clunker. The guy who sold me the engine was long gone. It was a good thing, too. The engine was like to burn up.

It didn't figure. The water pump was in perfect shape. The cooling chambers were clear. There was no obstruction. I went home baffled, dug up the papers that came with the engine, and pored over the parts list.

Suddenly I saw it, right on the picture of the engine: a round knob at the intake. There was nothing like that on my engine. It was listed as a horizontal check valve. I picked one up from a plumber in the morning for a buck and a half and stuck it on the intake line, and the engine began to drink water. I had a bargain.

I began to live for that engine. There was nothing else to monkey around with. No mast. No sails. Nothing. Just an old Doman—pardon me, Falcon—engine that sipped a gallon of gas an hour, was rated at twelve, and probably developed forty horsepower. I had done well by *Princess*.

So had my friend John. In a grand gesture of respect for the original character boats, he had come by with his trusty power sander, ground the deck and the cabin top to a pure finish, and covered it with mat glass. Then he poured on all the resin it would sop up. John would pretend to take money to do the job and then go out and spend it all on resin and glass. Thanks to him, I could forget about the deck.

Running down the river with the rest of the fishing boats, skimming under the bridges without a blast or a bellow, I decided to become a fisherman. To hell with sailing. Too much trouble.

I had the right boat for it, too. Ten-foot beam. Twenty-five feet long and only three feet of draft without ballast. She was fast in the water, steady in a blow, and altogether just right for an old geezer like me.

Just to make sure she stayed that way, I cut the king plank where the mast used to go through the deck and installed a sizable hatch. This was a must on a motorboat. The kids could crawl out forward in case of fire.

I went fishing. I bought every damn lure they made—and gave them all up for a #3 silver spoon that seems to be the one most fish like to have in their mouth when they meet the Great Fishmaker. I caught fish.

Sometimes it was a big mackerel that spoke Spanish. (I don't.) Then it would be a misguided congregation of blues. One day I got into a school that was so big I could have walked on their backs.

I couldn't haul them in fast enough. I never saw such a passion for eternity. I ran around Biscayne Bay, pulling them into the afterworld so fast that my arms ached. They hit the lure the instant it hit the water. They grabbed it in the air before it hit the water. They would have grabbed my thumb.

Suddenly I had the ultimate fish—the one you dream about—right on the end of a five hundred-pound test nylon hand line. Pulling just as hard as I could. Oh, baby!

It yawed at breakneck speed back and forth behind the boat, turning its great brown and white belly as it slewed. I couldn't tell what it was, but I was determined to land it. There were all kinds of plans and alternatives on board, but no gaff.

I began to head slowly toward the harbor, where I could beach *Princess* on a sand spit, jump ashore from the bow, and work that fish into shallow water.

I almost made it, when *whammo!*—the fish did an acrobatic flip, snapped a kink in the leader, and broke loose.

It broke my heart. I lost the big fish, and I lost my lure. The big fish went off to bask along some island strand.

The acid of the sea and of himself would erode the hook in three days and he would be free—free to live some more and smirk at little fish darting for their lives in the lucid depths of a Bahamian cove.

It served me right. I didn't need all that fish. I tied the boat to a mooring in Hurricane Harbor and went looking for a mast. I had to go and find that fish, or any other big fish. I had to find a lonely island in the sun.

There were all kinds of guys with the same idea. Like Hobart Cook, who had everything but was bound to find an island. An island in the Mediterranean. He had just bought a boat to find it with. She was a hundred-foot ketch, and she drew better than ten feet of water. Her name was *Symphony*, and she was being re-rigged over on Miami Beach when I came by looking for a mast.

The yard manager said, "Why don't you talk to Mr. Cook. He is stepping new sticks in his boat. He may be willing to let you have the old mizzen."

I went looking for Mr. Cook. I climbed the long ladder to the deck of that great bird of a vessel and stood in awe of her lines, her sheer, the teak, the mahogany, the workmanship, and the splendor. But no Mr. Cook. "You'll have to call him on the phone," said the yard boss.

I called Mr. Cook. I got him right in his cabin aboard the *Symphony*. I outlined my problem. "What kind of a boat do you have?" said Mr. Cook.

"I have a Friendship sloop."

"A Friendship sloop," said Cook. "What's her name?"

"*Princess*."

"Are you the guy that does all that writing about the boat?"

"I guess maybe I am."

"Hell, yes," he said, "you can have the mizzen."

"How much do you want for it?" I asked.

"Oh, any amount you want to pay."

"I'm a little broke right now."

"You can pay me any time you want to," Cook came back.

This began to look like the kind of negotiation that was made to order for me—"Pay any amount and pay it any time."

"I'll be over to get the mast," I said.

What I meant was, right now, before he could change his mind. I needed help.

It was Saturday. I roused Percy Manley, my neighbor with the ever-ready smile. Snapped him right out of his catnap. We headed for the harbor.

Princess seemed to sense something big. Her engine started at the first pull, and we headed out in a gusty gale for Miami Beach. It rained now and again. We ran up the bay under all the causeways and bridges. We ran afoul of a sand spit, ran aground, backed her off, and kept going. By three o'clock we were alongside Purdy Avenue on the Beach.

Hobart Cook was on the dock looking up at his great dream boat. I introduced Percy Manley and I introduced myself. I gave him a copy of *Princess–New York*. That book was getting to be one hell of a calling card.

"Where's the mast?" I asked.

"You'll find it over there under the shed."

It was there all right. All forty feet of it. The most beautiful hollow spar I had ever seen. It was on the hefty side, but it was complete with English cast bronze track, stays as big as your thumb in diameter, stainless-steel turnbuckles, roller reefing gear, a hollow boom with an inset aluminum track, and a special gooseneck. There must have been several thousand dollars tied up in that rig. I knew I could never afford to buy it. I looked at it sadly, wishing I could. Then I went back to level with the man.

I talked to him in the lovely saloon of the *Symphony*.

"That's a beautiful rig," I said. "I could never afford to buy it."

He looked at me. "Can you use it?"

"Of course I can use it."

"Well, go ahead and take it."

"You mean, just like that?"

"Yes, just like that." Hobart Cook held up the book I had presented to him. "You were going to give me this book, weren't you?"

Percy and I carried the mast to *Princess* and made it fast. We had a fair wind going back to the Key, and we even caught a fish. But before we left I went back and inscribed the book:

> *To Hobart Cook and* Symphony,
> *whose mizzen is now our main,*
> *gratefully,* Princess *and Joe Richards.*

8

I now had the pieces to make the dream. I had a mast for the boat. I had an engine for the boat. I had the boat. All I had to do was put the pieces together. The dream island waited somewhere east of Key Biscayne. Way out in the blue green.

There were interruptions. Little things like making a living. Buying a house. Sweating out a siege with an orthodontist. A tonsillectomy.

If I had been alone, I would have been lolling on that island long since.

You can travel faster if you travel alone. You can travel farther. You won't travel as well. The bigger the audience, the more convincing the show. The sea is an eternal prima donna. She has to have a sounding board. The family supplied it.

I could see the way the kids bounced to the irascibility of

brine, the morning light, the alchemy of mist. Their fun was the payoff for the pain.

Surprisingly enough, they were willing to help. The girl was the shipmate, maybe because she wanted to show her love for her old man or because girls are natural homemakers. Suzy kept the cabin neat, the lines coiled down. Seth goofed off, hunting lobsters on the harbor bottom.

We talked about the big adventure. About the emulsion of gay blue and terror called the Gulf Stream. About sailing vessels waltzing around in its insane embrace. There were five hundred in a single year wrecked along this coral strand.

Princess went out under power to Fowey Rocks to look around. We took a pounding in a dead calm. Green seas out of nowhere smashed across the deck. My wife said, "We better believe it."

We paid in pummeling for a close-up of the lighthouse. Back in Hurricane Harbor, we thought of a square-rigged ship in her death throes, of the jungle of twisted shrouds, torn canvas, and cordage. Of spars timbered, smashed bulwarks, and the ugly crunch of reef. We took a second look at what we had between ourselves and the deep.

The planks were fine. The keel, horn timbers, stem, and sternpost were dandy. The frames, replaced more than twenty years before, were almost gone. All but the ones aft that old man Kretzer had steamed up out of sour oak back in City Island. God rest him. They were solid.

All the rest were either cracked at the chine or fragmented at the floor. They had to go.

Suzy was all set to pitch in and help with any new foolishness that Daddy could dream up. We decided to reframe *Princess* right in the water. Maybe it had never been done before. We were all set to try. There were reasons.

The boatyard was hot, dirty, and expensive. It was also too far away. The key to the whole operation was that wonderful recent invention, the diving mask. The job went off like a frogman campaign.

Princess was drawn in along a sandy bank and lashed to the mangroves. The idea was to replace one frame at a time to keep her famous shape intact.

A lumberyard in Coral Gables came up with a quantity of oak strips two inches wide and better than a quarter of an inch thick. They had been milled for a boatbuilder. Elated with our luck, we bought all we could carry and dragged them out to the Key.

The first step was to remove one frame. That was a cinch. A couple of saw cuts, and the frame split right out with a rap from a hammer and chisel. The fastenings were left undisturbed, poking right up into the boat.

I went under *Princess* with a mask and a handful of tapered wooden plugs.

Suzy tapped the screws from the inside and I caught them on the outside, one at a time. I replaced each gushing hole with a wooden plug. We shipped barely a bucket of water. Back in the boat, I sawed off the protruding points of the plugs and pushed the first oak lamination down into place.

Suzy brushed a coat of waterproof glue on top of the first lamination and down went the second lamination. Another coat of glue on top of that and the third lamination was forced into place.

We wedged the new frame down from the overhead, and to hold it in place I went out and under, pulled the plug at the chine, and drilled a hole clean through with a quarter-inch bit. A quarter-inch bronze bolt went into the old screw hole in the chine plank and through the laminations of the frame. Suzy put the nut on the bolt and drew it up tight with a wrench. Seth came up with four lobsters, and we went home to dinner.

The next day we found that the glue had set and the frame was stiff. I went under again with a hand drill and a screwdriver and replaced all the plugs with bronze screws. Standing on the bottom it was cool, comfortable, and even calm. I replaced most of the screws with my nose out of water. The mask solved the problem at the keelson. We got good at it. We replaced two frames in a day. That's the way to work in the summertime in Florida. We had to work fast if we had any idea about getting to the island that summer.

We were still working by the time the kids had to go back to school. The mast turned out to be much too fat. You can't plane forever on a hollow mast without ending up with nothing but the hole. I quit in time, sold the mast for forty dollars, and went hunting for a thinner one.

About the time I latched onto that great big mast, the engine began to kick up. I've noticed that kind of thing about people. Inanimate things should be above all that.

The mast was a lively piece of Norwegian pine, and the engine was a heavy-duty rock crusher that shook the hell out of the hull when she wasn't hitting on both cylinders. Sometimes she wouldn't hit on either cylinder. Sometimes she purred. You never knew. At least, *I* never knew.

I tried to check it out. I had the carburetor rebuilt. I bought a new carburetor. Still the same old jazz. Sometimes she would run. Sometimes she wouldn't. The spark was beyond reproach. It would jump almost an inch.

It got to be a real headache. We would go out for an afternoon spin and most of the time I was down below, cranking, changing spark plugs, cussing the day it was born and I was born. My mood enveloped the family. That engine damn near broke up a marriage.

I did know something about an engine after all the years. She did have compression and she was in time. Then why in hell did she run and not run, purr and suddenly give up? I thought that maybe, when I sold the mast, the engine would behave. No such luck. If it had nothing to do with the age-old feud between power and sail, it had to be something else.

But what? Maybe, I thought, maybe it's the magneto. I knew it couldn't be, but there was nowhere else to look.

It was a Saturday morning that I took the magneto to the doctor, an old Bosch dealer in the old part of town. He picked up the little black dog and clamped it to the bench, put a pulley on the armature, connected the wires to a gap, and started up the

301

motor. There was a rheostat to set the speed, and a great speedometer on the wall.

At two hundred revolutions there was the big fat spark. At three hundred revolutions, nothing. At four hundred revolutions, nothing. At five hundred revolutions there was that big fat spark again. That's the way it went all the way up to fifteen hundred revolutions. Off again, on again. I had a real screwball for a magneto. It was the story of my life.

"Can you fix it?"

"I don't even know what's wrong with it, and I may never know."

"Better give it back to me." At least now I know what to expect. Not everyone can have an idiotic magneto. I was determined to hang on to this one. It was the smartest thing I ever did.

The magneto was cured. Completely. It was cured by Mr. Henry Shellenberger, a retired auto mechanic who went into the pool-service business out on Key Biscayne. Shelly is my kind of Einstein, Fermi, Steinmetz. A small-town mechanic with a touch of cosmic genius.

His diagnosis was simple, direct, unequivocal. He said, "The spring in the distributor has lost its snap. Take it out, straighten it out, and put it back. Then give the points another five thousands."

I did what he said. Then I put the magneto back on. The engine never missed another beat. It ran without a suggestion of a miss for years and years. It ran to hell and gone. It took on an aura of immortality. Nothing could stop it. Neither dirt in the distributor, water everywhere, or complete neglect. That old engine even helped me find the best damn mast you ever laid eyes on.

We were up the Miami River looking when I spotted a yawl alongside that was owned by a retired sea captain. Its masts had been covered with fiberglass. Both of them. The main had snapped right above the boom from some old imperfection that had festered under the glass.

The mizzen, being of the same vintage as the main, was suspect. The mizzen was discarded, and that whole section of the boat was given over to the damndest-looking fiberglass back porch you ever saw.

The vessel was a graceful forty-footer with the lines of an ocean racer, but with that thingamabob on the stern she looked real comfortable in a miserable kind of a way.

I asked the captain what had happened to the mizzen.

"There it is on the dock."

I went ashore and looked at it. It was just the right size, about thirty-four feet over all. It was covered with two layers of fiberglass, so there was no telling what the condition of the wood might be, or even what kind of wood. Here was the real pig in the poke. "What do you want for it?" I said.

"Dollar a foot." I might have guessed his answer. I had to take a chance. Even if it had a spot of rot here and there, I figured to cure it with a wooden fish and the new miracle glue. I shelled out thirty-four dollars.

He was so anxious to get rid of that mast, he offered to tote it out to the key in a borrowed motor boat.

I declined his offer. *Princess* took off with the doubtful mast as deck cargo.

The fiberglass came off like sections of stove pipe, and as heavy. Underneath it was a pristine spar of Maine spruce. Beautiful and unblemished, it had been wrapped in fiberglass like a Christmas present. *Princess* had a mast.

We were almost ready to go.

9

Max Brown is a friend. He is also a businessman. Max the business-man, with the best interests of both of us at heart, dragged me as far from the dream island as I could get. I dragged the family with me.

Up to the time Max came to Key Biscayne, life was a matter of making a living, rebuilding an old Friendship sloop, and taking advantage of whatever fate and nature had to offer. The ultimate aim was an island.

A palm tree on the island would help. A secure cove for *Princess* would be acceptable. And all the fish we could eat. We had a right to expect the fish. What we got was Max Brown.

Max was director of a big soap company. He came to Miami for a convention of soap manufacturers. There was an art gallery near the hotel where the convention was being held. A painting of mine hung in that gallery. Max saw the painting.

It took him back twenty-five years, to an old mansion in New York. Max and I and some assorted people had occupied the top floor of the mansion. It was a great place. You could look right over the top of Charley Schwab's palace, all the way down the river. A majestic sweep of city, shipping, and shore.

Somewhere in the warp and woof of this fabric there was a cut-rate boatyard where *Princess* was hauled. It was a long winter. In the spring we went sailing—Max and I and the girls.

Twenty-five years is a long time. The picture that Max was looking at in the gallery was *Princess* in full career. *Princess* nestled in Cos Cob. Becalmed off Port Jeff. Raft-up and reflection. That's the one Max bought.

We met in the posh place and talked about other times. "How in hell do you make a living down here?" said Max.

"You've got to be flexible."

"How flexible?"

"I paint. I write. I make movies."

"What kind of movies?"

"Little commercials. I invented a gizmo that records the process of art."

"How does it work?"

"Very simple. I draw with a magic marker on the lighted side of tracing paper and photograph it with a movie camera from the other side."

"Isn't there some sort of shadow?"

"Sure there is. But I got rid of it. That's the gizmo." I went out to my car, got some footage, and projected it for Max.

"Hey, that's great! We could use this kind of thing. Let me take this film to Philadelphia."

"With my blessings." He went.

So did we, three weeks later. *Princess* was put in wet storage up the river. The house on Key Biscayne was rented to a newly arrived Cuban refugee whose island had been taken away from him. The Cuban patriot confided that he had fifty grand in gold and jewels buried on his island. He was going back for sure.

We had a gold mine, too. That's what Max told us. We went to Philadelphia to dig. We dug for a solid year. All we got was a dozen Indian arrowheads that Seth found on a farm we rented, and a cow by the name of Mary. Suzy spent all her waking hours on Mary's back.

The invention was great for little merchants in Miami, but it was no contender in the big time. It was too inexpensive, too simple, but Max got a patent on the process.

I was shunted over to a TV chain. I did a newscast with art, as fast as the news came over the wire. If it set the world on fire, you could barely feel the heat. All we could think of in Philadelphia was Key Biscayne and *Princess*, waiting to take us to the island.

It got to be too much. We were chasing fool's gold. We abandoned the mine and took off during the first snow flurry of the second winter. Heading south was as much fun as it had been the first time we lit out.

We found *Princess*, mastless and somewhat afloat, in Nuta's boatyard on the Miami River. We had been away eleven months. She had been pumped only once in all that time. My friend Percy Manley had come by and said to Nuta: "If *Princess* sinks, we're both in trouble." Then he pumped her dry.

Her engine was like some iron island, almost awash in her own little sea. The cushions, Coast Guard approved, were sailing on a regular schedule from bulkhead to bulkhead on the oil-calmed *mare nostrum* of the cabin. She was a sight.

We took one look at her in the gloaming, pumped a few quick strokes to keep her afloat till morning, and headed for the causeway and our home on Key Biscayne. It wasn't much better out there.

The Cuban patriot had flown the coop. The windows were broken, and the place was a shambles. Our dream island suddenly took on a wonderful aura. That aura could invest any insulated place. We knew now what we were after, and why.

In the morning I went over and pumped *Princess* dry.

Princess had her innards scrubbed with a broom and a box of soap powder. I drained the water from the crankcase of the engine. She wheezed when I cranked her, but she still had compression. The valves, way up on top, were above the high-water mark. I replaced her oil, hooked on the magneto, added some gas, and cranked her up. After several tries, she barked into life. I let go the lines. We were glad to get out of there.

The components of the dream were still around. The mast, acquired before we went prospecting for gold, was still lashed to the backyard fence. We hauled *Princess* at Dinner Key, replaced an odd frame or two, and suddenly became involved in the usual major opus. *Princess* needed new garboards. She had to have them to go with the new keel and keelson. You know how ladies are.

I bought some beautiful white cedar. The port garboard was spiled off and the new wood cut to size. It went into place like downtown. The garboard had a forty-degree twist from end to end. It was no job for a beginner.

Then came the port plank, and the unsolicited help of a professional boat carpenter. He came along just as I was easing the after end of the garboard into the rabbet of the keel.

I had four clamps working for me, and a wonderful guy by the name of Lennie Agostino, who had fallen in love with *Princess*. *Princess* had a way of attracting the best people. When Lennie wasn't working on my boat, he was working on his doctorate in philosophy. I don't know what in hell the professional carpenter was working on, but just as Lennie was taking up on the clamps and I was paring away the last impediment with the thin blade of a razor-sharp jackknife, the pro said: "Here, I'll show you how to do it," and walloped the plank with a maul.

It split.

If I thought I could get a jury of small boatman for the murder trial, I would have brained that bum with the maul.

We took out that garboard, worked some epoxy glue into the crack, let it set for a day, and then warped it into place. While we had her on the ways, Lennie and I melted three hundred pounds of lead in a washtub and poured an outside segment of ballast to attach to the keel.

It was a highly successful smelting operation. We set up our open-hearth furnace in the driveway of our house on the Key. It consisted of four bricks to hold up the washtub, a small pile of charcoal briquets, a vacuum cleaner with the hose hooked up to blow, and three hundred pounds of scrap lead.

I built a form out of two-by-fours and painted the inside of the form with a loose solution of cement. We clamped an iron rod to the washtub in order to tip the tub and pour the lead.

When the briquets were lit and the vacuum cleaner began to blow, the heat was unbelievable. It melted down all the lead in less than ten minutes. We hauled on the iron rod, and every drop of lead poured into the casting form.

There was a lot of smoke but the die was cast, like they say, before the wood had a chance to burn. We were pretty proud of ourselves. We lugged the casting out to Dinner Key, jacked it up to the keel, and bolted it with bronze three times, up through the keelson and the keel.

Princess was launched at last. Lennie and I ran her over to Key Biscayne with the clunker pounding away like a compulsive blacksmith.

There was something wrong with that engine. It was too damn noisy. When we got to Hurricane Harbor, Finlay Matheson showed us what it was. He jumped down into the cabin, grabbed the fly wheel, and lifted. Then he let it go. It dropped almost an inch. "You have no main bearing," said Finlay Matheson.

There was no babbitt in the main bearing. It began to worry me. I asked Wes Hempstead about it.

"Better fix it," he said. "It will get worse fast."

Old man Hempstead, who was standing alongside, tapped my arm and winked. After Wes went back to work the old man said, "Don't worry about it. I've seen those old engines keep running long after the flywheel wore a groove halfway through the engine bed. Those slow-speed jobs can accommodate themselves to anything."

I thanked the old man. "Just keep on running it," he said.

Here were two schools of thought. I was caught in the middle. I went along with the perfectionists.

I yanked the engine out of the boat at Finlay's dock, dragged the main bearing into town, and had it poured by an old-time machinist. There were no inserts on this job.

When I got the engine all bolted together, it wouldn't turn over. I had to loosen up the bolts, take out the bearing, and scrap it some more. And more. And more.

At last I snugged up the bearing bolts to ninety pounds with a pressure wrench, and she would just turn over. I had an engine. Back in the boat she ran quiet and true. I was deeply indebted to Finlay Matheson.

10

I stepped the mast. It wasn't easy. It took more soul-searching than you can shake a stick at. Even if the stick is a thirty-four foot Maine spruce spar.

Princess, who was now pushing seventy-five, carried too much weather helm. I had tried for twenty-five of those years to figure out why she was rigged the way she was. It didn't seem possible that Wilbur A. Morse hadn't known any better.

All that canvas was great. It made a big show. Spread out on a broad reach or close-hauled, the tiller had to be hard over. She dragged half the ocean along.

You could take her off a reef in a hell of a hurry. Flatten out all that canvas and she would lay over and slide off a bar that had barely a foot of water over it. There are not too many sand bars on the Maine coast. There are plenty of rocks. So what the hell.

Maybe Morse really didn't know any better. Maybe nobody did in those days. But did I?

And if I didn't, who did? I talked to a marine architect. He said, "Put it there," pointing to a spot just forward of a beam on the cabin overhead.

I asked a boatbuilder. "I don't argue with marine architects," he said, "but if it was *my* boat I would put it just aft of that beam."

You just don't change the rig on a character boat that's been sporting the same style for seventy-five years without good and sufficient reason.

The reason was good enough but not quite sufficient. I took it up with my friend Lennie Agostino, who was bucking for a doctorate in philosophy. If there was a final answer, this would be the guy to have it.

"Lennie," I said, "where shall I step the mast?"

Lennie walked around the deck. He looked up an imaginary mast in the sky. He examined the real one, which was lashed to the deck, shining with varnish and festooned with halyards and stays. He spun the sheave for the mainsail halyard. He stroked his great black beard and spoke:

"Hell—step it anywhere. Let's go sailing."

That did it. I snatched the beam right out of the cabin overhead with a claw hammer, drew my trusty keyhole saw, and cut a mast hole midway between the two recommended positions. That is what is known as the philosophic approach. It works.

I felt as sassy as Alexander the Great when he unlimbered his cutlass and sliced the Gordian Knot. There was a sailor for you.

If the Friendship buffs raised too much hell about the way *Princess* was rigged, I could always hang a gaff on her. Leg-o'-mutton is the way a Friendship sloop should be rigged in the islands. I had the example of the Down East builder who showed

311

the Bahamian islander how to build a vessel like mine. They showed him how to rig it.

I wanted to know after all these years how well a Friendship sloop would handle with a modern Marconi rig.

I found out. The answer was, "Great!"

It took time to find out. After Lennie and I stepped the mast, I went looking for a sail. There was a used Dacron main kicking around Ratsey's that measured eighteen feet on the hoist. I needed twenty-four. When I unstitched the bolt rope along the luff, it stretched out to twenty-one. For twenty bucks they added three more feet along the boom.

Bruce Roberts, who can't stand a boat without a sail, gave me a beautiful Dacron genny. I gave him a seventy-pound kedge. If you can't compromise in this life, the least you can do is barter. I could spare the kedge. It was just right for his poop deck plunder boat.

I unlayed one shroud off *Symphony*, and it provided enough cable to rig *Princess*. The lay is still in that cable. No matter how great the strain, it never comes out. It is like a tempered spring stretched taut. It was just what *Princess* needed aloft. She has weathered three full hurricanes without parting a stay, two of them right on her mooring in the full brunt of the blow.

There were a lot of half-hearted experiments with borrowed canvas and odd scraps of sail. We tuned the stays. There was enough play around the cabin top so the mast could work. Lennie sewed a nice mast boot. It was a great day when at last *Princess* was fully rigged and ready to go.

She ran out of Hurricane Harbor like a lady with scarcely a touch of helm. When the wind increased to fifteen knots she developed a touch of weather helm. Up near gale force she never needed more than ten degrees of rudder.

The speed she picked up as a result of the proper placement of her center of effort was a revelation. *Princess* came alive in her old age.

Her mainsail was only one hundred and fifty square feet. It used to be four hundred and fifty with the gaff. The new genoa jib was comparable in size to the old one, but it was much taller. It was also set five feet further aft. She flew.

Princess always liked to strut her stuff. She was still no racing machine, but now she could step along with them. We often wondered as we shook her down, getting ready for the long passage to the island, what she would do in a race against a boat that carried her old arrangement of sail. One day we had a chance to find out, and we jumped at it.

Another Friendship sloop appeared in Hurricane Harbor. Her owner, an aircraft engineer, was full of fight. He and his salty little wife came swooping down, looking for us. He was thunderstruck when he saw what I had done to the sail plan. It made him all the more anxious to take us. Here would be the conclusive justification of the Friendship rig. He hauled up his vast main with the sanctimonious deliberation of the defender of the faith. First the throat halyard and then the peak. It made me a little homesick to watch him.

Our sail went up the track with a zip. Out we went into Biscayne Bay with a stiff southerly on our beam. *Princess* luffed and gave her old-fashioned sister the channel. We sheeted her in and drew alongside. We luffed and did it again. At last we couldn't resist the temptation—we sailed a ring around her.

Sailing down toward the yacht club, we did it again. We sailed around that poor boat on every tack and in every quadrant. When we were tired of running around her for the sport of it, we did it to study her lines.

Struggling to keep up with us, the old Friendship parted her outhaul. The last we saw of her, the captain was out on the bitter end of that silly boom—out over green water, hanging on by his teeth, trying to join the flaying ends of the broken outhaul.

His wife hauled on the main sheet until the old man had a foot on the deck. He finally made it. Then he turned tail and ran for the bridge going north. We never saw them again.

I got a letter from him one day saying that he had sold the boat. She was no bargain, poor girl. Somebody had sliced ten inches off her counter to get rid of the rot.

It was the summer of '62. School was almost out. We began the final preparations for the trip to the island.

We bought charts. There is something about a chart that fires the imagination. The kids had all the charts spread out on the living-room floor, looking for bights and coves and a likely island. It brought to mind the observation of Robert Burton, the religious recluse, who said in his *Anatomy of Melancholy:* "Methinks there is great pleasure in the perusal of charts."

We went back and got more charts from Bill Masterson, who runs Hopkins and Carter. Billy and I used to play stickball when we were kids back in Yonkers. It was all Bill could do to take my money. Sometimes he didn't. Seems like anyone looking for an island has a wild look in his eye. People tend to go easy on a guy like that.

We bought a big galvanized fisherman's pump from Bill, just in case. We bought an alcohol stove and an ice chest. We bought life preservers for all hands, and running lights.

I bought a sailing dinghy with a cracked side for five dollars and rebuilt it. John came up with a sail for it. We hauled and painted *Princess.* By hook and crook and the grace of God we got ready. School was out. We could hardly wait to get going.

I bought the current nautical almanac and polished up my old British sextant. We began to make lists. That's a sure sign of departure.

We made lists of dried food. Lists of canned goods. Lists of vegetables. Lists of bottled drinks. Lists of spare parts. Lists of medicine. Lists of clothes. Lists of gear. Lists of lists.

Figuring on a long passage across the Gulf Stream with no one to spell me at the tiller except Betty, who would have her hands full with the kids, we decided to ship an unpaid hand. We shipped Lennie. It paid.

When Lennie wasn't working on his philosophy doctorate or on *Princess,* he was helping his ma and three brothers run one of the swellest eating establishments south of the Mason-Dixon or any other line.

On the day of departure he arrived before dawn. With his

duffle bag and his big black beard, he looked like a movie pirate. The duffle bag felt kind of heavy for a change of clothes. We stowed it.

We dragged the dinghy up on the after deck between the double back stay and lashed her down. We rigged her little sail and she paid for her passage. She was loaded with all the necessities for a forced departure from the mother ship. Her sail, acting as a spanker in partnership with the jib, shoved *Princess* out of Hurricane Harbor before the mainsail was up.

There were three hours left of the outgoing tide. When we rounded the channel marker and caught the current heading out past Cape Florida, we wound up the engine. The idea was to get out far enough with the ebbing tide to avoid the fierce effect of its return.

Suzy and Seth were too excited to sleep. The sun came up in their faces. After we had passed the ghostly old lighthouse on the point, they at last bedded down in the lulling motion of the sea.

The wind was out of the south, and diffident. We were barely off the great steel latticework lighthouse at Fowey Rocks when the wind died. In the hopes of its revival, we kept the sails up and flapping. We ran the engine until noon.

The lighthouse on the point was land down before we picked up enough wind to curve the canvas. Little by little it picked up. It helped us pass the violence that is at home around Fowey Rocks. For all its ferocity, the Stream is a lamb compared to the goings on around those rocks.

Our course was southeast. Bimini lay due east. We allowed five points to compensate for the sluice of the Gulf Stream. The wind whipped up and we cut the engine. *Princess* in her new canvas complete with spanker went to it with a vengeance. Betty made sandwiches and cracked open some cans of beer, then sacked out with the kids. I went to sleep on deck with old Blackbeard holding *Princess* on course.

Flaked out between the weather shroud and the cabin side, I dreamed about a tropical island. I dreamed about a cove edged with sand as white as snow and as soft as fleece. I dreamed about a glade of palms and a high knoll from which with a glass I could see to the ends of the sea-covered earth.

I dreamed of a great wall of coral rock that lay like a jeweled breakwater against the northeast storm. I dreamed of the clear depths of a cove, woven with weed and interlaced with the color of fish, of torpid tortugas and the furtive trail of crawfish. I dreamed of dazzling bursts of sun and sea.

I woke. Lennie, the philosopher, was fast asleep at the tiller. *Princess* was sailing herself, heading southeast true.

II

It must be a ball to be a beautiful boat. What a life. Sooner or later some guy will go for you. Spend every spare dime on you. And every spare hour. He'll take you to the ends of the earth—if he can get away.

If he can't make it alone, he'll take the family along. And a friend of the family. Anybody with an eye for a boat could see what *Princess* was up to, pouring it on across the Gulf Stream at the age of seventy-five. Actually, she was an average of sweet sixteen when you considered all the new members that were installed in her over the last twenty-five years.

Maybe she was even younger. The only old things on the boat beside that fashion piece at her bowsprit—"WILBUR A. MORSE, BUILDER, FRIENDSHIP, ME."—were the captain himself and

317

an ancient valve-inhead engine that had driven her into the edge of indigo that marks the depths of the Gulf Stream.

Once the clear blue-green of the mainland bank was lost, *Princess* took over. Before that she didn't quite believe it.

Who ever heard of a seventy-five-year-old lady setting out across those waters? How could she be sure that she was sound enough? Had some guy really spent all his spare time over all those years putting her back in condition? Why did he do it? Was he some kind of a nut? Like a truly beautiful woman, a boat is totally blind to the beauty of her own lines.

Princess surged to the trough, lifted to kiss the comber, and ran the slope of sea, curling a silver bow wave into a trail of tress. To any water man watching her, it would have been the old story of Dante and his beloved Beatrice. *Princess* was still heading southeast true and sailing herself. There was no sense butting in. She knew her business. Better than Lennie the bearded philosopher. Better than I.

The sea grew from ripples to waves and from waves to combers. Then the waves blossomed with spume. By the time this white flower of the sea brushed and broke along our quarter, we were far and gone out of sight of land.

I put a restrainer on her tiller and my girl held to her course as if she had an Iron Mike. She balanced herself in the twenty-knot wind as if she had wheels and the wheels were locked to a track. It was luck and it was love.

After twenty-five years of ownership, you can sense things about a boat that a marine architect with a barrel of slide rules couldn't tell you. But there has to be love.

I leaned back against the dinghy, which was still chipping in with her main as a spanker, and watched the sun climb up through a garden of clouds to pass us on our meridian. Here was the chance to find out how far the current of the Gulf Stream had thrown us toward the north.

My boy made his trolling line fast to an after stay and fetched me the magic box with the angle-measuring device in it. My old British sextant had a bimetal scale, as required by English law. This was to compensate for the expansion of heat. It was hot.

The old mahogany sextant case had a ring of char where some absentminded mate had set it down on a hotplate at coffee time. I screwed the telescope into place and sighted the great ball of sun through the tinted filter. Then I brought it down with the mirror until it swung like a pendulum along the southern edge of the vast landless world.

"Lennie," I said, "I am going to teach you navigation. It will take exactly two minutes. At least the latitude part. When you know that, you will know at least as much as Magellan knew."

"Fire away," said Lennie. Seth was listening.

"The earth is an orange. The navel is the north pole. The slice at the center is the equator. All the rest of the slices are the great circles of latitude. The segments are the lines of longitude. Get it?"

They got it.

"The sun is so much bigger than the earth that its rays are all parallel when they hit the earth," I said. "For the purpose of navigation, the sun revolves around the earth. Over the equator, wobbling north and south according to the season. Right?"

"Right."

"When the sun is on your segment of the orange, it is dead noon. At dead noon you can find your latitude by measuring the angle between the sun and a point right over head called your zenith."

"That's the same as a line from the center of the earth up through the place where you are standing," said Lennie.

"Who wants peanut butter and who wants tuna fish?" said my wife.

"Time out," I said. We had lunch. The ball of sun was still climbing. The wind died. As soon as my wife got out of the cabin, we started the big red engine.

There were forty seconds left on the navigation lesson.

"If you stand on the equator, the angle between the sun's rays and your zenith is what?" I asked.

319

"Zero," said Seth.

"That's the latitude," said Lennie.

"What's the angle between the sun's rays and your zenith when you're standing at the North Pole?"

"Ninety," said Lennie, "and that's the latitude."

"How could you be standing at the North Pole in a boat?" said my wife, who had certain rights, too.

"When do we get to Bimini?" said Suzy.

"Anyway the angle between the sun's rays and your zenith is the latitude."

"How do you find the zenith with that thing?" said Seth.

"You can't. The zenith is ninety degrees from the horizon. So you measure the height of the sun."

"And subtract it from ninety degrees," said my wife, who did the income tax.

"It's now more than two minutes," said Lennie the philosopher.

"Joe always exaggerates," said Betty.

"You said we'd be in Bimini this afternoon," said Suzy.

"We will be if we haven't drifted too far north."

My boy took the sextant and aimed it at the sun. "It's rising very slowly now," he said.

The sun was almost on its shelf. It was almost on its top rung, where it hesitates for a magic interval between its morning rise and afternoon descent. That is the moment of midday. The original moment of truth. The height of the sun at this moment brought Columbus, Magellan, Cortez, Balboa back to Spain.

I took the sextant and followed the great red ball of sun as it slowly parted from the line of horizon. Slowly I turned the vernier to bring it down. At last it struggled no longer. It lay for a tenuous part of a minute on the top edge of its wheel in the sky. I had the topmost reading. The sun slowly sank in the afternoon.

We added the summer declination for the day and the hour out of the Nautical Almanac and applied the corrections. Then we subtracted the corrected reading from ninety degrees.

"We're too far north."

"How far?"

"About ten miles. We could miss Bimini altogether."

The wind picked up. It blew out of the southwest, which put *Princess* almost on a reach.

We had passed the axis of the Gulf Stream. Its force was no longer a dominant factor. As the force of the wind increased, *Princess* forged ahead to the limit of her lines. She didn't seem to need the advantage and the noise of the industrial revolution down below. We cut the engine and pointed her clipper bow more to the south.

The wind blew in great hot bursts. The dark stream, chopped down by the new direction of the wind, slowly built a new system of seas out of the west. We tore through the confusion of little waves making up for the drift. We made our easting.

From the west and source of the wind, a great bank of clouds on a collision course was being stashed on seven levels for the heroic abstraction of sunset. It broke the ferocity of the glare, and some of the crew came out of their early afternoon stupor.

Seth took the tiller and Suzy went out on the bowsprit, where she could kick the tops off the waves. Betty snapped the top off the soft drinks, and the wind blew through our shirts.

Lennie lay under the dinghy and snored.

I pulled in the line with the lure and disentangled a scrap of seaweed. It seemed unbelievable—we hadn't had a strike all day. It was the second of July, and it was slowly spent as the sun stepped down.

The wind grew stronger at day's end, and we were flying. Still no Bimini. We put her head due east and began to look for a radio tower, a lighthouse, anything. The clouds colliding in the west in a prism of incipient nightfall threw a false loom across the sky to the area of our expectant landfall. It was almost dark, and still no Bimini. We had been sailing for eleven hours. A longitude sight at this point would sure be nice, but we had no chronometer to work one. All we had for a longitude was five pair of eyes. All looking.

We were so busy looking that we missed the sight of a

marlin fisherman that roared up behind us until his high bridge almost threw a shadow across us. Here was a guy with all the gadgets anyone needs to know where he is. Radar. Loran. Direction finder. Fathometer. Ship-to-shore and shore-to-ship.

As the great sleek fish hunter came abreast, we shouted and waved a bright life jacket. The master cut the throttle and the hull streamed like some mighty shovel-nosed sea creature, settling to her water line.

"Where's Bimini?" we shouted like a bunch of lubbers.

A lovely thing in a bikini uncoiled herself from the old man and climbed the towering lookout. Up on that flying bridge, she was where one of us might have been if we had had brains enough to rig the shrouds of *Princess* with ratlines.

"There it is," she called, ship to ship, pointing like a dreamy figurehead making a supplemental buck as a lookout for a short-handed whaler. The fisherman roared off.

We kept going, following his wake. At last he was out of sight, and as night came down it provided a backdrop to a point of red that took the place of his masthead light. It was the light on the radio antenna on Bimini. This was the first look *Princess* had of a foreign port in forty years.

Years ago some guy by the name of Robert Ayer took me to lunch at the Harvard Club and told me how his father had bought *Princess* from a fisherman and had her cuddy enlarged, and how he sailed her Down East across the Bay of Fundy to Yarmouth. You find out these things about a girl after you've lived with her for years.

Princess, thoroughly reconstituted, was nice enough to act as if this was her first trip abroad. She picked up the stiff southerly and made a run for it. Lennie took the tiller, and the rest of us went forward to share the first look at a Caribbean island.

All we saw for what seemed hours was the same red light and, after a while, another, like the running lights of ghost ships running away from us in the black night.

At last there were other lights, down low. Then, off on the port bow, the light of Great Isaac flashing four times every fifteen seconds.

According to the chart, its visibility was eighteen miles. We had two more hours of running. Or more. We ran.

The crazy Gulf Stream must have still been pushing, away over there where it had no business to be. When you realize the size and the impact of such a jet, there is hardly any wonder there are all kinds of silly slipstreams, back eddys, and offshoots. We had to shift our course to the south again to counter the pull to the north. Those last two hours were the longest hours of all.

At last the white lights lifted onto a hill, and we came along an edge of land, a ridge. It looked like all that was left of some vast Caribbean continent. Or perhaps the outcropping of a new one. We dropped our hook in the lee of a bump of land and went to sleep.

12

Princess lay all night in an open roadstead off Bimini. She swooped into every phosphorescent sea at the end of her cable as she ran the endless unrecorded miles of a vessel at anchor. I watched in the blackness of the night and wondered how many times around the world all those miles would tally to in the life of a boat.

I thought of all the boats and all the hours and all the miles that were spent at a mooring or a dock, going nowhere. And all the poor slobs who were spoiling to go, and all the romantic places they would never get to.

As *Princess* surged against the sea I hit the sack, tired as hell and just a little smug. At least I had come this far. We were anchored off a foreign port. I sailed into sleep, and the first green fire of a tropical day cut the crystal water.

In the last hour of darkness the wind went into the east. We were in the lee of land. The anchor was holding on a hundred feet of chain. *Princess* swung gently between the soft persuasion of the wind and the nudge of the current. I slept late.

Lennie slept on deck under the dinghy. The kids, chattering on the cabin top, woke him. When I came on deck the sun had come over the hill and the day was unfolding like some kind of blue-green flower, shiny and clear.

Lennie and Seth were over the side. Big bearded Lennie and my kid were somewhere down below in a sea so transparent that it was a wonder they didn't figure it for air and toss their masks away.

The water was so clear that you could see the floor of coral at forty feet as if it was the Bimini-blue bottom of our bathtub back on Fiftieth Street.

There was the anchor, caught in kelp. There was a school of jack, followed by a pokey grouper. There was a little fellow with a yellow diving mask trailing a big guy with a black mask and a coal-black beard.

We had breakfast ready for them when they lifted their Hawaiian slings, laid them on the deck, and jumped on board.

Suzy was watching the coral ridge through the glasses. She ran her eyes along the sugary sand, over the little houses on the hill and down to the point. She sensed the whiteness of everything against the bluest of blues and the jet-black people that made it sing. We could hardly wait to get ashore.

Bacon and eggs off Bimini is like bacon and eggs anywhere else where the air is totally free of dust, the sky made of nothing but blue, and the water simply a deeper shade of sky that seems to support the boats in a tricky gambol.

Princess was a long way from Pugsley Creek. This was no Eastchester Bay. To goof it up with the thought of polluted rivers and contaminated bays would have been to spoil our breakfast in particular and to louse up the feast in general.

We sat there, munching in stupefaction and wondering why a native of this place would ever emigrate. Or how long it would be before the rest of the world was climbing on their backs.

There was no one on their backs on that fine third day of July. Not even the scenery stiff who usually arrived early in the afternoon and left before dark. The vessel that made regular runs between Miami and Bimini was in drydock over on the mainland. It had run aground and sprung some planks in her bottom trying to negotiate the millrace of the new channel. You could see the reason from a hundred yards away.

We elected to run around the point and we found the feeble little range lights that could bring you into the harbor of Bimini at night. If you know where it is. Or how to find it.

There isn't enough in Bimini at night to make it worth the danger. It is better to come in during the hours of daylight. Then there is a lot to see. The sunlight on the shoal danced in the exuberance of the surf, and the sea bounced in all the shades of shell. We ran the violent current into the limited harbor, bearing close along the docks of the eating dives. We caught hold of a piling at the Angler's Club and gas dock.

A very formal immigration officer in a uniform that smacked of a British bobby checked us in. He made all sorts of vital notations on a form that was flapping on his clipboard in the determined easterly while we rocked on the dock in the persistent reverberations of a day, a night, and half another day in a little boat.

At last he ran out of red tape, and he gave us a great white smile, as if the whole business was a big joke dreamed up by some clown in the Foreign Office for the amusement of the natives.

We walked the streets of the little colonial town. Bimini looked like Miami might have looked in the eighties. Or Coconut Grove. There were little wooden inns and tiny shops filled with tourist trash and all the junk made in Podunk that traveling people buy to send back where it came from. There were shops that sold food at twice the mainland price, and shops that sold liquor at less than half of it.

We walked along the cusp of a ridge that was at least as high as the outcroppings along Bayshore Drive in Miami. From that height you could see the long shoals to the southeast that spawn the fish and all the tiny uninhabited islands that lay between Bimini and Gun Cay.

That was the way to go. When we got down to *Princess*, the kids had found the aquarium that some dress manufacturer had donated in his dotage. The sharks were nicely fenced off. So were the porpoises. There was none of the dog-eat-dog freedom that you find in the garment district. We waited in the shade of the palms for the bread to bake in the smallest bakery in the world. It was worth waiting for. We found a freshwater shower hidden in the head of the gas dock. We left Bimini showered and/or shaved. *Princess* was loaded with Dutch beer, ice, newly baked bread, and fresh water. The wind was on the port beam and strong. We sailed due south.

We sailed half the afternoon against a current that must have been the first cousin of the Gulf Stream. The wind at least was in our favor. We skirted Turtle Rocks, bearing to the west lest the current carry us in among the shoals. We ran close aboard Piguet Rock, scaring the gulls into tiny scudding flecks of white that were lost among the covey of clouds.

It was a long two-hour run by the time we came abreast of Holm Cay and headed for the lighthouse on the south end of Gun Cay. The sun was deep in the west. An oblique ray of light like the burst of sun in a painting by a groovy old master struck on a clean, white patch of beach. It came on so strong that we stared in silence. *Princess*, sailing herself, edged over to the east, heading tentatively in between the north end of Gun Cay and a friendly little rock that rose just north of it.

The place looked friendly. We let her go. The kids were out on the bowsprit, and so was Lennie with a lead line, when we entered the tiny cove. The entrance from the west was unobstructed. The bottom was visible. There were no pinnacles of coral, and the bottom shoaled gently toward the beach.

As we wheeled in the cove and came about, *Princess* made

an unmistakable curtsey and dropped her hook. Her sails shivered in excitement as we let them go. This was her pad. She was home.

This was the island we had been looking for. The Caribbean island that had everything. It fitted the dream as if it had been poured into it.

There was the cove of sand cupping the clear water. It was shaped like a boomerang, and soft as down. There was the lithe little grove of palms, and to the north against the weather was the reef of rock jeweled by the sea. There was even an abandoned little house on the hill above the cove. The place was alive with fish.

As the kids went over the side I thought of all the islands and all the coves and all the wartime places here and in the Pacific that I had found and left. I held my wife's hand and wondered if she minded having *Princess* along.

So far as *Princess* was concerned, it was hardly as cozy as it would have been without my wife, the kids, and Lennie. But it was all she could ask for in the way of an island.

We put on our masks and joined Lennie and the kids in the water. No configuration of canyon and cliff, no volcanic panorama, no cascade of water spilling into a deep and misty valley, no outdoor wonder can beat the kind of merchandise we were looking at. Betty and I finished the day chasing shadow and substance, shimmer and shade—all the cockeyed wonder of underwater life. It was better than Bonwit's window on the night before Christmas. The kids were more businesslike.

They speared a mess of snappers, blues, and crawfish. Lennie came up with a baby octopus. We showered with water from the cistern beside the house on the hill, and Lennie opened his great big sea bag.

Out of it came a caldron, his pet saucepan, and spices for which the conquistadores would have sailed halfway around the world. We had bouillabaisse on the beach and a seafood smorgasbord to put to shame the cuisine of the great Agostino himself.

Down the beach a little motor boat pulled in from Lauderdale. They were real polite. They declined to join us. They squatted to the lee and tasted ham sandwiches with their tongues while their noses devoured the aroma. Lennie, full of Dutch beer and his own masterwork, curled around the driftwood fire and fell asleep as the sun went down. There was a full moon. Naturally.

The next day was the quietest Fourth of July we had ever known. It was one of the quietest days we have ever known.

There was no way to celebrate the victory over the British except by occupying this tiny patch of heaven that we had neglected to take away from them. The motorboat left in the morning and we were alone. We had a sneaking suspicion that other people knew about this place, but we paid it no mind.

We lolled in the sun and chased the phantom fish for fun and food. We searched the grottoes of the reef for lobsters, and we dove for conch. We ate the pure white meat of it raw with a touch of lime juice. Lennie found some turtle eggs. The kids from Lauderdale had destroyed most of them, but we had a seafood omelet for breakfast. The day slipped away full of everything but war and business and scientific achievement and crime.

It was too good to last.

Suddenly, out of nowhere, there were a half dozen Boston Whalers on the beach. They were full of boxes and baskets and umbrellas and drums and guitars and God knows what else.

The umbrellas popped open, the tables were unfolded, and the bongo drummer began to swing it. And from everywhere came boats. Great big fancy marlin-fishing boats, a hundred of them, clustering around *Princess* in the tiny harbor like a free day at the boat show.

There were boats and people and calypso music, and mountains of food and drinks. For two bucks each, we were happy to join the gang. The kids ate free, lost among the people and the people and the people.

This was the day of the annual outing of the chowder-chomping, whiskey-belting, hell-for-leather Marlin Fishing Club. Our little island was the scene.

We made it.

13

The price of peace and quiet must be periodic bedlam. If you don't believe it, take a look at the world. Or at our island in the blue Caribbean. It was jumping.

The bongo kids from Bimini in their red silk shirts were swinging. Their calypso was so hot that even the fish were popping right up between the hundred marlin-fishing boats in the cove. Half-crocked anglers were doing the twist, the watusi, and the dead man's float with the other stoned crabs. A man with a chef's hat was hawking hamburgers, with or without. A soupy-eyed account exec was giving away prime time. The brokers and the bankers were rolling in the sand, losing more loot than Blackbeard had buried. It was wild.

We had never seen so much food. Seafood, shore food,

fancy store food heaped on tables. The legs of the tables sank into the sand to the mean high-water level. Hot and cold, roasted and baked, barbecued, diced, pickled, basted, beaten, shirred, and stirred. Fried, filleted, sautéd, parsleyed—every edible plant, fish, bird, or animal. It was the phantasmagoria of a starving island castaway, the final fantasy of a fat gourmet.

Here was the ultimate desert island with all the fixings, a rush-hour Eden. And in the very center of this blast of madness and mirth lay *Princess*, sedate and bemused.

In the shade of a palm frond, on a throne of wire grass, with the best of beer oozing from every pore, I contemplated the anomaly. Beyond the immediate sphere of smorgasbord lay the lovely limits of the island. The ultimate refuge. The reward for all the strain. I tried to remember what it had taken.

The city, the dark and dismal rooms, the lonesome crowds, and the cold, wet streets. The long gray days of winter. A layer of snow on the deck of *Princess*, hauled on the frozen banks of an ice-clogged river, and the long ordeal of rebuilding. Rotten frames, nail-sick planks, a spongy stem, and soft horn timber. I felt again the bluster of spring and the sudden humid summer. And the worry and the work.

Here at last was the sun and the sea, the clearness and the clean. And here too were all the silly people who were part and parcel of the other world, leaping, laughing, bragging, and brawling.

And there in the very vortex of that sandy shindig lay *Princess*, the brainchild of a backwoods Brancusi by the name of Morse. She had been plucked from anonymity by a painter who had given as much of himself to a boat as he had given to the pursuit of his art. Not that anybody gave a damn.

To those people *Princess* was just another Bahama Island vessel. Prettier than most, but still just an island boat. Crowded around her were scores of sleek and shiny fish hunters. The rake of a sheer, the touch of a tumble home, or the suggestion of a clipper bow had been borrowed, begged, or stolen just a little bit from *Princess*.

Like all things of great and transcendent beauty, *Princess* could afford to give. Imitation is the sincerest form of flattery, and *Princess* had pointed the way to a new breed of boats. Whether it was her Down East builder himself or a branch of the family who had come to Abaco to build the same hull was of little moment; there was *Princess* among her step-children. She was as proud as Punch. The rest of us were just punchy.

It was the Fourth of July on a tropical island, and our boat had everything but an air conditioner and room enough for everyone to get in out of the sun. Who cared? The kids reveled in it. Suzy was chasing Seth, hide and seek among the anesthetized anglers. Lennie looked at all the food and shrugged. I looked at all the boats and shrugged. Betty shrugged, pulled her big straw hat over her face, and went to sleep in the sand.

Suddenly they were gone: the people, the boats, the bongo band, the umbrellas, the tables, most of the chow. All gone. Here was our silent island again, with a gift from the other world. They had left us a case of Dutch beer, a box of ice, and enough salad, hamburgers, hot dogs, and rolls to feed us for a week. For the rest of the time we could count on fish.

The days went by in a vast swirl of sun and sea and the breathtaking color and magic of the underwater world. We ventured out of the cove and dove along the great white coral floor of the sea. We met all the fish and we took what we needed. We met some well-fed sharks who were bigger than we were. We went back to the cove.

It blew hard out of the northeast one night so we took *Princess* around to the southwest lee of the island, where the bottom was a carpet of dark sea grass. It blew all day. We took the hint, hauled the hook, and ran the channel at the south end of Gun Cay and down along the arched back of Cat Cay to the sheltered arm of the harbor.

There was a store and a shower and a nice dock for two dollars a day. We walked across and climbed the hill for a look around. Then we explored the island.

Cat Cay was a dream island of an advertising nabob who

had lured wealthy manufacturers into his fold with the promise of a permanent place in his slightly commercial heaven. Then it happened the way it has happened in all nirvanas since man began to tamper with the wilderness. The ad man died and went to his reward; his Caribbean island heaven went to hell.

On this pistol-shaped island just south of our own little heaven, the big get-together building with its ballroom, Tudor architecture, stained-glass windows, and woody gentlemen's bar had gone downhill. The fancy cottages along the hooked road of paradise were paintless and peeling. Someone was struggling to keep the grass cut, but the swimming pools were cracked and stagnant and the tennis courts were overgrown with the boisterous flora of the bush. The golf course was neck and neck with the jungle. The bloom was off the rose, blown off by a couple of hurricanes or new, more fashionable enthusiasms.

This particular heaven needed a new deity, a young and lively god with a lot of old sell.

There was something heartwarming in the patina of disintegration. For anyone who wants an untouched island there is comfort in the fact that the works of man are almost as temporary and fugitive as man himself. Perhaps someday the Indians may think twice before they hand over twenty-four bucks for the vine-covered ruins of Manhattan. There's a pleasant thought for the day. All it takes is time.

A tiny eight-place amphibian flew into Cat Cay twice a week. The plane was a honey. It was a Grumman Goose, and nobody loved it better than its captain, Irving Jones. To hear Jones talk, I could believe his little bird had all the kindly characteristics of an airborne *Princess*. That in the moments of stress, when it's up to the ship, she always came through. I have known times when *Princess*, sensing the urgency of the circumstance, has taken over and sailed herself, as if the hand of old man Morse was on her tiller.

That's the way it was with the little Grumman Goose. There was an obvious romance going on between that pilot and his plane. You could see it in the loving care Jones showered on his ship. She knew it, too. You could sense it in the way she rose and stepped from the crest of a roller that came in across the sixty miles of shallow sea; the way she wheeled and banked above the mast of my boat in the sea-clear sky.

Her fat little tumble home and the flawless lines of her hull made her the sister ship of all sea-kindly vessels, the airborne counterpart of my Friendship sloop.

We were running out of time. The stuff you buy with luck or love. Time is coin of the realm. Any realm. We had to go back for more. Back to our island on the edge of the city.

It was time we did. Seth had filled every crawfish in the jetty with the fear of God, or whatever it is that sends the tropical lobster into hiding. Suzy had climbed every hill and explored every cove in Cat Cay. Lennie had gone full circle in his fabulous culinary repertoire, and we were back to spaghetti with marinara sauce. Betty had come as close as she dared to the color of a coffee bean.

As for myself, I am a studio painter, which only an artist can understand. If there had been another island in the chain, we would have given it another week. The Berry Islands were more than a hundred miles to windward. It was blowing hard. The wind was too good to waste.

We stowed some store food and soft drinks, and squared away for sea. We said goodbye to the pilot, the storekeeper, and the master of the dock. The mainsail went up alongside. We tacked to the jetty, came about, and passed through the harbor entrance on a starboard tack with the big jib coming up puffed out like the cheek of the wind god.

It's a bouncy run along the lee shore in an easterly from the harbor of Cat Cay to the high rock corner that holds the light on Gun Cay. And there's always a bad rip in the channel with the tide horsing through. We jibed over in the race and ran north for one last look at that idyllic spot—the lonely little dream island that belongs only to us and the world.

We came into the cove with confidence. We had lived in it

for a solid week, and we knew every curve and configuration of the bottom. It was a kind of enchanted ol' swimmin' hole.

The white beach beckoned in the cloud-strewn light of early afternoon. The fronds of the coconut palms reached out to us in the gathering easterly. The basin of the cove glistened in the same gemlike clarity as it had the day we found it.

Now we were sure that it would never change. That we could come back any time, tomorrow or a hundred years from now, and it would be the same. It would be as clean as the swimming hole of our childhood so long as the river ran, the big river called the Gulf Stream.

As we pivoted in the dead center of our dream island and picked up the wind, wing and wing, we shot out of that incredible rim of coral rock that mothers the softest, whitest, cleanest beach in the world. We waved again to the place which is known as Honeymoon Harbor.

Then we headed for home.

14

We should never have left the dream island. It was a mistake. Once you have established a beachhead, invest the land.

If you can't beat the natives, join them. Retrench. Set up a provisional government. Spike the beaches. Arm the heights. The worst thing you can do is turn tail and run.

That's what we did. We ran. We were chicken. There was a fair wind. The Gulf Stream was not too obstreperous. By the time the fates had dug up a whipping wind to teach us a lesson, we were home.

The last hour off Key Biscayne, close hauled and heading for the sea buoy with a twenty-knot tanker cutting across our tail and *Princess* pounding into a cross sea, gave us a taste of what it could be like. A few more hours of that and we would have been damn sorry that we didn't go native.

No island could be that bad. Even for property owners, members of the PTA, citizens. As such we live in greater dread of the doctor, the super-grocer, the orthodontist, the truant officer. We are cultivated cattle with about as much chance of survival in a primitive paradise as a popsicle has in purgatory.

Heroes we ain't. Pioneers? Hardly. Long ocean passages in a tiny boat, hanging onto the tiller through weeks of rain, days of adverse winds, hours of cresting seas until the brain is reduced to a hard nut, is strictly for the other guy.

We like to read about the hero. We watch a Western stung with the adrenalin of participation as the steely-eyed gunslinger moves in for the kill. When virtue triumphs, we reward ourselves with cold cuts and another can of beer.

Sure—we found the ultimate island. It is known among the natives and marlin fishermen as Honeymoon Harbor. We left it to the birds, the turtles, the fish, and—God forbid—the honeymooners.

That was the awful part about it. We should have stayed. Reinforced the garrison. Established ramparts. Who knew, but by the time we got back the place would be all gooped up with newlyweds? We lived in dread through the long school year. The weather was in our favor.

The winter months in this area abound in an easterly that turns the Gulf Stream into a wet hell. The boys who brave it in pursuit of the big fish couldn't care less about an island. Unless it has a gin mill and a built-in blonde. Winter was our time to haul, paint, and prepare for the passage.

I pulled a bad plank, one of the two top planks, which in a Friendship sloop are fashioned of oak. I bent in a new one made of tidewater cypress, which is almost as hard as oak and is also a better water wood. I did the job right at the dock with a styrofoam float snugged up for a working platform. Anything to beat the boatyard.

Seth went up the mast with a can of paint. Suzy scrubbed

Princess down and painted the interior. Betty sewed a dandy awning for the hot summer sun, and I built a swimming ladder. The days went by.

We made an occasional run down the Keys. We poked in among the mangrove wilderness, and hunted shells along the beach and pirate treasure in the bush. We caught fish. We gloated in the special privilege of having a boat in the water all the year. The season called summer came early.

The preparation for the second foray to the island began at the supermarket in May. Betty began hoarding cans of beans, cans of soup, cans of juice, beer, and Chinese food. There is nothing like a can of cold chicken chow mein with a touch of salty soy sauce on a hot day. The silverware, the spices, and all the galley jazz were stowed. The last thing would be the bedding and the perishables. The very last to be stowed would be the most perishable of all. Us.

The dock looked like the 'tweendecks of a steerage ship on the day of departure. There were boxes of canned goods, bags of towels, sacks of clothing, hampers of food, and chests of ice. Over all was heaped the bedding and the sails. Strewn about under the stately royal palms and the feathery poincianas in the misty light of early morning, it looked like a crazy composite canvas by a French romantic painter and an American of the ashcan school.

To top it off, Seth and Suzy had arrived at an age when sniping at each other seems like the end-all of life. They were about as much help getting squared away for sea as a couple of jackanapes.

At last the baggage was all below, and the little vessel headed out with the kids still beating at each other.

"Seth," I said, "did you bring the sextant?"

"Yes," he said.

"Where is it?"

"Down below."

"Make sure." Seth went below and turned the cabin into a shambles looking.

"It ain't here," he announced.

"Last time I saw it, it was on the sea wall," said Suzy, sticking out her tongue at Seth.

We turned the vessel around at the channel marker and went back into the harbor to look while Seth prepared a new onslaught on Suzy. I blew my stack.

The blast echoed in the silent harbor in the early morning. Sure enough, the sextant was on the sea wall. We plucked it off and made another start, but the mood of the passage was set.

It was a long, hard haul. The wind was no bargain and the sun, unobscured, beat down all day, doubling in intensity as the angle of incidence met the angle of refraction. It was hard to tell which was worse.

A noon sight, way out of sight of land, showed us too far north again. We ran the engine at full throttle heading southeast by east all the long afternoon. The heat in the cabin was unbearable.

The late afternoon sun beating in under the sails was the clincher. There was no way of hiding from it except by ducking forward of the house or down behind the dinghy, which was lashed on the fantail. The fumes of the engine ran along with us in the lazy air.

Night put her soothing hand on us and brought along a southerly that gave the engine a breather. The red antenna lights on Bimini appeared in the southeast long after dark and we started up old faithful again lest we miss the island altogether. At last we came in along the western edge of Bimini and dropped the hook. This was the third passage *Princess* had made between Key Biscayne and the first of the Caribbean Islands. There didn't seem to be any way of making the passage in under fourteen hours, sail or power.

I was bushed. The heavenly respite from the ordeal of steering can come only with the wind. Under power, *Princess* had to be held by the tiller like any other motorboat, all day and half the night.

The kids were spoiling to go ashore in the morning.

We ran in at seven o'clock and I hunted up the immigration

Charley. I found him walking down the main drag in his full regalia. He was most obliging. He made out the form and checked out everything. Then he handed us a bill for four dollars.

"What's that for?" I asked.

"Two hours overtime at two dollars an hour," he said. "The hours of regular service are from nine to five."

I paid the four dollars and thanked the lucky stars that I hadn't come hollering for him in the middle of the night. It was a good thing to find out. For four dollars.

Seth went skindiving with another kid in the opalescent harbor while the girls went shopping. I hit the sack and slept.

I was half asleep when I heard them discussing their acquisitions on the cabin top. Suzy had a beautiful straw hat, and my wife had the cutest thing to put under grandma's teapot.

"Wouldn't it be cute if it exploded?"

Seth came up with a dandy snapper on a spear. We went down along the waterfront, where an old time English settler had a little vessel full of fresh-picked conch. We watched him bang the hole with another shell between the second and third ring on the bottom to relieve the suction and cut the muscle. Out came the lovely white meat of the conch. Right out of its spiral ivory tower.

The old man showed us how to cut away the inedible part. Seth asked, "Do you skindive for these?"

"Lor' no," he said in a Cockney brogue. "We tongs 'em. Too many shark, you know." His veined hand, gnarled by the sun, the sea, and the years, came at us with a knife upon which was skewered a square of conch meat.

We ate.

The drench of the sun was off the afternoon when a brisk easterly began to snap the British colors on the government house. We began to think of our own little island borrowed from the British. We shoved off with the bargain booze, the Bimini baked bread, the straw hats, and all the rest of the tourist debris.

We swung into our private heaven at the dinner hour with the tingle of fulfillment and the slightly hysterical glee of realization. It was just the way we left it. The cistern on the hill was full, the lobsters had quadrupled, and the fish had also multiplied. We climbed the hill above Honeymoon Harbour and looked around. There wasn't a newlywed in sight.

We built a fire on the soft white beach and ate the gifts of the sea roasted on a fire kindled from the gifts of the forest. Wood that might have come all the way from the lush banks of the Amazon or Zanzibar.

By morning it began to blow from the east and the north. It was cool and brisk and wonderful and we got a taste of how marvelous it must be in the winter months.

The wind had that cold North Atlantic flavor. It felt like it meant business. It did.

By nightfall it was whooping in over the shoals. We moved around to the western lee in the morning. It still came in so rough that it damn near dumped us when we rowed into the abandoned house for a couple of buckets of water and a bath.

We had a real tempest in our teapot. In the hopes of a decent night's sleep, we hightailed it for the cover of Cat Cay harbor. We had to power through the pass.

By the time we got in, there were several other vessels at the dock, all in out of the nasty east wind, with more to come. It blew for ten days.

It blew at gale force mounting at times to hurricane velocity. The woman in the little cutter abandoned the cruise and flew home in the beautiful amphibian, sending back her son to help daddy with the boat. The crew from Chicago on the *Shark* sweated it out for days. A huge schooner tied up in the corner with another sloop. It blew from the east by north without variation or restraint. It was the longest damn blow I have ever known.

We pitched so badly, bridled between the piers, that we got out with our bedding and slept on the dock. The only relief we had from the everlasting bellow was to go over the backbone of the hill, slide down the dune, and bask in its protection.

There were lobsters beneath the coral rocks that kept the kids busy, and a wooden staircase that went up and up to the crown of the hill for another slide down the dune.

We did the island again. This fabulous island of fabled people was still on the skids. We saw the autographs of the Duke and Duchess, the impresario, the ball player, and the plutocrat in the casino of the baronial manor. The English thatched-roof cottages along a primrose path that flirted with the jungle looked like an abandoned movie set. The shacks of the hired natives in the bush stood out in strange and vindictive contrast. One could almost hear strains of "After the Ball Is Over."

The club pool and the beauty shop were closed, and yet, of all things, there was a water cooler, full of mountain water. Plugged in, too. Ice cold and plenty of paper cups. Sign of hope.

And things to see. The old lighthouse on the southwest corner of Cat Cay and the pumping station built in the massive style of the Dutch mill. The shooting trap and the tennis courts. Cat Cay must have been one hep place in its heyday.

The *Shark* left first, at dawn, with the fierce easterly behind them. We watched them through a glass from the hill as they galloped into the heaving Stream, pounding and rearing in the seaway. By noon the wind had moderated some, and we got the urge to get underway.

I was watching *Princess* surge in her harness, working as hard at the dock as she might have in a violent passage, and I said, "What the hell."

Then everybody said, "What the hell."

Betty added, "Wait till I get my carton of frozen water from the kitchen on the hill." And we were off.

We came through the passage wing and wing, with the staysail set to take some of the pressure off the big genny. We passed Honeymoon Harbor with scarcely a backward glance. We were too busy.

We made time. This was the kind of action that *Princess* was built for. Maybe not with a woman and two kids on board, but Gun Cay was land down by three in the afternoon, and we were far out in the Stream by nightfall.

It was work. You can use a big rudder running down wind. *Princess* had it. There was no danger of a broach so long as I could hang on. We were running free with the wind on the starboard side, and the giant seas were getting bigger every moment. The vast rollers towered above us in the phosphorescent dark.

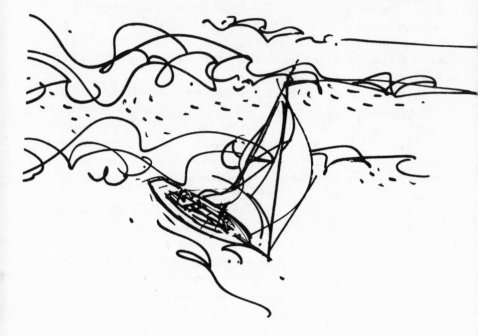

We whipped along, barely ahead of each cresting catastrophe, with every rag set and drawing. They were stretched to the tearing point. By nine it was blowing a full gale. As the vessel tore ahead with all that canvas, I feared for the mast. It was time to take in sail. But how?

To let go of the jib sheets in a sea that towered thirty feet above us would have created a flapping havoc. The genny was good as it was, backed up with the staysail. The answer was to get the mainsail down and run before it with the head sails.

The main halyard was cleated to the mast about four feet above the emergency hatch forward. I could duck under, come up the hatch, and let it go, but I didn't dare trust anyone else with the tiller. I waited. *Princess* tore ahead into the blackness.

The waves came roaring up behind us like stampeding buffaloes climbing all over each other. I thought of the kids below, kind of sick, and my wife on the verge of it, and I wondered if we would make it.

We had to make it. Of course. But the ache in my arm from nine hours at the tiller and the overwhelming fatigue brought on by the blow and all the sleepless nights had me in a corner. I looked out at the ferocity of all that water and I said, "Terrifying."

Betty, sitting in the hatchway heard me. "What?"

"It's kind of fun," I said.

"I heard you the first time," she said.

"We've got to get that mainsail down. Do you suppose you could crawl under, come up the hatch, and let it go?"

"I'll try."

"It would be too tricky to leave you with the tiller and do it myself. I'll put a line on your waist. Tell the kids to hang onto your legs."

Betty crawled forward below, trailing her lifeline. The kids went with her and held on to her legs. She reached up and let the mainsheet halyard go.

"Mommy is shaking like a vibrating machine," Suzy called. She was.

Down came the main like Uncle Harry's drawers all tangled up in the family wash. It twisted around itself and the boom. We breathed again and snugged in the main sheet.

Princess still tore ahead to the limit of her lines but it was easier now. All we needed was the sight of the light on Fowey Rocks. We kept going, heading southwest. It was near midnight. Eleven hours and no sign of the light. Not even a loom.

"You don't suppose something's wrong with the light? Maybe it's out."

"Fine time for that."

"Can't understand where it can be. We've been running southwest for eleven hours and we must be making six knots. That makes sixty-six miles. It's only sixty miles to Bimini. So where's the light?"

"There it is!"

And there it was, right on our starboard beam. We changed course but fast. There was no way of telling how far we were from the outlying coral rocks off Elliott Key. Probably spitting distance. It was close.

Princess played ducks and drakes with a half dozen ships getting in. At last we were under the wing of the big light on Fowey Rocks and heading for the sea buoy. Now we knew that even the Gulf Stream, that mighty torrent, can be stopped in its tracks and even made to back up in the face of a heavy and persistent easterly.

I was on the ropes. Seth came up like a good sailor and took the tiller. *Princess* grazed bottom on the soft sand of harbor point, which was nothing but funny with the tide coming in.